Mommy Angst

MOMMY ANGST

Motherhood in American Popular Culture

Edited by Ann C. Hall and Mardia J. Bishop

PRAEGER

An Imprint of ABC-CLIO, LLC

A B C · C L I O

Santa Barbara, California • Denver, Colorado • Oxford, England

Library of Congress Cataloging-in-Publication Data

Mommy angst : motherhood in American popular culture / edited by Ann C. Hall and
    Mardia J. Bishop.
        p. cm.
    Includes bibliographical references and index.
    ISBN 978–0–313–37530–9 (hard copy : alk. paper) — ISBN 978–0–313–37531–6 (ebook)
1. Motherhood—United States. I. Hall, Ann C., 1959- II. Bishop, Mardia J.
HQ759.M848   2009
306.874'30973—dc22   2009020716

13 12 11 10 9   1 2 3 4 5

This book is also available on the World Wide Web as an eBook.
Visit www.abc-clio.com for details.

ABC-CLIO, LLC
130 Cremona Drive, P.O. Box 1911
Santa Barbara, California 93116-1911

This book is printed on acid-free paper ∞

Manufactured in the United States of America

To our children, Sarah, Zachary, Jack, Matthew, and Leia

CONTENTS

INTRODUCTION

Ann C. Hall
Mardia J. Bishop

Americans are anxious about motherhood, and American mothers are anxious about nearly every aspect of their lives: their careers, their families, their bodies, their children, their mothering abilities. One of the important reasons for this anxiety is the culture's desire for a simple, reliable definition and representation of motherhood, one that answers all questions, addresses all situations, and, perhaps, requires nothing on the part of the American culture in return. Americans want a "mom" definition of motherhood—a nurturing, accepting, easy definition. Mothers, moreover, are the reservoir of American expectations, so it is no wonder that when Americans say "mother," there are a host of images and expectations associated with the term. For mothers in American culture, the deluge is overwhelming.

In order to fulfill the desire for a definition or simple representation of motherhood, mothers in pop culture are frequently represented in particular ways. Most recently, the "supermom"—the mother who could do it all, with a smile, with a perfect figure, and on a budget—was the cultural ideal. Those who complained earned the most oppressive label in American culture, "the bad mom," the postmodern equivalent of a scarlet letter. In other instances, perhaps in an attempt to perpetuate the competition among women so common in patriarchal structures, stay-at-home moms are pitted against working moms, with both sides feeling inadequate as a result of the comparison. Under these circumstances, women who once competed with one another for a man, now compete with one another for the title, "good mom."

From the perspectives of media studies, literature, psychology, economics, film, politics, and history, this collection exposes the cultural anxiety over motherhood as demonstrated by these representations of motherhood in news, film, television, and other media. The chapters also interrogate various expectations regarding motherhood and the ways in which motherhood is used for and against women. *Mommy Angst* resists codifying representations of mothers because it only serves to divide mothers from one another, distorts the maternal experience, and ignores the fact that the mothering experience is different for different women. The chapters demonstrate how the icons of motherhood attempt to control motherhood and mothers, while paradoxically presenting multiple representations of motherhood. In other words, despite the evidence to the contrary, the American media and culture long for a singular definition and representation of motherhood as deeply as they long for a time when mothers stayed at home and baked apples pies. But, as we all know, this longing is illusory; there was really no such time, at least not for women of color or women of a certain socioeconomic status. The desire for the illusory produces anxiety on both the cultural and the individual levels because it cannot accommodate the realities of motherhood in American culture. These chapters investigate the cultural reasons or motivations for many of the unsatisfactory expectations and icons prevalent in American popular culture.

Scholarly work on the question of motherhood has clustered around certain trends. E. Ann Kaplan's *Motherhood and Representation: The Mother in Popular Culture and Melodrama* offers psychoanalytic interpretations of film and discusses cultural "master discourses" regarding motherhood from the nineteenth century to the 1990s.[1] Other scholars attempt to address the feminist perspectives on motherhood, basically correcting the idea that motherhood and feminism were mutually exclusive.[2] And Sharon Hays's *The Cultural Contradiction of Motherhood* examines the "intensive mothering" that appears in society, but her analysis looks at the economic and historic perspectives on motherhood, not their popular culture expressions.[3]

The 2000s see an increasing interest in motherhood, particularly in terms of economics. Ann Crittenden's thorough *The Price of Motherhood: Why the Most Important Job in the World Is Still the Least Valued* examines how motherhood costs women a great deal in terms of financial security and personal wealth.[4] *Consuming Motherhood* is a collection that looks at the relationship between consumerism and motherhood—how patterns of motherhood and consumerism shape each other.[5] Neil Gilbert in *A Mother's Work* argues that women's choices regarding work and family are influenced by capitalism, feminism, and government policies.[6]

Judith Warner's wonderful *Perfect Madness: Motherhood in the Age of Anxiety* (2005) examines the pressures women face to be perfect, but does not interrogate the ways in which the media perpetuates its desire for a singular maternal trope.[7] Warner focuses on particular women's experiences and her own culture shock when she returned from France to the maternal madness of America, which inspired the book. She rightly concludes that despite the many changes in women, society, and media, women's roles as mothers and wives have not changed much since the publication of the landmark feminist book by Betty Friedan, *The Feminine Mystique*. *The Motherhood Manifesto: What America's Moms Want and What to Do About It* by Joan Blades and Kristin Rowe-Finkbeiner also bases its conclusions and arguments on personal stories from women across America, in this case the economic and mental hardships associated with American motherhood.[8] And while the book outlines many problems, it also indicates moments of successful and supportive maternal environments across America. Gail Heidi Landsman uses a similar method in *Reconstructing Motherhood and Disability in the Age of "Perfect" Babies* by talking to mothers of disabled children and addressing their feelings, as well as the pressures placed upon them by the media, which, again, tends to blame mothers for their children's failings, emotional and physical.[9]

The latest scholarly works on motherhood and popular culture were published in the early 2000s. *Mothering, Popular Culture and the Arts* was published as a special edition of the *Journal of the Association for Research on Mothering*.[10] The journal included poetry and fiction, as well as critical analyses of the representation of motherhood in popular culture. The collection was eclectic and useful, but there was no theorizing about the multiplicity of media, representations, or perspectives. *The Mommy Myth: The Idealization of Motherhood and How It Has Undermined Women* by Susan Douglas and Meredith Michaels, who are media specialists, provides such theorizing regarding various media—primarily television, radio, and print.[11] They examine the ways in which the icon of the Perfect Mother has created impossible standards for mothers to achieve. They label the idealization of our contemporary icon of motherhood "new momism" and argue that it works to propagate a conservative agenda, pushing the responsibility for child care solely on the mother, making child rearing a personal issue instead of a social one, creating mommy wars between good moms and bad moms, and defining the ideal mother as stay-at-home, Caucasian, and upper class. Our collection expands on Douglas and Michaels's work, examining additional media (the Internet, movies, novels, political publications) and various maternal representations. In addition, and from the perspective of different disciplines, this collection attempts to interpret and explain the diverse and conflicting images of motherhood in popular culture. Consequently, this collection offers timely and fresh perspectives.

As we worked on this collection of essays, moreover, we found there was reluctance in the literature as well as the drafts of the essays themselves to discuss the maternal. Ironically, in a collection on motherhood, some essays seemed to veer away from the topic. Given the scholarly work on motherhood and popular culture, we conclude that there seems to be a resistance to making any general statements about motherhood, perhaps because we have been so conditioned by our cultural expectations regarding motherhood—there is only one way to think of mother and that is favorably, a "natural" outgrowth of our connection to the maternal. Of course, intellectually we know that this is not true; we know that our understanding of motherhood is culturally defined and influenced by our media. And yet, it was remarkable that as the drafts of the essays began to appear, many of them began examining motherhood in particular areas, but then neglected to examine the mother at all. Upon revision, of course, the focus returned, but it seemed as if the topic itself was more challenging than others. Or, as in popular culture, the mother in these essays appeared on the surface and then disappeared. *Mommy Angst* will hopefully resurrect the maternal for many readers, as well.

Though Warner is correct in concluding that motherhood and the cultural expectations regarding this feminine role have changed little, she and other authors admit that there are differences between motherhood in the 1950s and motherhood in contemporary America. In the recent elections cycles, for example, more and more women are proudly showing off their motherhood credentials. In a recent column in the *New York Times Magazine*, Lisa Belkin defends Caroline Kennedy's bid for a New York senatorial appointment in maternal terms, noting that she served on important boards, wrote several books, and raised money for New York schools, while she was on what society calls a "mom sabbatical."[12]

In what can only be an appeal to the Puritan work ethic that founded this country, Belkin shows that Kennedy's maternal work has value in terms of running for political office. Motherhood is not ethereal; it has its practical uses. Motherhood is utilitarian. Of course, every mother who has taken a "mom sabbatical" knows, leaving the workforce, but not really leaving the workforce has a high cost. As Anne Crittenden notes, "social policy does little to insure these risks [poverty] or reward mothers for their economic contribution [child rearing]. Nannies earn Social Security credits; mothers do not. They earn a zero for every year they spend caring for family members. This means motherhood is the single biggest risk factor for poverty in old age."[13] But the fact that women are now using motherhood as a resume-builder reflects a change in culture, albeit small and, as we shall see later, such a strategy is not without its dangers.

In addition to the changes in political climate, media have changed in the last 10 to 20 years, and it is important not to underestimate the power and influence these new media have over our perceptions and expectations about motherhood. Information, images, symbols, and icons are streamed overnight, beamed into our homes, and sent to our BlackBerries at an amazing rate and speed. Further, given the fact that more mothers are working than ever before, it seems important to examine the maternal images that bombard the culture, which depict and idealize stay-at-home moms. According to Warner, the "mommy mystique," the cultural belief that women are totally responsible for their children, their happiness, their everything, depletes women so that "we have little left for ourselves. And whatever anger we might otherwise feel—at society, at our husbands, at the experts that led us to this pass—is directed, also, just at ourselves. Or at the one permissible target: other mothers."[14] Consequently, it is time to examine motherhood and its representations in the twenty-first century, perhaps with the hopes of making American culture more supportive of mothers.

Katherine N. Kinnick's chapter "Media Morality Tales and the Politics of Motherhood" examines representations of mothers in contemporary culture, with an appropriate nod in the direction of mother-media pioneers like Donna Reed and June Cleaver. According to Kinnick, media moms are more than sheer entertainment; their representation dictates public policy and "workplace practices." Though there is a great deal more diversity to maternal representation on television than in the 1950s, Kinnick demonstrates that many are "remarkably similar, reinforcing the same 'morals,' lessons, and stock characterizations." Specifically, media representations still idealize motherhood as the sole raison d'être for female existence, pit bad mothers against good ones, and continue to reinforce the view that maternal problems are personal, not social or political problems.

Marjorie Worthington's "The Motherless 'Disney Princess': Marketing Mothers out of the Picture" illustrates similar findings—mothers are still represented traditionally. Here, however, not only are the mothers absent, virtually erased, the princesses, the supposed stars of the Disney films, are also denied personal identity and power. Using the relatively new marketing practice of "bundling," Disney makes all princesses identical, thereby erasing any difference. Worthington analyzes Disney's new marketing strategy and shows that not only does bundling increase profits, it also increases problems for girls and their mothers—discouraging female friendship and bonding, as well as disallowing mothers as trustworthy allies. She then addresses the phenomenon of "chastity balls," finding that just like Disney, chastity balls reinforce the idea that mothers cannot be trusted to raise their daughters on their own.

Similarly, Manuel Martínez's "Motherhood, Memory, and Mambo: The Case of the Missing Cuban American Mother in Contemporary American Popular Culture" examines the phenomenon of absentee mothers in Cuban American literature. The representation is ambivalent at best. He establishes the tendency of novels and television shows to idealize the Cuban homeland as maternal. The maternal, then, would appear to be a positive force, but not so. When it comes to the female characters in Cuban American pop culture, the mothers are either absent or marginalized.

Craig N. Owens examines the hyper-mother, the mother who exists too much. His essay presents the darker side of maternal representation, arguing that the mother/mother-in-law has become the monster of contemporary culture on the level of a medieval creature in "Of Mamothers and Behemothers-in-Law: Toward a Twenty-First-Century Bestiary." Using the work of Kristeva and Foucault, Owens specifically analyzes the 2005 film *Monster-in-Law* to show the cultural maternal stereotypes and how they work in contemporary culture.

In "Killer Instincts: Motherhood and Violence in *The Long Kiss Goodnight* and *Kill Bill*," Angela Dancey examines the idealized vision of motherhood and violence in the two Tarantino films. She notes, "as violent professional killers who are also mothers, these warrior moms incorporate social roles that are culturally and ideologically incompatible.

Through this exaggerated incongruity, each film attempts to negotiate the cultural anxiety surrounding motherhood and career through the typically masculinized framework of the action genre." She finds that despite being a warrior-mom, the mother-child relationship is presented as a "natural one." Further, once mother and child are bonded, the maternal tames the violent behavior of the heroine.

The "hip mama" syndrome is represented in Robin Silbergleid's "Hip Mamas: *Gilmore Girls* and Ariel Gore." Silbergleid illustrates the ambivalent messages of both the works. Both present teenage pregnancy as a feminist triumph—independent, young women, rearing their own children, overcoming adversity and patriarchal oppression on their own. It appears that these "hip mamas" are now the feminist icon, but as Silbergleid's chapter shows, things are not always what they seem. Teenage pregnancy may be "hip" but only if you are white and wealthy.

Ann C. Hall's essay, "Running the Home, House, and Senate: Political Moms Pelosi, Clinton, and Palin," examines the way in which female politicians use motherhood as a criterion for elected office. Nancy Pelosi, Hillary Clinton, and Sarah Palin all played the motherhood card differently, but by examining their campaigns and their media coverage, it is clear that while women may use maternity, they must do so with care. Americans are still very conflicted over working mothers, particularly if they are in positions of incredible power. Hall finds that despite the powerful positions, Americans expect political moms to take care of the home front first.

Mardia J. Bishop's "The Mommy Lift: Cutting Mothers Down to Size" examines the anxiety mothers feel over their post-baby bodies and the latest acceptable cultural practice associated with manipulating the body— the "mommy lift." She argues that this cosmetic surgical procedure serves as a cultural symbol for the role of women, particularly mothers —they are creatures that must be nipped, tucked, and snipped into submission—literally cut down to size. She concludes with an economic perspective, encouraging a new economy that is not based on the physical downsizing of women.

Alina Bennett offers a provocative look at maternity in "The Bioethics of Designing 'Disabled' Babies." She demonstrates that American culture is an "ableist" culture, one that disadvantages the disabled. Disabled mothers, then, are pressured to produce, if at all, nondisabled babies. Her chapter examines the possibility and implications of affording the disabled the opportunity to introduce their own disability into their child's genetic profile. Her chapter clearly demonstrates that reproductive, technological innovations have the potential to make biological motherhood obsolete.

Kathleen L. Riley's " 'Real' Motherhood: Changing Perceptions of Adoption in American History" offers a more traditional but no less controversial approach to reproduction by examining the changing perceptions of adoption in American culture. She shows that in the past, expectations regarding motherhood were so specific that even adoptive mothers in American culture were considered "second best," not the "real thing." Thankfully, recent trends are focusing on "what satisfaction mothers have 'found' in the search for their children, as opposed to what may have been 'lost' along the way." There is still a great deal of anxiety over the authenticity of adoptive mothering. Riley demonstrates that children, as well as adoptive mothers, must reconcile their relationship in the shadow of the "real," therefore "better," biological mother perpetuated by culture and media.

Dennis Hall's "Moms.Com" clearly illustrates the high level of anxiety associated with motherhood by the sheer volume, diversity, content, and overwhelming presence of "mom" on the Internet, as well as the "marketability" of moms. Addressing nearly every eventuality, the Internet sites are there to serve, answer, and support. But many are also there to encourage people to buy, thereby highlighting the consumer culture associated with motherhood. He concludes the essay with a close analysis of a particular and local set of Internet sites.

Jessica Prinz's "Jewish Mothers: Types, Stereotypes, and Countertypes" offers an extensive look at the Jewish mother in American culture. She includes jokes, literature, poetry, and film, paying particular attention to the following works: *Maus*, *A Call to Remember*, *A Secret*, and *Mother Economy*. She observes that "widely divergent views somehow co-exist: the stereotypes established in jokes and the countertypes conveyed in more complex and serious works of literature and art." She concludes that sometimes Jewish mothers represent American culture, and sometimes they interrogate American culture, but whatever the case, in reality or in fiction, "these female character[s] . . . deserve our ongoing attention, and perhaps, also, admiration."

These chapters, then, illustrate that there is a great deal of ambivalence regarding maternity on a variety of levels. On the Internet, in film, in television, in novels, in politics, and in the operating room, mothers pose a problem for our culture. It is our hope that the essays will also provoke and promote some anxiety regarding our culture's relationship to motherhood, both figurative and literal. That is, the American cultural tendency to praise the maternal in theory but abuse it in practice. We hope that this anxiety will lead to some change and a less ambivalent relationship to mothers in American culture.

NOTES

1. E. Ann Kaplan, *Motherhood and Representation: The Mother in Popular Culture and Melodrama* (New York: Routledge, 1992).

2. Lauri Umansky, *Motherhood Reconceived: Feminism and the Legacies of the Sixties* (New York: New York University Press, 1996).

3. Sharon Hays, *The Cultural Contradictions of Motherhood* (New Haven, CT: Yale University Press, 1996).

4. Ann Crittenden, *The Price of Motherhood: Why the Most Important Job in the World Is Still the Least Valued* (New York: Henry Holt, 2001).

5. Janelle S. Taylor, Linda L. Layne, and Danielle F. Wozniak, *Consuming Motherhood* (Piscataway, NJ: Rutgers University Press, 2004).

6. Neil Gilbert, *A Mother's Work: How Feminism, the Market, and Policy Shape Family Life* (New Haven, CT: Yale University Press, 2008).

7. Judith Warner, *Perfect Madness: Motherhood in the Age of Anxiety* (New York: Riverhead, 2005).

8. Joan Blades and Kristin Rowe-Finkbeiner, *The Motherhood Manifesto: What America's Moms Want and What to Do About It* (New York: Nation, 2006).

9. Gail Heidi Landsman, *Reconstructing Motherhood and Disability in the Age of "Perfect" Babies* (New York: Routledge, 2009).

10. Andrea O'Reily, ed., *Mothering, Popular Culture, and the Arts* (Toronto: Association for Research on Mothering, 2003).

11. Susan Douglas and Meredith Michaels, *The Mommy Myth: The Idealization of Motherhood and How It Has Undermined Women* (New York: Free Press, 2004), 4.

12. Lisa Belkin, "The Senator Track," *New York Times Magazine,* January 4, 2009, 9.

13. Ann Crittenden, qtd. in *The Mommy Manifesto* by Joan Blades and Kristin Rowe-Finkbeiner (New York: Nation, 2006), 4–5.

14. Warner, *Perfect Madness,* 33.

CHAPTER 1

Media Morality Tales and the Politics of Motherhood

Katherine N. Kinnick

Grab your remote and fast-forward through the decades of "Motherhood, According to TV." In the 1950s and 1960s, June Cleaver served up lemonade and cookies and vacuumed her home in heels and pearls. In the 1970s, Mary Tyler Moore gained respect in her male-dominated newsroom, but seemed to forfeit lasting love and motherhood in the bargain. In the 1980s, Clair Huxtable, Elise Keaton, and Maggie Seaver showed us moms could effortlessly juggle prestige positions as attorneys, architects, and journalists while keeping their primary focus on raising large families of polite, endearing children. In the 1990s, Martha Stewart upped the ante of the domestic arts to impossible heights that separated the truly devoted mothers from those who still purchased store-bought birthday cakes and Halloween costumes. And now it is the new millennium, where reality shows like *Wife Swap* and *Supernanny* show us moms performing poorly and the damage they are obviously doing to their sugar-guzzling, back-talking kids.

As innocuous and trivial as some media content appears on the surface, studies of entertainment and news content on television and in movies, magazines, and advertising show us that media portrayals matter. The depiction of gender roles in the media has been a major vein of media scholarship since the 1970s, establishing links between media representations and attitudes toward women and women's causes, treatment of women in the home and in the workplace, and women's own aspirations. This, of course, has implications for women's political agendas.

Young people identify the mass media as their principal source of political information and a significant influence on their political opinions.[1] But media scholars emphasize that political discourse is found not just in the expected places—in the news and opinion pages and politically focused media like talk radio and *Meet the Press*—but in entertainment programming and advertising.[2] By what all of these media choose to emphasize and valorize, as well as what they leave out, media play a profoundly important role in constructing societal norms and expectations for women at all stages of their lives. This chapter examines the predominant cultural narratives about motherhood told by American media, and their implications for public policies and workplace practices impact not just mothers, but children, families, and the greater society.

In the years since the women's rights movement of the 1960s, American women have made undeniable progress in achieving greater parity with men educationally, occupationally, and economically, as well as in personal relationships. Although "soccer moms" gained notoriety as an influential "new" voting bloc in the U.S. presidential campaign of 2000, women have long been the majority of voters, exceeding the number of male voters in every presidential election since 1964.[3] Nevertheless, the political priorities of women and mothers, such as paid maternity leaves, affordable, quality child care, and family-friendly policies in the workplace, have yet to become national priorities. The last child care bill approved by Congress was vetoed by President Richard Nixon in 1971. It is no secret that women remain a small percentage of elected officials, and as of 2008, only one U.S. Supreme Court justice was female. Despite the history-making 2008 democratic presidential candidacies of Hillary Clinton and Barack Obama, two candidates whose own life stories should have sensitized them to women's issues, with the exception of universal health care, very little attention was paid to issues of concern to women by any of the presidential candidates or the media. Governor Sarah Palin, a surprise choice for the Republican vice-presidential candidate, stood out for her novelty as a working mother of five. Yet, working mothers, who constitute 60 percent of all mothers and 38 percent of the U.S. workforce,[4] continue to be viewed by some campaign planners and government officials as a narrow special interest group, not as the majority of women.

Since the 1980s, the expanded media offerings made possible through cable and satellite television and niche magazine publishing have meant that the stories told by the media about motherhood have become more ideologically diverse from the days of Donna Reed and June Cleaver. Some genres, networks, and particular shows lean toward portrayals that are sympathetic toward liberal or feminist views, and others idealize traditional, conservative values. For example, *ER*, *NYPD Blue*, and *Law & Order* have been categorized as "progressive" dramas, whose story lines show women working as equals or superior to men, although sometimes struggling with gender-related issues in the home and workplace. Conversely, "traditional" dramas, including *Touched by an Angel*, *Walker, Texas Ranger*, and *Dr. Quinn, Medicine Woman*, emphasize women in the home rather than the workplace and in nurturing roles.[5] Other examples of media with traditional takes on motherhood include Dr. Laura Schlessinger's syndicated radio advice show, which she begins with the mantra "I am my kid's mom"; mothering magazines, including *Parents* and *American Baby*; and the many childbirth and child-rearing reality shows on cable TV, like TLC network's *A Baby Story*, featuring a different couple's trip to the delivery room each week. Hit shows that valorize large families include TLC's enormously popular *Jon & Kate Plus Eight* and the Discovery Health Channel's *18 Kids and Counting*, documenting the Duggars, an Arkansas family who had their eighteenth child in December 2008. Of course, the proliferation of Internet blogs and Web sites offers something for everyone at every point in the ideological spectrum—from homeschooling moms to stay-at-home dads and gay couples raising children.

Despite this greater diversity in media offerings from years past, media scholarship continues to provide evidence that the stories told by mainstream television, movies, magazines, and advertising are remarkably similar, reinforcing the same "morals," lessons, and stock characterizations.[6] This chapter focuses on the predominant stories told about motherhood, repeated in various forms, across a wide variety of media channels. Unfortunately, there is much in these stories that serves to undermine women's power and progress. First, the media idealize and glamorize motherhood as the one path to fulfillment for women, painting a rosy, Hallmark-card picture that ignores or minimizes the very real challenges that come along with parenthood. Second, media narratives often cast motherhood in moral terms, juxtaposing the "good mother" with the "bad mother," who frequently is a working mom, a lower-income mom, or someone who does not conform to traditional gender roles of behavior, ambition, or sexual orientation. Third, media frame the issues, suggesting how the public should think about them. In particular, by focusing on the individual level rather than the societal level, media stories frame problems facing mothers as "personal problems" rather than problems needing systemic, public policy solutions. Occasionally, women turn the tables on media and effectively draw on their status as mothers to bring attention to political issues that would otherwise be ignored. Thus, as media scholar Todd Gitlin has argued, the stories emphasized by media are not so much a reflection of the real world, as a value-laden repackaging of it that perpetuates gender myths.[7]

LACK OF AUTHENTICITY

It may not seem like a difficult question, but ask a group of mothers "What TV mom is most like you?" and consider their choices: domestic perfectionist Bree Van De Kamp of *Desperate Housewives*, who faked a pregnancy to spare the family the humiliation of her daughter's teenage pregnancy and plans to raise the baby as her own? Nancy Botwin, the widowed soccer mom who sells pot to help make ends meet on Showtime's series *Weeds*? Kelly Carr, a somewhat bitter, wisecracking, yet deep down lonely, single mom on Fox's sitcom *Back to You*? Reality TV's Kris Kardashian Jenner, who boogies with her 20-something socialite daughters in Las Vegas on their own E! reality show, *Keeping Up with the Kardashians*? Emilio Suarez, the kindly, nurturing, always cooking for the family father on *Ugly Betty*? Oh, that's right—he is not a mom. Finding a relatable mother on television may not be so easy, but at least these female characters may make women viewers feel better about their own lives and mothering skills. Today's mother is no June Cleaver, but the emphasis on outlandish plots ignores the real dramas linking politics and motherhood, like family-work-life balance, the glass ceiling, and latchkey children.

The Myth of Easy, Breezy, Beautiful Motherhood

Lack of authenticity is an issue not just in television but in other media as well. Celebrity-focused magazines like *People* and *Us* and "news" shows like *Entertainment Tonight* and *Access Hollywood* routinely feature profiles of new celebrity mothers and their babies. Inevitably, these stories emphasize pregnant Hollywood moms "glowing" (not nauseated and swollen) and feeling sexier than ever.[8] We see over-the-top baby showers, adorable baby gifts, and designer nursery décor. Once baby arrives, we see celebrity moms back in their size two couture within weeks (remember postpartum supermodel Heidi Klum strutting the runway in bra and panties on CBS's 2005 *Victoria Secret's Fashion Show*—a prime-time special—just two months after giving birth to her second child?)

Interviews and photos of celebrity moms and their chubby-cheeked offspring paint an idealized picture of maternal bliss, with mothers declaring a new purpose and contentment, a satisfaction unmatched by fame and fortune.[9] In fact, the word "bliss" occurs repeatedly in the headlines of these stories. "Nicole & Keith's Baby Bliss!" gushed *People's* July 23, 2008, cover story about actress Nicole Kidman and her new baby.[10] Beside it on newsstands was *OK!* magazine's cover story, "Jamie Lynn's Baby Bliss!" a tad harder to believe given that it was profiling 16-year-old unwed actress Jamie Lynn Spears and her 19-year-old boyfriend.[11] While becoming a mother is certainly a transformative event for most women, media coverage depicts these transformations as nothing short of miraculous. Motherhood, according to the celebrity weeklies, instantly transforms wild-child celebutantes like Nicole Richie into devoted mothers who crave nothing more than outings in the park with baby. Angelina Jolie and the aforementioned Duggars cannot seem to get enough of babies—so more is always better.

The media fixation on celebrity moms has led many to question whether these rosy versions of motherhood have anything to do with an uptick in U.S. birth rates since 2006. The Centers for Disease Control reports that U.S. teen pregnancy rates—long the highest in the Western world—are rising again after years of decline, with one million teenage girls now becoming pregnant each year.[12] After controlling for other factors, a longitudinal study reported in *Pediatrics* found that teens at greatest risk of early sexual activity and pregnancy are those with the highest consumption of television, movies, music, and magazines.[13] In fact, it is not just teenagers having more babies. Federal data show that American women of all ages from 14 to 42 have bought into the baby boom, with the nation's birth rate increasing in 2006 and 2007 to reach the highest level since the baby boom of 1957.[14]

A rare departure from the media's overly glamorized version of motherhood aired on NBC during a brief-lived 2008 summer series. *The Baby Borrowers* challenged teen couples who thought they were ready for parenthood to care for babies, toddlers, teenagers, and the elderly, with the gleeful promo slogan: "It's not TV—it's birth control!" Media depictions of maternal bliss also mask the fact that in reality, the incidence of depression is estimated to be three to five times higher in mothers than in other populations.[15]

As children age, most *real* parents are engaged in far from glamorous daily routines of scheduling and schlepping; cajoling, bribing, and threatening; breaking up squabbles; scrubbing out stains; supervising homework; and trying to instill a taste for green vegetables. Yet television commercials and TV shows depict supermoms who do it all, trading brief-cases for babies for little black dresses as they move through their days with a bounce in their steps and perfectly coiffed hair. A major criticism of an otherwise exceptional series, *The Cosby Show* (1984–1992), was that it made parenting a large family and holding down a demanding job look effortless. Work-life balance? No problem. Who is going to be there to watch the kids when attorney mom has her big case and dad is at a medical conference? Never came up. Flextime or job sharing at work? Don't need 'em. Despite demanding careers, Clair Huxtable, as well as fellow sitcom moms Elise Keaton, an architect, and Maggie Seaver, a reporter, appeared relaxed, cheerful, playful, balanced—not to mention slender and attractive. As such, these shows fueled the myth of the super-mom: that doing it all, and doing it all with ease and style, was not only possible but was the new standard for modern moms. More so, these shows were evidence that women could do it all without accommodations from the workplace, government-sponsored social supports, or even maid services or fast food.

"Missing Mom Syndrome"

Lack of authenticity is also found in what we do not see in the media. Not just the crying babies, temper tantrums, and moody, cursing teen-agers, but sometimes, mom herself is missing. Despite the fact that the vast majority of single parents in the United States are mothers,[16] televi-sion and movie plots have more frequently focused on single fathers than single mothers.[17] The preponderance of missing mom shows harkens back to *Family Affair*, *My Three Sons*, *The Andy Griffith Show*, and *Court-ship of Eddie's Father* in the 1960s. The trend gained steam in the late 1970s and 1980s with hit sitcoms *Diff'rent Strokes*, *Full House*, and *My Two Dads*, as well as the blockbuster movie *Three Men and a Baby* (1987). Media researcher Angharad Valdivia notes that many of the single fathers in contemporary family movies are widowed or "inherit" children through unlikely circumstances (*Ghost Dad*, 1990; *Curly Sue*, 1991; *Fatherhood*, 1994).[18] Despite a few exceptions, notably television's *One Day at a Time* (1975–1984), *Grace Under Fire* (1993–1998), *Judging Amy* (1999–2005), and *Reba* (2001–2007), a single mother apparently is not enough of a "concept" to carry a show, unlike the endlessly entertain-ing fish-out-of-water tale of men struggling to perform unnatural acts of child care and housework.

The missing mom theme is also notably present in a long string of Disney movies, from classic fairy tales including *The Little Mermaid* (1989) and *Beauty and the Beast* (1991) to *A Goofy Movie* (1995), *Finding Nemo* (2003), *Herbie: Fully Loaded* (2005), *Chicken Little* (2005), and *Ratatouille* (2007), prompting a groundswell of Internet postings pondering, "What does Disney have against mothers?" [19] The trend continues today with programming targeting young viewers, including the Disney Channel's megahit series *Hannah Montana*, the CBS sitcom *Two and a Half Men*, and Dreamwork's *Kung Fu Panda* (2008).

The message, according to these media portrayals, is that mom is replaceable, but a good father is essential, and single dads who fulfill this role are heroic. This message is reinforced in magazine articles and news features profiling single fathers. A 2002 study found that television news stories about stay-at-home dads "valorize men for learning parenting skills and adapting to stay-at-home paternity," when these are things that millions of single mothers do on a daily basis without recognition or fanfare. [20]

Something else media rarely shows us is the parent who does not conform to societal norms. While thousands of gay and lesbian couples are raising children, we tend to see their stories only when a sensational custody case or legal challenge arises, not in the everyday circumstances of raising a family. For many Americans, whose only opportunity to observe these households is through the media, the absence of such images perpetuates stereotypes, negates the real struggles of these families, and ensures that issues do not rise to the top of the public policy agenda. What the media does not show us may be just as important as what it does.

CAUTIONARY TALES

Career women, beware: working may be hazardous to your relationships. Media morality tales frequently suggest dire outcomes for women who decide to climb the corporate ladder rather than focus on marriage and motherhood.

Career Women Sacrifice Personal Happiness

One of the oft-repeated "morals of the story" is that career-focused women pay a price: in this formula, career success means negative impact on family and romance. Women in prestige positions, like news anchor Murphy Brown and attorney Ally McBeal, reach the top only to find that they are lonely and unfulfilled, in a way that can only be resolved by having a baby, husband or not. Openly ambitious women are often portrayed as villainous ice queens and dragon ladies: Alexis Carrington on *Dynasty* (1988–1989), Rosalind Shays on *L.A. Law* (1986–1994), Julie Cooper on *The OC* (2003–2007), Wilhelmina Slater on *Ugly Betty* (2007–present)—if not murderous psychos—Glenn Close's character, Alex, in the film *Fatal Attraction* (1987). Middle-class working women, like Mary Tyler Moore (1970–1977), Laverne and Shirley (1976–1983), and later, Elaine on *Seinfeld* (1989–1998), also struggle to find romance. This theme is repeated in magazines and news coverage. Magazine articles targeting working mothers often underscore work as a threat to family relationships, with headlines like, "Don't let work get between you and your marriage." [21] Kaplan's 1990 content analysis of images of mothers in women's magazines found that photos gave the impression that careers were antithetical to motherhood, with women pictured as either mothers or as career women, but rarely both.[22] *Backlash* author Susan Faludi cites a 1986 ABC News Special Report, "After the Sexual Revolution," that mentioned the "costs" and the "price" of feminism, particularly referring to working women, 13 times.[23] "The more women achieve in their careers, the higher their chances for divorce," warned host Richard Threlkeld.[24]

Career Women Face an Uphill Struggle

Of all 1997 popular magazine articles dealing with working mothers, more were negative than positive, focusing on problems of working women, including those related to child care, work-life balance, and demanding workplaces.[25] When women are shown as career-focused (as opposed to Clair Huxtable's family focus, in spite of her career), as in dramas like *ER*, *Law & Order*, and *NYPD Blue*, story lines often portray many of the realistic difficulties faced by women in male-dominated workplaces, such as fighting to be treated as an equal or to gain the respect of male subordinates.[26] These narratives have both positive and negative consequences. Seeing characters we care about confront problems facing working women helps to humanize these issues and emphasize the personal impact of public and workplace policies. Research suggests these dramatizations may lead to greater opinion change than overt political content, such as reading an editorial on a topic.[27] On the other hand, repeatedly witnessing working women's trials and tribulations and sexist or hostile work environments certainly is not an appealing advertisement for women weighing a career track versus motherhood, particularly one in a male-dominated environment. If the struggle is that difficult, why put yourself through it?

DEFINING THE "GOOD" MOTHER

Both entertainment and news media narratives frequently cast mother-hood in moral terms, contrasting the "good" mother with the "bad" mother, and thus both prescribing and proscribing norms for maternal behavior.[28] The good mother, the noble mother-saint, makes her family her highest priority, continually sacrifices her own interests for the good of her family, and conforms to expected gender roles of femininity. The bad mother (and frequently, the single woman who cannot find a husband to become a mother) is depicted as self-centered, neglectful, preoccupied with career, or lacking in traditional femininity. We see the ideal of the nobility of motherhood emphasized in television dramas featuring female characters in domestic, caregiving roles, like *Touched by an Angel* (1994–2003) and *Dr. Quinn, Medicine Woman* (1993–1998).[29] Media experts Holbert, Shah, and Kwak found these shows are often set in the American heartland and emphasize religious themes. In contrast, career women are most often found in urban dramas set in traditionally male-dominated environments: law offices, hospitals, police departments. View-ership studies of these shows reveal political implications. There is evidence that viewers selectively choose to watch the programming that fits with their own ideological preferences (selective exposure theory) and that this programming further reinforces their preexisting beliefs and values. Holbert, Shah, and Kwak found that viewers of traditional dramas like *Touched by an Angel* were less likely to support women's rights than those who viewed urban dramas featuring professional women.[30]

The "family values" rhetoric of the 1990s contributed to the delinea-tion of a moral hierarchy for mothers. As the dissolution of the family through out-of-wedlock births and high divorce rates was pinpointed as the cause of a multitude of domestic problems and the moral decline of America, stay-at-home mothers in male-headed nuclear families cemented their position at the top of the hierarchy as "good" mothers. Working mothers, whose numbers had swelled by 40 percent between 1985 and 2005, clearly, were part of the problem.[31] But worse were will-fully single mothers, like television's Murphy Brown (1988–1998), who chose to become mothers outside the confines of marriage, what author Jane Mattes calls SMC—Single Mothers by Choice.[32] As then-Vice President Dan Quayle famously pointed out in 1992, these mothers' "lifestyle choices" were different from the sympathetic characters who became single mothers through the death or desertion of their husbands, as seen, for instance, on *The Partridge Family*. Near the bottom of the hierarchy are mothers we see most frequently in news stories, rather than entertainment media. Here we find the single welfare mother. Unlike middle-class stay-at-home moms, welfare mothers who do not work are not viewed as noble for staying home with their children, but as lazy and irresponsible for their reliance on the public dole in order to support their children. A highly publicized example of a mother falling into this category is Nadya Suleman, the California woman dubbed "Octomom" after giving birth to octuplets in 2008, bringing her total number of children to 14. Rather than being embraced by the media and diaper companies like the McCaughey septuplets and other multiple-birth families before her, the single woman with a sketchy employment history and an anonymous sperm donor was lambasted by the press as morally, and perhaps mentally, bankrupt. Race and gender often intertwine in these stories. Social policy scholars James Avery and Mark Peffley found that African American mothers were overrepresented as welfare recipients in negatively toned stories that depicted welfare reform efforts as a failure. Subjects who read these stories tended to blame the mother and favor stringent eligibility limitations.[33] Occupying the bottom rung of the hierarchy are mothers who murder or abuse their children, or who allow such acts to occur.

"Good" Working Mothers Always Stay Focused on Family

Media portrayals reveal a culture deeply conflicted about working mothers. As Generation X daughters were told, "you can do anything you want to do!" and encouraged to go to college, professional women became more visible on television in the 1980s. But in order to keep a character who is a working mother out of the "bad mother" zone, television shows made clear that her top priority is her family, even if she is a professional woman with a demanding career. Thus, we rarely saw corporate attorney Clair Huxtable or architect Elise Keaton at work, let alone bringing work home.[34] Their careers were more akin to props than central plot devices and did not distract them from their primary focus on their families. In film, Valdivia notes that the "good" single mom (the one who did not become that way by choice and lovingly sacrifices for her children) often is rewarded at the film's end with a man who falls in love with her and her children, as in *Jerry McGuire* (1996), and promises to restore the traditional nuclear family.[35] Even celebrity moms seem to know that the politically correct way to handle interview questions about juggling work and home is to emphasize that they are either taking time off from Hollywood or bringing their babies with them to the set. These depictions of working women whose primary focus is on their children maintain the image of the noble, self-sacrificing mother, but at the same time, contribute to a cultural bias against real women seeking employment or promotions. Employers may question whether a mother will be willing or able to give 100 percent to the job, the way a man presumably would.

Pity the high-profile mother who does not conform to this family-is-my-priority model. When attorney Cherie Blair, wife of former British Prime Minister Tony Blair, continued to work after giving birth to her third child in 2000, she was blasted in the British press as a bad mother. "Cherie Blair 'bad role model,'" proclaimed a BBC News headline.[36] Similarly, Hillary Clinton has had to defend her choice to remain active in political affairs after becoming a mother, leading to her infamous statement on ABC News' *Nightline*, "Well, I could have stayed home and baked cookies and had teas," which, of course, angered all the women who had chosen to do exactly that.[37] By contrast, Barbara Bush and Laura Bush, two of the most popular first ladies of recent times (both more popular than their husbands in national polls),[38] adhered to traditional mother-wife roles and kept their political opinions to themselves.

In the 2008 U.S. presidential election, it is noteworthy that both Democratic candidate Barack Obama and Republican vice-presidential candidate Sarah Palin paraded their children on stage at every televised opportunity. Parenthood was used as a strategy by both sides to relate to the average American family. A biographical video about Michelle Obama was produced by the Obama campaign and aired nationally before her speech to the Democratic National Convention. It emphasized her role as a mother, while glaringly omitting her impressive professional accomplishments. Thus we learned that "The last thing I think about before I go to bed at night and the first thing I think about when I wake up in the morning is these girls," but not that she earned degrees from Princeton University and Harvard Law School. While the Obama campaign was proving that race no longer matters, the Michelle Obama video was a crushing blow to many educated professional women that said loud and clear, if you are a woman, motherhood is *all* that matters. Politically, it was also likely a strategy to ensure that Mrs. Obama would not be cast in the same mold as fellow female attorney Hillary Clinton, whose open ambition drew parallels in the public mind to television's scheming— and dangerously intelligent—villainesses.

For her part, Sarah Palin called to mind the perky supermoms of 1980s TV, assuring us that handling five kids and a vice-presidential career would be a piece of cake; yet begging the question, "if she's really a good mom who puts family first, how can she carry out the unrelenting duties of the second in command?'' In an otherwise historic election, the experience of these women shows that the pressure on American women to conform to traditional stereotypes has not abated. Whether Democrat or Republican, liberal or conservative, a desire for the political spotlight must still be defended with the familiar refrain of the "good mother," assuring the American public that family will always come first.

Good Mothers Embrace Domesticity

Conforming to traditional gender roles is central to the media construction of the good mother. Cooking and cleaning are embraced by good mothers, even those who work outside the home. Mothers who fail to embrace the cult of domesticity, as seen in *Roseanne* (1988–1997) and in *Married with Children*'s (1987–1997) Peg Bundy, derived much of their humor by flaunting a shocking lack of interest in domestic duties. As modern conveniences and prepackaged foods have made household chores easier than ever for American mothers, the rise of Martha Stewart's magazine, television, and mail-order empire suggested easy was not good enough. The renewed interest in the domestic arts reflected a cultural idealization of the 1950s, consistent with "family values" rhetoric, while at the same time elevating domesticity to a competitive art form that would allow affluent mothers to showcase talents that lesser mothers would never achieve. Currently, the ABC reality show *Wife Swap* repeatedly juxtaposes women who refuse to do housework, relegating it to their children and husbands, with more traditional mothers. It is often clear from these narratives who the "good" mother is, and who is lazy, spoiled, and warping her children.

There is evidence that the media's emphasis on women's identities as mothers and homemakers, rather than professionals, experts, or leaders, does impact young women's aspirations. One such study found that the professional status portrayed by female actors in 1980s television commercials influenced the career achievement goals of female college students.[39] The authors found that viewing sex-stereotyped commercials depicting cooking, cleaning, and child care caused college women to emphasize homemaking in descriptions of their long-term aspirations. Women who saw reversed-sex role commercials were more likely to emphasize independence and career-related goals. More recent experimental research with college students in 2004 confirms that exposure to stereotypic commercials reduces women's likelihood of choosing leadership positions when given actual group tasks. Female subjects who saw gender stereotypic commercials were more likely to choose support roles than leadership roles when given a choice in a group task, and to predict domestic rather than professional roles for themselves in the future.[40]

MEDIA SPIN AND POLITICAL SETBACKS

News media are critical not just in bringing issues to our attention, but in framing *how* the public, not to mention our bosses, government agency heads, and elected officials, thinks about them. In *Backlash*, Susan Faludi makes the important point that media framing is *not* a vast conspiracy. Rather, "like any large institution, [the news media's] movements aren't premeditated or programmatic, just grossly susceptible to the prevailing political currents." [41] She notes that the press "acted as a force that swept the general public, powerfully shaping the way people would think and talk about the feminist legacy," and coined terms like "the man shortage," "the biological clock," "the mommy track," and "postfeminism." [42]

Choosy Mothers Choose to Stay Home

An important example of media framing is found in how media have covered the phenomenon of well-educated, professional women who leave lucrative careers to become stay-at-home moms, what media researcher Mary Douglas Vavrus calls "opting out." [43] Vavrus's analysis of news stories, from a seminal 2003 *New York Times Magazine* cover story to subsequent cover stories in *Time*, in *Fortune*, and on *60 Minutes* and *The Today Show,* as well as local news outlets, found that the stories emphasized personal fulfillment and the "tug of motherhood" as the reason for leaving the workplace. Ignored were structural issues such as the expense of child care, demanding workplaces marked by inflexibility, insistence on 24/7 accessibility as well as "face time" in the office, 60-hour workweeks, and gender discrimination against mothers in wages and advancement. The rhetoric of personal choice, long a pillar of women's movement ideology, is co-opted by these stories' headlines: The *New York Times Magazine* asks, "Why don't women run the world? Maybe it's because they don't want to." [44] The *Fortune* article, entitled, "Power: Do Women Really Want It?" notes that "Apparently it's not that women can't get high-level jobs. Rather they're choosing not to." [45] The *Chicago Sun-Times*'s headline: "Is the 'Glass Ceiling' a Matter of Choice?" [46]

In framing the decision to stay home as a choice, these stories negate the reality of mothers who essentially were pushed out, were reluctantly sacrificing their careers, were "satisficing" to make the best of their situations, or who simply said, "Take this job and shove it!" Vavrus notes that the question of whether a father or mother should stay home with children indeed is rarely a "choice." Rather, because of the wage gap, the practical decision is nearly always that "the mother's smaller salary is sacrificed since it would go largely—if not entirely—to paying for childcare." [47]

A point that Vavrus's analysis overlooks is that the cultural pressure to be perceived as a "good" mother may lead mothers to emphasize to reporters the politically correct reason for staying home (for the love of baby) rather than acknowledging that a career was not all it was cracked up to be or that they lacked the political clout in the office to negotiate work-life accommodations. In addition, while having a professional career was a symbol of glamour for young women in the 1980s, today, for many women, stay-at-home motherhood has become the new status symbol—indicative of both financial success (my husband makes enough that I can stay home!) and the truly devoted mother. Called "neotraditionalists," [48] these largely affluent mothers have helped shift the focus of the modern family to the children, ushering in a new era of consumerism and "intensive mothering" [49] to meet the child's every need. Businesses unheard of 30 years ago, from Baby Einstein infant videos to Kindermusik and tutoring franchises to Gymboree exercise studios for toddlers, have morphed into multimillion dollar empires. When working mothers who do not have the luxury of quitting compare themselves to this new superclass of stay-at-home moms, they may develop an inferiority complex. In a recent survey by the Pew Research Center, mothers who worked full time rated themselves lower on the question, "How good a job do you feel you've done so far as a parent?" than mothers who worked part time or who stayed home.[50] Since the opting out stories first made headlines in 2003, the number of women in the workforce has fallen to its lowest point since 1996. Today's economists now suggest that the media-framed story of women choosing to opt out probably (oops!) was less a factor in the national statistics than a declining economy.[51] The political damage, however, and the personal damage to ever more guilt-wracked working mothers, was done.

Feminism Is No Longer Needed

On a personal level, when women tell others that they have chosen to quit their jobs because they want to stay home with their children, they are able to save face, suggesting empowerment and control over this decision, while keeping their explanations in the realm of the positive—even evoking envy—and maintaining the image of the "good" devoted mother. On the other hand, saying that you are quitting because you just could not make career and motherhood work may be interpreted by others as a personal failure—you could not cut it—you are not the superwoman you once presented yourself to be. The downside of these personal narratives is that they let the real villains—corporate inflexibility and discrimination against mothers—off the hook.

On the larger political level, the media's framing of the opting-out movement as a choice suggests that the feminist movement and affirmative action politics are no longer necessary. The reason there are fewer women at the top or in the highest paying careers is not that there is discrimination or a glass ceiling, but that women are choosing not to pursue them. Furthermore, the logic goes, if the most talented, highly educated women choose not to climb the corporate ladder, then clearly, staying home must be the best choice for all women who can afford to do so. Since women *can* reach the top if they really want to—just ask all 13 women heading Fortune 500 companies[52]—feminism is a moot point. Not helping matters is that feminism has been depicted in popular culture as antithetical to feminine qualities. Women's studies professors routinely commiserate that feminism has become a new "F-word" among college students, who are loathe to call themselves feminists, even if they support the movement's ideals.

Motherhood Issues Are Personal, Not Political

One of the more troublesome tendencies of media is to treat concerns of women as personal, rather than political, problems. Having trouble with sexual harassment at work? Watch how you dress. Can't take time off when your child is sick? Be creative! Find a faux grandparent in the neighborhood. Stressed out? One women's magazine headline from 1999 offered a solution: "The Healing Power of Housework. Stressed out? On the edge? About to lose it? Do a load of laundry." [53] The advice is never to lobby employers to redesign corporate policies stuck in the 1950s. *Working Mother* magazine's long-running monthly feature "How She Does It" profiles the personal career paths of successful women, but maddeningly keeps the focus on women who have managed to succeed *despite* the system, rather than those who demonstrate that women can *change* the system.

Vavrus contends that because mothers' dilemmas are presented as personal, they are not linked to larger social issues or the well-being of society as a whole, "making a systemic solution unlikely." [54] "Decisions about mothering have public, long-range consequences," she notes,[55] yet while women ought to be advocating public policy (yearlong maternity leaves, anyone?) the dominant narrative in media suggests that taking on the status quo is futile, so why not just change yourself instead? Content analyses of leading women's magazines find that the only sphere of influence for women consistently emphasized in women's magazines is the home. Among the issues to get the least attention are the economy, global conflict, poverty, the environment, and media practices themselves.[56]

WHAT MEDIA DO NOT TELL YOU CAN HURT YOU

In addition to framing how the public thinks about motherhood issues, what is not covered in the press ensures that these issues will be relegated to the political back burner. Some of the biggest public policy stories for mothers that media are not covering include the following.

Maternal Profiling

Contrary to popular belief, there is no federal prohibition on asking about marital or family status in job interviews. Only 22 states and Puerto Rico specifically prohibit employers from inquiring about applicants' marital status.[57] In a 2007 editorial, the *Media Report to Women* noted, "The ability of employers to discriminate against working mothers without penalty in many states should be a big, big news story," but it remains in obscurity.[58]

Even if employers do not ask about family status, evidence suggests that inadvertently disclosing it in the hiring process may be the kiss of death for mothers, but not for fathers. In a revealing 2007 study, Cornell University sociologists used pairs of fictitious resumes of ideal job applicants, varying only parental status, to determine if mothers were being discriminated against in the hiring process. Half the resumes revealed parental status through a single, seemingly innocuous line: "Officer, Parent-Teacher Association," and a cover letter that indicated that "I am relocating with my family." In the first phase of the study, evaluators reviewing the resumes rated applicants who were mothers as less competent and committed, and recommended nearly $12,000 less in starting pay than for women who were not mothers. In phase two of the study, the resumes were tested in the real world, sent to a real employer found through the classified ads. Non-mothers were twice as likely to receive call-backs as mothers.[59] According to the authors, these findings reflect the incompatibility of cultural norms for mothering that "prioritize meeting the needs of children above all other activities" and the norm of the "ideal worker," who should be unencumbered by competing demands.[60] It is noteworthy, however, that no negative effects were found for the fictitious fathers in the study. In fact, fathers were rated as being more committed to work than non-fathers and were recommended for the highest starting salaries of all.[61]

The media has largely ignored maternal profiling, as well as a new legal term, family responsibility discrimination, despite a 400 percent increase in family responsibility discrimination lawsuits since the mid-1990s.[62] The University of California's Center for WorkLife Law notes that workplace discrimination against mothers is so common that the glass ceiling should really be called "the maternal wall."[63]

The Experience of Low-Income Parents

Media stories tend to reflect the biases of their middle-class authors, and to target the middle- to upper-income parents who can afford to buy the products of advertisers. Media stories thus often focus on dilemmas related to choice and consumption (the news weeklies' annual "how to choose the best college" issues, women's magazine tips for "12 enriching vacation destinations for your child this summer"). Conversely, media tend to ignore the challenges experienced by millions of working-class parents, who are the least likely to work for firms with family-friendly options[64] and for whom child care is the fourth largest household expense after housing, food, and taxes.[65] So rather than planning an educational vacation trip, these parents are worrying about issues that do not appear in the media, like how to find part-time or weekend child care, or how to cobble together and pay for summer care for school-aged children from summer camps, church programs, and grandma.[66] Low-income parents have the most to gain from political solutions, like guaranteed paid maternity leave or a nationally regulated and federally subsidized child care system, but these concerns rarely receive the media spotlight or are "humanized" in the way that the trials and tribulations of professional women are in television's hospital and legal dramas.

The Political Possibilities

Perhaps mothers would be more likely to press for political solutions and institutional changes in the workplace if they knew what the possibilities were. But with little in-depth or sustained media attention given to commonsense proposals offered by think tanks and women's groups in this country, or solutions that are working in other parts of the world, American families are kept uninformed and disempowered, and the business community is not challenged to change the status quo. Among the proposals not getting coverage are the following:[67]

- Allowing new mothers without paid maternity leaves to receive unemployment benefits while they are out with baby
- Banning new credit cards or mortgages for parents delinquent in child support payments
- Allowing hourly workers to choose to be compensated for overtime in the form of time off, instead of extra pay
- Eliminating state and local taxes on children's necessities, like diapers, school supplies, and car seats
- Allowing workers to use sick leave to care for an ill child, partner, or parent (as is available now in California)
- Offering tax incentives to employers for family-friendly policies such as benefits for part-time workers and flexible working hours
- Enacting a federal law to give employees three days annual paid leave to attend to family needs, like children's doctor's appointments and teacher conferences
- Reforming the marriage penalty tax that taxes married couples at a higher level than two single people with the same income
- Encouraging schools to provide affordable afterschool care to better match the hours of the workday
- Providing tax deductions to offset college costs
- Expanding free or subsidized prekindergarten programs
- Encouraging employers to create "on-ramps" to make it easier for women to return to the workplace after time off for family care

The media are doing a poor job of showing the business community that "job flexibility for working parents reduces costs, not raises them," says *Media Report to Women* editor Sheila Gibbons. "Evidence keeps mounting that working mothers are at the breaking point because businesses fail to grasp that acceptance of working mothers and flexibility for them reduces costs, not raises them. The tension between stressed-out working mothers and wary business executives persists in part because influential media are not delivering the information about the upside often enough." [68]

The news media and business press also give short shrift to stories that put U.S. policies into global perspective. While Americans may be generally aware that things are better for mothers in Scandinavian countries, they may not be aware of how far the United States has slipped away from the pack as other countries have responded to mothers' needs. Thus we are not informed of the extravagant possibilities (Sweden's yearlong leave for new mothers at *90 percent* pay; the Netherlands' law requiring that part-time workers be paid at the same hourly rate as full-time workers, allowing many mothers to scale back their work hours; Denmark's publicly financed preschools, serving 95 percent of three- to six-year-olds;[69] Argentina's [and 11 other South American countries'] gender quota law, requiring 30 percent of congressional candidates put forward by their political parties to be women[70]). Nor are we told that the United States and Australia are the only industrialized counties that do not guarantee paid maternity leave, or that even smaller, poorer nations are surpassing us—Brazil and Kenya give workers 12 and 8 weeks of paid maternity leave, respectively.[71] We are not informed that, over the past three decades, government regulations of the workweek in most industrialized nations have caused average annual work hours to fall substantially—except in the United States, where average annual work hours now exceed even Japan's, and the issue has never been seriously debated as a solution to work-family balance.[72]

MOTHERS USING MEDIA

The politics of motherhood in the media is not just about how media represent mothers. Sometimes, it is about how mothers use media to pursue their own political goals. Often, these mothers consciously or unconsciously draw on motherhood stereotypes to make their stories more compelling to the public. It is precisely because of these stereotypes that the figure of the protesting mother has enormous symbolic power.

In patriarchal societies, the protesting mother is unexpected. She is stepping out of the private sphere into the historically masculine public sphere. She is speaking out rather than remaining quiet. Annelise Orleck, who has studied activist mothers, notes that there is a belief in many cultures that "bearing and raising children alters a woman's consciousness in an essentially conservative way, quieting and grounding even the most rebellious of women." [73] Activist mothers' violations of these gender norms command attention.

Activist mothers have inspired many noble causes, from tightening laws against drunk driving and demanding investigation into toxic waste at Love

Canal, to protesting human rights abuses in El Salvador and Argentina and deforestation in Kenya. But history also shows mothers whose activism is directed toward less noble causes. Scholar Sara Ruddick points to fervent Ku Klux Klan mothers, Nazi mothers, and homophobic mothers. "Maternal roles, identities and symbols serve them all," Ruddick notes.[74]

Many activist mothers fall into the mold of grieving mother-saint. Like Candy Lightner, founder of Mothers Against Drunk Drivers, and Beth Twitty, mother of murdered teen Natalee Holloway, who in the aftermath of her daughter's disappearance was featured nightly on CNN's *Nancy Grace* show, these mothers are often embraced by the media as they seek justice for their own children and other victims. The cultural stereotype that mothers' worlds revolve around their children (more so than men) makes them especially sympathetic spokespersons when they lose a child. Cindy Sheehan, mother of a soldier killed in the Iraq War, benefited from this public sympathy in the initial months of her antiwar campaign. President Bush's refusal to meet with her as she camped outside his Texas ranch in a 2005 publicity stunt was viewed by many as a public relations blunder. Going up against grieving mothers in the court of public opinion is rarely a winning proposition. Cultural taboos against violence toward women also mean that officials understand the worldwide negative publicity that can result if they try to forcibly remove grieving mothers from a protest site. The CoMadres of El Salvador, a group of mothers who denounced the disappearances and murders of husbands and sons during the civil war of 1981–1992, were allowed to occupy the presidential palace for four days in 1984, successfully drawing world attention to these human rights abuses. Similarly, in Argentina, the Madres of the Plaza de Mayo "literally paraded their suffering," [75] wearing photographs of missing loved ones around their necks while marching in noisy protests in Buenos Aires during the World Cup soccer tournament of 1978. They successfully drew the attention of foreign journalists to the disappearances of thousands of children during the nation's "Dirty War" of 1976–1983, and continued weekly marches on behalf of the missing until 2006.

In addition to invoking sympathy, motherhood provides credibility. Ironically, speaking "just as a mother" often carries more weight than speaking as a policy expert or a feminist leader, because it is viewed with less suspicion. In her memoir, Cold War peace activist and mother Amy Swerdlow remembers making a conscious decision to present herself as a concerned mother, rather than a political activist, because "I believed that my genuine motherly concerns would be received and understood by non-political women, the media and public officials." [76] For nearly three decades, the Madres of the Plaza de Mayo shrewdly kept their campaign independent from other political causes, because they knew that "their voices as mothers were the most powerful weapons they had for winning some measure of justice and recognition for their children's deaths." [77] By contrast, the tide of public opinion shifted against Cindy Sheehan as she increasingly appeared to step out of the "just a mom" role and present herself as an activist, aligning herself with liberal filmmaker Michael Moore and criticizing Bush's policies on issues unrelated to the Iraq war. Some media-savvy mothers' organizations in the United States coach their members to focus on their personal stories and to downplay their political roles,[78] as in, "I'm just a housewife from Topeka." As noted earlier, this strategy was employed in downplaying Michelle Obama's Ivy League credentials.

In the experience of this author and my colleague Sabrena Parton, even when mothers want to present themselves as experts, the media may ignore their credentials and focus on their identities as mothers. Early in our careers, we tried to persuade Wal-Mart to remove a misogynistic World Wrestling Federation toy from its shelves. The toy featured two burly WWF action figures packaged with a Barbie-like head in between them, with the words "HELP ME" permanently scrawled backwards across the Barbie head's forehead. The packaging featured a photograph of wrestler Al Snow holding a similar female mannequin head on a stick. When we got nowhere with local Wal-Mart managers, we brought our story to the media. While we presented ourselves as college professors with expertise on gender and media issues, our identities as mothers of young children, not as college professors, were repeatedly emphasized in national and local news stories. The research evidence we offered about pop culture's cultivation of misogyny, and even statistics on domestic violence, rarely made it into the stories, except in the op-ed piece we wrote ourselves.[79] The symbolic power of motherhood won out over the credibility of college professors. On several occasions, we were asked by reporters if we were members of a feminist group. While we answered truthfully that we were not, we recognized that being identified as card-carrying feminists would actually have discredited our positions. After the story was picked up by the Associated Press and appeared nationwide, the toy was pulled from the shelves by not only Wal-Mart but by other major national retailers as well. A victory, to be sure, but a disquieting lesson about the cultural imperatives that continue to require mothers to adhere to motherhood stereotypes and established media frames in order to draw media attention to their causes.

CONCLUSION

Popular culture has always been more than information or entertainment. In Valdivia's words, it is "a site of struggle over meaning and values."[80] As shown here, media representations of mothers not only reflect deep cultural tensions about the "proper" roles for women, but also demonstrate the media's ability to undercut or bolster a group's political power, and transmit values and stereotypes to future generations. The media's myths and morality tales, as well as its lack of attention to political and structural solutions to problems facing mothers and families, have largely impeded the fulfillment of the vision of the women's movement. Eminent media scholars Gaye Tuchman and George Gerbner maintain that media's slowness to reflect women's concerns, particularly those related to the increased participation of women in the workforce, and failure to present women's issues as legitimate political problems requiring political solutions, reveal the politics of cultural resistance.[81]

In the political arena of the twenty-first century, the media's role in the politics of motherhood is more influential than ever. The sheer amount of time that Americans spend with media, and their reliance on television, in particular, as the dominant source of public discourse about political and social issues, mean media representations impact our views and priorities to an unprecedented degree. Ideologies of motherhood act as a hidden political force, "often accepted unconsciously, assumed to be true, yet highly valued and vigorously defended."[82] When the dominant ideologies we see in media are based on gender stereotypes, they legitimate gender discrimination in the evaluation and advancement of women.

Hollywood entertainment media must provide more realistic and more frequent depictions of the experiences of the majority of American families: families with two working parents, mothers who work out of necessity, and those headed by single mothers. News media need to correct the gender bias that trivializes work-life balance issues as "women's issues," as well as the class bias that ignores the special challenges, institutional inflexibilities and potential systemic solutions for working-class caregivers. Politicians need to give more than lip service and sound bites to "family values" and "working families" in election campaigns. In the midst of the 2008 U.S. presidential campaign, a female blogger summed up the frustrations of many women and families:

[Of course] I am interested in when we will get out of Iraq and how we will deal with global terrorism, but I am just as concerned about how the next president will deal with the lack of family leave and affordable childcare. I think that a candidate who articulated a comprehensive plan to help twenty-first-century families to better balance work and home would win by a landslide.[83]

None of this change will happen without individuals voicing their concerns to media, elected officials, and employers. Recognizing the political consequences of media myths and stereotypes is the first step to changing the ending of the story for the next generation of American mothers.

NOTES

1. Steven H. Chaffee, "Mass Communication in Political Socialization," in *Handbook of Political Socialization,* ed. Stanley Allen Renshon (New York: Free Press, 1977), 223–258.

2. See, for example, Celeste M. Condit, *Decoding Abortion Rhetoric: Communicating Social Change* (Urbana: University of Illinois Press, 1990); Bonnie J. Dow, *Prime-time Feminism: Television, Media Culture, and the Women's Movement Since 1970* (Philadelphia: University of Pennsylvania Press, 1996); and R. Lance Holbert, Dhavan V. Shah, and Nojin Kwak, "Political Implications of Prime-Time Drama and Sitcom Use: Genres of Representation and Opinions Concerning Women's Rights," *Journal of Communication* (2003): 45–60.

3. Center for American Women and Politics, "Gender Differences in Voter Turnout" fact sheet, www.cawp.rutgers.edu (accessed June 29, 2008).

4. United States Department of Labor, Women's Bureau, *Women in the Labor Force in 2005*, http://www.dol.gov/wb/factsheets/Qf-laborforce-05.htm.

5. Holbert, Shah, and Kwak, "Political Implications of Prime-Time Drama and Sitcom Use."

6. See, for example, Susan Faludi's chapter, "Teen Angels and Unwed Witches: The Backlash on TV," in her book *Backlash: The Undeclared War Against American Women* (New York: Crown, 1991), 140–168; Elizabeth Hadley Freydbert, "Sapphires, Spitfires, Sluts and Superbitches: Aframericans and Latinas in Contemporary Hollywood Film," in *Critical Readings: Media and Gender*, ed. Cynthia Carter and Linda Steiner (Berkshire, U.K.: McGraw-Hill, 2004), 265–286; Richard Butsch, "Ralph, Fred, Archie and Homer: Why Television Keeps Recreating the White Male Working Class Buffoon," in *Gender, Race and Class in Media, 2nd Ed.*, ed. Gail Dines and Jean M. Humez (Thousand Oaks, CA: Sage, 2003), 575–585; and Sally Steenland, "Content Analysis of the Image of Women on Television," in *Women and Media: Content/Careers/Criticism*, ed. Cynthia Lont (Belmont, CA: Wadsworth, 1995), 180–187.

7. Todd Gitlin, *The Whole World Is Watching: Mass Media in the Making and Unmaking of the New Left* (Berkeley: University of California Press, 1980).

8. See Susan J. Douglas and Meredith W. Michaels' chapter, "Attack of the Celebrity Moms," in their book *The Mommy Myth: The Idealization of Motherhood and How It Has Undermined All Women* (New York: Free Press, 2004), 110–139.

9. Ibid.

10. Michelle Tauber, "Nichole & Keith's Baby Bliss!" *People*, July 21, 2008, 62–66.

11. Mary Ann Norbom, "Jamie Lynn's Baby Bliss," *OK!*, July 21, 2008, 44–51.

12. Gardiner Harris, "Teenage Birth Rate Rises for First Time Since '91," *The New York Times*, December 6, 2007, www.nytimes.com/2007/12/06/health/06 birth.html.

13. Jane D. Brown, Kelly Ladin L'Engle, Carol Pardun, Guo Guang, Kristin Kenneavy, and Christine Jackson, "Sexy Media Matter: Exposure to Sexual Content in Music, Movies, Television and Magazines Predicts Black and White Adolescents' Sexual Behavior," *Pediatrics* 117 (2006): 1018–1027.

14. See Gardiner Harris, "Teenage Birth Rate Rises," and Sharon Jayson, "Is This the Next Baby Boom?" *USA Today*, July 16, 2008, http://www.usatoday .com/news/nation/2008-07-16-baby-boomlet_N.htm.

15. Deirdre D. Johnston and Debra H. Swanson, "Invisible Mothers: A Content Analysis of Motherhood Ideologies and Myths in Magazines," *Sex Roles: A Journal of Research* (July 2003): 21–33.

16. According to Census data, 84 percent of single parents are mothers. U.S. Census Bureau, *Custodial Mothers and Fathers and Their Child Support: 2005* (Washington, D.C.: U.S. Department of Commerce, August 2007), http:// www.census.gov/prod/2007pubs/p60-234.pdf.

17. Susan Faludi, "Teen Angels and Unwed Witches: The Backlash on TV," in *Backlash*, ed. Susan Faludi (New York: Crown Publishers, 1991), 140–168.

18. Angharad N. Valdivia, "Clueless in Hollywood: Single Moms in Contemporary Family Movies," *Journal of Communication Inquiry* 22 (1998): 272–292.

19. For example, see Kristin Lems, "Disney's Dead Mothers Club," www.cwlu herstory.com/Salon/kristin.html. For a listing of Disney movies with no mothers, stepmothers, orphans, and mothers who are killed or captured, see "Disney Mothers," http://en.wikipedia.org/wiki/Disney_mothers.

20. Mary Douglas Vavrus, "Domesticating Patriarchy: Hegemonic Masculinity and Television's 'Mr. Mom,' " *Critical Studies in Media Communication* 18 (2002): 354.

21. Johnston and Swanson, "Invisible Mothers."

22. E. Ann Kaplan, "Sex, Work and Motherhood: The Impossible Triangle," *Journal of Sex Research* 27 (1990): 409–425.

23. Faludi, *Backlash,* 82.

24. Ibid., 97.

25. Anna M. Smith, "Mass-Market Magazine Portrayals of Working Mothers and Related Issues, 1987 and 1997," *Journal of Children and Poverty* 7 (2001): 101–119.

26. Holbert, Shah, and Kwak, "Political Implications of Prime-Time Drama and Sitcom Use."

27. Ibid.

28. See Valdivia, "Clueless in Hollywood," and Mary Douglas Vavrus, "Opting Out Moms in the News," *Feminist Media Studies* 7 (2007): 47–63.

29. Holbert, Shah, and Kwak, "Political Implications of Prime-Time Drama and Sitcom Use."

30. Ibid.

31. According to the U.S. Census Bureau, the number of U.S. preschoolers with working mothers rose to more than 11.3 million during this time period.

32. In a speech delivered in 1992, Dan Quayle said, "it doesn't help matters when prime-time TV has Murphy Brown—a character who supposedly epitomizes today's intelligent, highly paid, professional woman—mocking the importance of a father, by bearing a child alone and calling it just another 'lifestyle choice.' " See Jane Mattes, *Single Mothers by Choice* (New York: Three Rivers, 1994).

33. James M. Avery and Mark Peffley, "Race Matters: The Impact of News Coverage of Welfare Reform on Public Opinion," in *Race and the Politics of Welfare Reform*, ed. Sanford F. Schram, Joe Sass, and Richard C. Fording (Ann Arbor: University of Michigan Press, 2003): 131–150.

34. Steenland, "Content Analysis of the Image of Women on Television."

35. Valdivia, "Clueless in Hollywood," 284.

36. "Cherie Blair 'Bad Role Model,' " *BBC News*, February 29, 2000. http://news.bbc.co.uk/1/hi/uk/660867.stm.

37. *Nightline* transcripts, March 26, 1992; correspondent: Jackie Judd; anchor: Ted Koppel, http://www.pbs.org/wgbh/pages/frontline/shows/clinton/etc/03261992.html.

38. Jeffery M. Jones, "Laura Bush Approval Ratings Among Best for First Ladies" (Gallup Organization poll report), February 9, 2006, http://www.gallup.com/poll/21370/Laura-Bush-Approval-Ratings-Among-Best-First-Ladies.aspx.

39. F. L. Geis, Virginia Brown, Joyce Jennings Walstedt, and Natalie Porter, "TV Commercials as Achievement Scripts for Women," *Sex Roles* 10 (1984): 513–525.

40. Paul G. Davies, Steven J. Spencer, and Claude M. Steele, "Clearing the Air: Identity Safety Moderates the Effects of Stereotype Threat on Women's Leadership Aspirations," *Journal of Personality and Social Psychology,* 88 (2005): 276–287.

41. Faludi, *Backlash,* 77.

42. Ibid.

43. Vavrus, "Opting Out Moms in the News."

44. Lisa Belkin, "The Opt-Out Revolution," *New York Times Magazine,* October 26, 2003, 45, as reported in Vavrus, ibid.

45. Patricia Sellers, "Power: Do Women Really Want It?" *Fortune* October 13, 2003, 80–100, reported in Vavrus, "Opting Out Moms in the News."

46. Cathy Young, "Is the 'Glass Ceiling' a Matter of Choice?" *Chicago Sun-Times,* November 6, 2003, 16, reported in Vavrus, "Opting Out Moms in the News."

47. Vavrus, "Opting Out Moms in the News," 53.

48. Johnston and Swanson, "Invisible Mothers."

49. Sharon Hays, *The Cultural Contradictions of Motherhood* (New Haven, CT: Yale University Press, 1996), 4.

50. Cited in Maya Rupert, "The Working Wounded: Most Women Don't Have a Choice to Stay Home with Kids," *The San Francisco Chronicle*, August 12, 2007, C-6.

51. Louis Uchitelle, "Women Are Now Equal as Victims of Poor Economy," *The New York Times*, July 22, 2008, www.nytimes.com/2008/0722business22 jobs.html?scp=1&sq=%22women%20are%20now%20equal%20as%20victims %20of%20poor%20economy&st=cse.

52. Jenny Mero, "Fortune 500 Women CEOs," http://money.cnn.com/galleries/2007/fortune/0704/gallery.F500_womenCEOs.fortune/ (accessed July 22, 2008).

53. Johnston and Swanson, "Invisible Mothers."

54. Vavrus, "Opting Out Moms in the News," 54.

55. Ibid.

56. Johnston and Swanson, "Invisible Mothers."

57. Sheila Gibbons, "Discrimination Against Working Moms Apparently Not Newsworthy," *Media Report to Women* 35 (Winter 2007): 24, 22–23.

58. Ibid, 24.

59. Shelley J. Correll, Stephen Benard, and In Paik, "Getting a Job: Is There a Motherhood Penalty?" *American Journal of Sociology* 112 (March 2007): 1297–1338.

60. Ibid., 1306.

61. Ibid., 1332.

62. Mary C. Still, *Litigating the Maternal Wall: U.S. Lawsuits Charging Discrimination Against Workers with Family Responsibilities* (San Francisco: University of California Hastings College of the Law, Center for WorkLife Law, 2006).

63. Ibid.

64. As reported by Charney Research, a professional polling organization, in a national survey report conducted for the National Parenting Association, *What Will Parents Vote For?* (New York: National Parenting Association, May 2000), 6.

65. David E. Bloom and Todd P. Steen, "Minding the Baby in the United States," in *Who Will Mind the Baby*, ed. Kim England (New York: Routledge, 1996), 25.

66. Rupert, "The Working Wounded."

67. Many of these policy ideas have been suggested by the National Parenting Association. See *What Will Parents Vote For?*

68. Gibbons, "Discrimination Against Working Moms Apparently Not Newsworthy," 24.

69. Douglas and Michaels, *The Mommy Myth*, 267.

70. Alexei Barrionuevo, "Political Tango, Women in the Lead," *The New York Times*, November 4, 2007, www.nytimes.com/2007/11/04/weekinreview/04 barrionuevo.html?scp=1&sq=political%20tango%20women%20in%20the%lead &st=cse.

71. Ibid.

72. Janet C. Gornick, Alexandra Heron, and Ross Eisenbrey, *The Work-Family Balance: An Analysis of European, Japanese and U.S. Work-Time Policies* (Washington, DC: Economic Policy Institute, 2007), 1.

73. Annelise Orleck, "Tradition Unbound," in *The Politics of Motherhood: Activist Voices from Left to Right,* ed. Alexis Jetter, Annelise Orleck, and Diana Taylor (Hanover, NH: University Press of New England, 1997), 3–20.

74. Sara Ruddick, "Rethinking 'Maternal' Politics," in *The Politics of Motherhood: Activist Voices from Left to Right,* ed. Alexis Jetter, Annelise Orleck, and Diana Taylor (Hanover, NH: University Press of New England, 1997), 367.

75. Amy Swerdlow, *Women Strike for Peace: Traditional Motherhood and Radical Politics in the 1960s* (Chicago: University of Chicago Press, 1993), 375.

76. Ibid., 236.

77. Meghan Gibbons, "On the Home Front: The Politics of Motherhood," *The Washington Post*, October 16, 2005, B03.

78. Ibid.

79. Katherine N. Kinnick and Sabrena Parton, "Gruesome Toy Sends Wrong Message to Kids," *The Atlanta Journal-Constitution*, October 31, 1999, G5.

80. Valdivia, "Clueless in Hollywood," 277.

81. Gaye Tuchman, "Women's Depiction by the Mass Media," in *Turning It On: A Reader in Women & Media*, ed. Helen Baehr and Ann Gray (New York: St. Martin's Press, 1997), 11–15.

82. Johnston and Swanson, "Invisible Mothers," 24.

83. Yvonne Bynoe, "Presidential Candidates Ignore Working Mothers," October 11, 2007, www.alternet.org/story/64712/.

CHAPTER 2

The Motherless "Disney Princess": Marketing Mothers out of the Picture

Marjorie Worthington

As any parent of young girls knows, the Disney Princesses are everywhere, sold separately—and together—as dolls, toys, party accessories, even underwear. Much as college-age women once discussed which of the *Sex and the City* characters they most resembled, three-to-six-year-old girls constantly define and redefine which princess they want to be, whether it be *Aladdin's* Jasmine, Ariel from *The Little Mermaid*, or the more conventional Sleeping Beauty or Cinderella. Meanwhile, parents roll their eyes and commiserate in whispers about how "the Princesses" have invaded their homes. Of course, this parental dismay arises in part because the Disney films in which these princesses appear are both highly entertaining and patently patriarchal—a deadly combination for anyone trying to raise strong, confident daughters. The young princess characters are often extremely passive, domestic, and demure, content simply to wait, do housework, or read until their prince appears to whisk them into a happy ever-after. Although the later, more contemporary princesses are a *bit* more active in seeking their own happiness, they are still inexperienced and usually far too young (like 16!) to be making any long-term decisions about becoming permanently tied to a prince, charming or otherwise. Taken one at a time, these princess characters are dubious enough role models. But what are the effects on our daughters when the princesses combine forces in an unavoidable and, to young girls, irresistible barrage of images, as has been the case since 2001 with the creation of the brand "Disney Princess"?

What I am referring to is the relatively recent marketing ploy of "bundling" the princesses as practically identical entities. Not only does this deny each character her individuality (implying that all princesses, and in turn perhaps, all little girls, are the same, or at least they should be), but this assemblage of a veritable Princess Task Force packs an even more powerful rhetorical wallop, a wallop young girls are ill-equipped to understand, much less resist. It is dismaying enough to see these girls identifying so strongly with characters whose only desire is to marry, but there is something even more sinister in this mass marketing of the Princesses as a group, something that goes even deeper than the usual feminist arguments against such characterizations of young girls and something that serves as a challenge to the fundamental role of a mother in a young girl's life.

At first, this combined marketing of the Disney Princesses seems somewhat odd, considering that it includes characters spanning over 60 years. One might wonder what characters so temporally far apart could possibly have in common, given that women's opportunities have expanded so greatly since 1937 when *Snow White and the Seven Dwarfs*—Disney's original foray into the animated princess movie—was released. Upon reflection, however, what is most odd is that these various princess characters are actually so *similar* and that their desires to find true love and marry a prince are still so culturally relevant. Perhaps we have not come such a long way after all, baby. For these princesses are so alike as to be almost interchangeable: they are all beautiful, about 16 years old, spirited, have beautiful singing voices, are friends to cute, small animals, and, with rare exceptions, *they have no mothers*. Instead of portraying the mother/daughter relationship with all its contradictions, conflicts, and camaraderie, the Disney films sidestep the issue altogether by removing the mother figure. The motherless Disney Princess has been discussed by Disney watchers and scholars before, but my interest lies with this question: what message does the synergistic grouping of these motherless characters into a marketing juggernaut send about the value of mothers and motherhood? When their favorite characters have no mother, and this lack is neither lamented nor even commented upon, what conclusions will our daughters draw about mothers' importance in their lives, and about their own importance in our culture, should they choose to become mothers themselves?

Before Disney Princess became the brainchild of marketing executives, the general image of the princess character was well known from the films, and many critics noticed their similarities. Rebecca-Anne C. Do Rozario discusses the evolution of the Disney Princess as a character (not a marketing tool), claiming that there are "two pivotal eras of Disney feature animation." [1] The first includes the early films like *Snow White and the Seven Dwarfs*, *Cinderella*, and *Sleeping Beauty*, which were released when Walt Disney himself ran the studio, and the second era was when Michael Eisner was CEO of Disney and the creative group sometimes referred to as "Team Disney" created films like *The Little Mermaid*, *Aladdin*, and *Beauty and the Beast*. The earlier films portray the young princesses as beautiful, sweet, long-suffering, and passive. Although each is really a princess (Snow White and Aurora) or a rich man's daughter (Cinderella), they are all forced by their female malefactor to accept greatly straightened circumstances, which often involve the doing of housework. But these young women succumb cheerfully and tunefully, confident that their princes will come as long as they wait and remain pure. As I said earlier, one might think that times had changed so much since 1937 that this image of the passive and high-pitched princess would no longer be relevant to contemporary girls. Not so, apparently, since Snow White is one of the "primary princesses" who is always included in the marketing materials (as opposed to sprightly and spirited Tinkerbell who has been removed from princess merchandise and demoted to a "secondary princess").[2]

However, there have been some noteworthy changes to our current princesses from the older models. Perhaps because of the changing times and resistance to the traditional passive princess ideal, films from Disney's latter era often make more liberatory gestures, at least in the beginning: *The Little Mermaid's* Ariel wants to explore a new world, as does *Aladdin's* Jasmine, while Pocahontas resists traditional marriage to the prince of her community, and Belle from *Beauty and the Beast* dreams of escaping the "provincial life" of her small village. Mulan actually goes to war disguised as a man and becomes a hero by saving the Emperor and her friends. These young women strain under their circumscribed circumstances and work actively to alter their fortunes, to make their dreams come true. But these princesses' active stance to gain their independence and to achieve something with their lives is quickly projected onto the desire to marry the prince of choice, as he is portrayed as the vehicle through which those dreams might come true. For example, Aladdin takes Jasmine on a magic carpet ride where she can see "A Whole New World," the Beast offers Belle a library full of the books she loves, Ariel's desire to walk on the earth and "get some answers" transforms into a desire to marry Prince Eric and become "Part of [His] World," while Mulan rejects the Emperor's offer of a position in his government and returns home to care for her father and be wooed by her superior-officer-turned-suitor.

While it is sad and alarming that these films provide no alternative role for the young woman other than marriage,[3] Disney alone cannot be faulted for perpetuating a plotline that has dominated western culture for centuries. The fairy-tale source material for these films usually involves a wedding at the end, while the romantic comedy, with a similar required ending, is one of the most popular genres of contemporary film. In other words, the Disney Princess films simply follow the imperative of traditional narrative that requires unmarried female characters to get married. That is not to say, however, that this "marriage plot" is not damaging to young girls; it is damaging in that it forecloses other possible life choices by limiting girls' ability to see what else they might do with their lives. As Brenda Ayres argues, "The purpose of both Grimms' and Disney's fairy tales is to frame females into a patriarchally acceptable portrait of a womanly ideal." [4] Or, as Jack Zipes says about *Snow White and the Seven Dwarfs*, "one shared aspect of the fairy tale and the film is about the domestication of women." [5]

In addition, the heterosexist marriage plot surely causes untold anguish to young girls who may be struggling to come to terms with their homosexuality in a cultural landscape that is quite hostile to that possibility. However, while this heteronormative story line is standard across the board in most children's—and adults'—narrative, it is given a great imprimatur by Disney's embrace of it. As many critics have noted, Disney's dominant position as not just a reflector or purveyor but creator and arbiter of popular culture means that their films become the norm and the standard by which our culture measures itself. A close look at Disney's practices, both in film and in the marketing of its characters, is therefore necessary, given Disney's unprecedented and far-reaching influence.

In other words, Disney does not follow the trends, it sets them. So, there is a unique resonance with audiences when Disney films repeatedly ignore or erase the mother figure and replace her either with the evil stepmother or the void. In this sense, Disney perpetuates the notion that "Western patriarchy is constructed on a history of matricide, and on the expropriation of women from the mother's genealogy to the father's." [6] Disney Princess films, with their missing mothers, their caring fathers, and their young girls in need of parental guidance and—eventually—husbandly control, play out that exact scenario over and over again. Furthermore, as I will argue later, these patriarchal messages become as focused and potent as a laser beam by the omnipresent marketing strategy known as "Disney Princess."

It should be noted that, in the films from the earlier period, not only are mothers missing, but fathers too. In general, parental influences are scarce in the first era of the Disney Princess. Snow White, Cinderella, and Aurora, from *Sleeping Beauty*, each have loving fathers who are either ineffectual or dead, and Aurora's mother is equally unable to help her daughter when her life is threatened. Neither Snow White nor Cinderella have a mother; their fathers are said to be widowers who remarry the evil Queen and Stepmother, respectively, and then die. These early princesses are three young girls out in the world alone without caring parental protection. Instead, what they *do* have is a menacing mother surrogate who tries to kill them or at least keep them from happiness. These dark female figures have been dubbed by Elizabeth Bell as "femme fatales," and they do adhere to the noir tradition in that they are darkly beautiful and menacingly evil. Always jealous of their young charges' beauty, the Stepmother in *Cinderella* and the wicked Queen in *Snow White and the Seven Dwarfs* keep the girls in the scullery and out of the world. As Do Rozario puts it, this older woman character becomes a "wicked maternal substitute, simultaneously erasing the mother and replacing her with a negative image." [7] Aurora in *Sleeping Beauty* is also kept away from the wider world, as her parents, to protect her from the wicked fairy Maleficent's curse, send her to be raised in the woods by her three fairy godmothers. So these princesses are shut away from society with no parental figures to help them gain access to it or to navigate through it. And for Cinderella and Snow White, the only mother figure they know is cruel and dangerous.

Furthermore, these films place the older, middle-aged, mother-like woman in direct competition with the younger. The femme fatale does not provide guidance and love but rather threatens and feels threatened by her daughter. The older woman wants what the daughter has and what had, until recently, been hers: the power of great beauty—apparently the only power a woman can wield with impunity. Never mind that these older women, *Snow White and the Seven Dwarfs'* Queen and *The Little Mermaid's* Ursula the Undersea Witch, to name just two, are highly powerful and extremely sexualized. They are not satisfied with their lot and they lust after the youth and beauty of the young innocent girl. As Elizabeth Bell puts it: "The teenaged heroine at the idealized height of puberty's graceful promenade is individuated in Snow White, Cinderella,

Princess Aurora, Ariel, and Belle. Female wickedness—embodied in Snow White's stepmother, Lady Trumaine, Maleficent, and Ursula—is rendered as middle-aged beauty at its peak of sexuality and authority." [8] These equations of the young beauty with goodness and purity and the older woman with jealousy and evil give a very stark indication of society's viewpoint: as the older woman becomes less beautiful and the young girl becomes more so, the older woman loses social value, despite the fact that she is at that moment (as Bell argues) at the height of her social power and sexual maturity. According to these films, unless a woman is "the fairest one of all," she is worthless and, subsequently, evil.

Another clear message, then, is that older women—women of motherhood age, at least—are not to be trusted; sure, your stepmother might *say* you can go to the ball, but we know she never meant to keep that promise. Or, more urgently, "Don't eat that apple, Snow White!" One can only wonder whether this image of the evil and jealous older woman might discourage girls from viewing mothers as role models and loving sources of wisdom, and rather encourage them to see us as threats. What is the reaction to this pervasive image of femininity consisting of a battle between young women and old? Instead of espousing a world where women band together and support one another, these films contribute to an image of female relationships in which women mistrust one another and can therefore never come together to resist patriarchal forces. In other words, these films promote the divide-and-conquer atmosphere that patriarchal society fosters among women.

In the later princess films, fathers fare much better than in the earlier ones, in that they are allowed to live(!) and have loving, if not perfect, relationships with their daughters. Ariel from *The Little Mermaid*, Belle from *Beauty and the Beast*, Jasmine from *Aladdin*, Pocahontas, and Mulan all have strong relationships with involved fathers. True, these fathers do not always understand them—indeed, the father not understanding the daughter is often the driving narrative conflict in these films. But none of these girls has a mother, except Mulan, and Mulan's mother is merely a minor character who cares only about getting her married; Mulan's primary relationship is with her father (her greatest desire in becoming a warrior was to bring honor to her family and "keep my father standing tall"). Karen Brooks puts it this way: "Patriarchy replaces, oppresses and even elides matriarchy in the Disney galaxy." [9] Indeed, unlike the early princess films where the fathers are dead or absent, the only relationship that matters at the beginning of these contemporary princess films is that of father and daughter.

While it is encouraging that these young princesses have such loving relationships with their fathers, even though these kings do not understand their daughters (and, we might ask, what father *does* understand his 16-year-old daughter?), for the most part, these fathers are either highly patriarchal and demanding or bumbling and ineffectual. In the former category, Mulan's father tries to force his daughter into an unwanted marriage, and Ariel's tries to keep her from pursuing her dream of becoming human and, in a truly terrifying scene, destroys her cherished possessions. In the latter category, Jasmine's father falls under the spell of an evil advisor who wants to marry her, while Belle's is trapped by a Beast and allows his daughter to take his place as prisoner. As loving as they may be, these Disney kings are portrayed as ill-equipped to guide their daughters to adulthood.

And, *Mulan* notwithstanding, these girls have no mothers to turn to for guidance about how to become an adult, about how to negotiate between the expectations of a father, the dictates of society, and her own desires. There is a femme fatale figure in *The Little Mermaid* and a Grandmother Willow character in *Pocahontas* (a sort of Fairy Godmother in the form of a willow tree), but otherwise, no adult female characters to guide the princesses into womanhood or to serve as an example of what womanhood might be like. Not only is there no mother figure, but her absence is never explained.[10] In fact, the only other film besides *Mulan* that even *mentions* a mother is *Pocahontas*, when an elder claims that she has "her mother's spirit." Mothers have been so effectively erased from these later films that their absence is never remarked upon by the characters and, perhaps more importantly, their absence is therefore never noticed by the spectators, young girls. The fact that Disney seems to revel in killing or erasing mothers has been widely discussed,[11] and both eras of princess film are consistent in their erasure of the mother figure. As Geoff Shearer puts it, "removing the mother provides an adversity in the plot for the central (young) character. Mother characters, by nature, elicit too much strength. By being there as the one to run to when things go wrong they steal the thunder. Much easier to kill them off—the earlier the better—and let the audience concentrate on the child. And it works. Over and over again."[12] And it does not just work in terms of the plot, it works to mold the young princess into the ideal bride. Despite or, I would argue, because of this lack of a mother, all our favorite princesses grow up to be perfect domestic-goddesses-in-waiting, waiting for you-know-who to come along and take them from their father's house to the prince's castle. And not only are there no mothers in these films, but also few women in general. So, while the femme fatale has been removed from the most recent princess films (a positive step, perhaps), what has been left in her wake is a gaping absence of female characters. Sharon Lamb and Lyn Mikel Brown point out: "Disney girls don't have girlfriends and very little family";[13] as Princess Jasmine from *Aladdin* exclaims to her father, "I've never even had any real friends!"

Well, now she does, sort of. Since 2001, Jasmine has appeared with her sister princesses on thousands of products marketed around the world. The "Disney Princess" line of merchandise features several of the princesses pictured together: Jasmine, Ariel, and Cinderella on one pair of underwear, for example, and Snow White, Sleeping Beauty, and Belle on another. (While they are included on the official "Disney Princess" Web site, Pocahontas and Mulan appear far more rarely on the merchandise. There are several possible and alarming reasons for this, discussed below.) The harnessing of the combined power of the princesses to achieve heretofore unheard-of marketing synergy was the brainchild in late 2000 of Andy Mooney, Chairman of Disney Consumer Products Worldwide. While attending a Disney ice show, Mooney had his epiphany when he noticed that many of the little girls in the audience were dressed as princesses: "They weren't even Disney products," he noted with surprise, "They were generic princess products they'd appended to a Halloween costume." [14] Soon, Mooney determined, there would be Disney products galore, and being a "generic princess" would no longer suffice. Enter "Disney Princess." Mooney spearheaded a line of over 25,000 princess products, aimed at girls aged three to six, which caused Disney's merchandise sales suddenly to explode after years of decline. "Disney Princess" is now a $4 billion franchise and has broadened to include everything from toys, books, underwear, bedding, music CDs, electronic and video games, and even *Disney Princess Magazine*. Coming this fall is a line of "Disney Fairy" items that will feature Tinkerbell and will be aimed at slightly older girls (in that they are sassier and wear much shorter skirts). Another recent innovation is the Disney Princess Bridal line which features—what else—wedding gowns inspired by your favorite Disney Princess!

According to Disney executives, the real innovation for "Disney Princess" was the "bundling" of the characters together so that girls do not have to choose their favorite princess (and thereby limit their purchasing), but rather can have products that feature *all* of the princesses. Mooney says that before this line emerged, "*Princesses* had to stay in their own mythological worlds. No two of them could share the same environment.

Having them live together was a pretty controversial subject matter at the time. But young girls and mothers voted with their dollars. They believed in the unifying attributes of *Disney princesses.*" [15] But, however "unified" their attributes may be, this is not some kind of Princess labor union or consciousness-raising seminar; the princesses may be marketed together, but they are not friends. It is one of the mandates of the portrayals on the merchandise that the various princesses do not actually interact with—or even look at—one another. So, although they appear together, their eye lines never meet. The ostensible reason for this is to maintain the integrity of their unique "mythological worlds," but the effect, especially on straight-to-video stories about them, is that the princesses do not meet one another and do not play together or provide support to each other.

It is intriguing to consider, though, what might be the result of such a princess summit meeting: "You mean *you* had a mean stepmother also? *You* had to do all the housework, too? Why is it that each of us almost died and then were rescued by a prince and married by age 16? Were there no other options available to us? *And where are our mothers???*" There is no sense in "Disney Princess" that the princesses are in cahoots with one another, winking and chuckling over some secret plan for world domination. Because they never interact, there is little hope that the princesses could turn to one another for help and comfort or band together to challenge the system that makes such draconian, yet oddly similar, demands of them. No, each princess's plight is unique to her and she faces it alone, without the guidance of a mother and without the support of those other princesses standing right next to her on that pair of underwear. The Disney Princesses line does not change their fate, nor does it facilitate any questioning about that fate or provide alternative ways of facing it; Disney Princesses are alone in a crowd.

Some other, more obvious criticisms leap to mind when contemplating the concentrated power of this gang of princesses. First of all, the Princesses are everywhere, making them impossible to ignore and therefore, for very young children, impossible to resist. As Lyn Mikel Brown states: "When one thing is so dominant, then it's no longer a choice: it's a mandate, cannibalizing all other forms of play. There's the illusion of more choices out there for girls, but if you look around, you'll see their choices are steadily narrowing." [16] Furthermore, by marketing to very young girls, critics contend, Disney is sending the message that the most important consideration for a girl or woman is being rich and beautiful and getting married by age 16. Exacerbating this criticism, the princesses have undergone something of a make-over for their new marketing role: "Tomi-Ann Roberts, a professor of psychology at Colorado College, complains that the princesses have become more sexualized, with more skin showing and bigger heads, eyes and breasts." [17] This "Barbie-ization" raises concerns both about exposing ever-younger children to this sexualized imagery and about bombarding young girls with representations of impossibly perfect bodies, encouraging them to be dissatisfied with their own. These issues, while extremely important, are not confined simply to the Princess line, but rather manifest themselves in an alarming number of toys for girls. There are, however, specific problems related to the "princess packaging" in particular.

For example, another concern that others have raised with regard to the individual films but that deserves further scrutiny in terms of the princess posse is their racial homogeneity. Most of the princesses are white, and even the ones who are not, usually have highly Caucasian physical characteristics. What is more, the nonwhite princesses play only a minor role in the larger marketing scheme. When more than one princess is depicted, on a lunch box or bedspread, it is exceedingly rare that one of the nonwhite princesses (Mulan or Pocahontas) is included. Jasmine, of unspecified Middle-Eastern descent, appears more often, but is still overshadowed by her white sisters (I know this from personal experience: since Jasmine is usually my daughter's princess of choice, we often find ourselves fruitlessly searching bargain bins or Band-Aid boxes for her image).

There are several possible reasons for this lack of racial diversity in the Disney Princess product line, none of which is reassuring. There is the obvious racial bias, to which Disney seems still to be in thrall. As evidence for this bias, or at the very least, Disney's blindness to racial issues, one need only point to the history of the upcoming film *The Princess and the Frog*, the first film to feature an African American princess. Originally, the princess, whose name is now Tiana, was going to be named Maddy and was to be a housekeeper in a fancy hotel. Despite the fact that this princess-as-scullery-maid plotline has been worn thin by other films (see *Snow White and the Seven Dwarfs* and *Cinderella*), it apparently had not occurred to Disney until various consumer groups protested that it might be somewhat racially insensitive to depict the African American girl as a *maid*. It is this kind of insensitivity—fairly shocking at this late date—that might keep Disney from marketing its princesses of color as aggressively as the others. Another possible reason for the underrepresentation of Mulan and Pocahontas in the princess clan is that, as Peggy Orenstein says, these two, in their warrior garb and Native American animal-skin dress, respectively, are decidedly lacking in "bling potential." And Disney has determined, rightly or wrongly, that fancy dresses and jewels are what little girls want from their princess characters. Indeed, when she is included at all, Mulan is quite often depicted in the fancy bridal attire that made her so uncomfortable at the beginning of the film.

The third, and just as alarming, reason why Mulan and Pocahontas might be left out of broad circulation is that these two films do not adhere to the traditional princess story line. These two young girls are strong and defiant and the films *do not end with a wedding*! True, by the end of *Mulan*, it is implied that she will end up marrying her superior officer, but until this point, she has proven herself to be a formidable warrior—and a cross-dressing one, to boot! And Pocahontas does not marry John Smith at the end of the film. He has been injured and needs to return to England for medical attention. She decides not to accompany him, stating instead that her people need her to lead them. This is decidedly not what a good little passive princess would do. I cannot help but wonder whether it was the combination of all these things—the characters' strength and leadership qualities, their remaining single at the end of the film, in addition to their race—that made them unsuitable for inclusion in the upper echelons of Disney Princess-dom. In other words, although Disney has in recent years made films that portray strong and capable female characters, these characters do not make the cut in terms of marketing. When it comes to presenting young girls with toys and materials for their own personal developmental play, the demure and passive, good-girl princess wins the day.

For the princesses featured in Disney Princess movies *are* good girls, for the most part. They want to make their fathers happy, and they rebel only to the extent they must in order to win the hearts of their dream princes. For the most part, the princesses featured in Disney's marketing are rule followers: Cinderella *does* leave the ball at midnight, Snow White is happy to keep house for the dwarfs, and Belle bravely volunteers to take her father's place as the Beast's prisoner, thus paying the price for his trespassing. Jasmine and Ariel want to marry their loves, but the laws of man and nature, respectively, do not allow it until their *fathers* change that law and enable them to be together. In other words, these girls, feisty though they may be, do not overtly challenge patriarchal society, but rather turn to that very authority to grant them what they wish. And, of course, by marrying, they replace one patriarchal authority figure with another, more age-appropriate one.

The fact that adherence to patriarchal values is a primary tenet of the Disney Princess can be seen on the official Web site: disneyprincess. com.[18] Among other things, the site provides brief but telling descriptions of each princess. For example: "By the time Sleeping Beauty is awakened from her slumber by the Prince, she has been transformed from a sheltered girl into a mature young woman ready to become a bride." The Web site does not explain exactly how *sleeping* can mature a person, but the site reveals what some parents may actually wish, that their daughters could simply sleep through their difficult adolescent years and awake just in time for their weddings, having magically "transformed" into brides. In this scenario, sleeping takes the place of living, experiencing, and making one's own mistakes, something *Sleeping Beauty* suggests girls should not be trusted to do.

The Web site makes clear that the "Disney Princess" product line purveys a different viewpoint than the films from which it is derived. For, often, the "Disney Princess" site reasserts parental (patriarchal) authority, even when it means departing from the plot of the film. For example: "Although Mulan is as lovely as a blossom, she can't seem to behave like the gentle daughter she is supposed to be. In fact, she's quite a tomboy, whose spirit leads her into situations that defy the traditions of her society. She loves her family, but her behavior risks bringing dishonor to the family." What is striking is that this description focuses on Mulan's transgressions rather than her bravery and her accomplishments (or her crossdressing!); the film's implied lesson that a woman can do whatever a man can, even become a fierce warrior, becomes on the Web site a cautionary tale about disgracing one's family. Another example states, in part: "Headstrong Ariel means to follow the rules, but rarely succeeds. Like many teenagers, Ariel does not feel 'understood,' and is forever trying to make her friends, and especially her father, see things her way. . . . By the time Ariel's wish to be human is finally granted, she realizes that there is something to be gained from a father's wisdom." Here, the patriarchal overtones are even more overt and depart from what happens in the film; instead of saying that Ariel convinces her father to allow her to marry Prince Eric, the Web site implies that it is the *King* whose wisdom saves the day, thus reasserting the father's authority. Indeed, anyone who has seen *The Little Mermaid* might be a bit confused by this Web description, since Prince Eric rescues King Triton by killing Ursula the Sea Witch and the King's "wisdom" is somewhat lacking throughout his interactions with his daughter. The Web site exposes the cultural anxieties that in part motivate the Disney Princess: the threat of the autonomous (and possibly sexual) unmarried female who rejects paternal authority. The most marketed princesses are those who are the least threatening in that regard, and the Web site attempts to reinscribe any of the stronger characters' princess-tual transgressions.

But what are the cultural implications of the combination of individual princess power into an unprecedented marketing engine against which the youngest girls have no defense? As a mother myself, I cannot help but be concerned that the figures with whom young girls most identify are princesses who must always be beautiful, obedient, and good, and, perhaps most disturbingly, who must struggle to negotiate their way in a patriarchal world with no mothers to help and support them. Indeed, their mother-figure is often menacing and evil. What does it say about our society that such characters are so ubiquitous as to be unavoidable, so popular as to be all-consuming?

I would argue that this princess bundling belies a contemporary cultural anxiety that contemporary mothers cannot be trusted to guide daughters to their proper destiny of virgin bride. The suggestion is that the best young women—the true princesses—are those who grow up without a mother and outside any feminine community. Female figures (like mothers) who might want more for themselves and their daughters than the traditional marriage plot have been conveniently removed, often replaced with kindly but highly traditional and marginally powerful fairy godmother figures who use what power they do have in the service of the patriarchal dictate of bringing that wedding about. The result is that there is no depiction, in the films our daughters love, of a healthy mother/daughter relationship (or mother/son, for that matter). Because the films not only remove the mothers, but effectively erase them by not even mentioning them (we never find out what happened to Cinderella's, Snow White's, Belle's, Jasmine's, or even Aladdin's mothers), the films imply that mothers are simply not relevant to the lives of young girls. The underlying reason, I would suggest, is that mothers are unpredictable and powerful figures; they cannot be included in the neat Disney narratives because they might throw a wrench into the works, either by actively encouraging their daughters to question patriarchy and explore options besides marriage or, simply, through their very presence, demonstrating the impossibility of "happily ever after."

The lack of mother figures in these films has a cumulative effect that we should not ignore. As Lynda Haas argues, "the media's repeated erasure of the mother's place and her origins is a kind of ideological dominance accomplished on the unconscious (as well as the conscious) level." [19]

When they do not see examples of strong mother figures—or any mother figures at all—in the media, girls internalize the notion that a mother's role must not be very important. The implications of this are far-reaching, both in daughters' relationships with their own mothers and in their considerations of their own futures and whether or not they want to be mothers and therefore be deemed irrelevant to society. Haas goes on to suggest that, "Because the mother's place is silently elided in traditional readings of myth, a requisite cultural taboo has also been placed on the relationship with the mother." [20] And indeed, that does seem to be the result: a taboo, not only on the portrayal of the mother/child relationship, but of the considerable influence a mother can and does exert on the raising of children. The role of the mother, by being erased in these media, is threatened with devaluation by the culture at large. And we can see this devaluation at work in our culture, which has been increasingly influenced by the radical religious right.

One striking real-world example of the increasing perception that a mother's role is irrelevant and perhaps even dangerous when it comes to raising daughters and preparing them to be proper members of patriarchal society is the current "Purity Ball" craze. In events held across the country, fathers are now bestowing "purity rings" on their teenage daughters in (arguably) creepy ceremonies where the girls promise to abstain from sex and the fathers promise to "protect their virtue." The next best thing to putting one's daughter to sleep until she becomes a "young woman ready to become a bride," the Purity Ball ceremony overtly states that the virtue of the daughter is to remain under the protective aegis of the father; he will guard her purity and she will promise to remain a virgin until marriage. At one of the longest running and most popular "Father/ Daughter Purity Balls" in Colorado Springs, Colorado, the fathers make the following pledge: "I, (daughter's name)'s father, choose before God to cover my daughter as her authority and protection in the area of purity." [21] These ceremonies are touted by supporters as touching moments between a father and a daughter, where he can make her feel like a princess to his king, and where he can bolster her self-esteem so that she does not feel the need to turn outward for male validation, thus risking her pride and all-important chastity. The "Purity Movement" has numerous Web sites that sell products ranging from Purity rings and kits for holding your own Purity Ball to "Commit-mints" that can be handed out at such events. The movement has its roots in the Promise Keepers movement (whose rallies exhort men to reassert "servant leadership" of their households) and encourages fathers to take an active interest in their daughters' lives and to protect them from a highly sexualized culture. Some critics wonder whether getting so deeply involved in one's daughter's sexuality is perhaps *too* active an interest, and indeed some Purity ceremonies seem a great deal like weddings. Other critics note that the effectiveness of such abstinence efforts has been called into question; some studies show that girls who participate in such ceremonies are no less likely than their peers to engage in premarital sex and that the median age for such a first sexual encounter is about 15.[22]

For my argument, it is also important to note that, just as in the Disney Princess films, there is no role for a mother in these ceremonies, except as a supposedly proud and definitely *silent* witness to the proceedings. As Randy Wilson, coordinator of the Colorado Springs event says, "The mother's role is to enjoy the event and to support the father's commitment to integrity in their homes."[23] Fathers dance with their daughters, make pledges and bestow rings; daughters promise their fathers to remain "pure." Mothers, if they attend the ceremony at all, are to "enjoy" and "support," not "guide" or "lead" or even "talk to" their daughters about the role sexuality should play in their lives. Perhaps this is because sexuality is apparently supposed to play *no* role at all until, much like a Disney Princess, the daughter can be safely and chastely transferred from the custody of her father to that of her husband. In this scenario, there is no need for sex education that would inform young girls about their reproductive choices and responsibilities, and, perhaps more poignantly (although no less dangerously), there is no room, indeed no *need*, for the traditional "birds and bees" talks between mother and daughter. For, who knows what a mother might say in those talks. Why, a mother might claim that there is more to sex than duty, that a woman's sexual pleasure is not only possible, but is her right; she might even suggest that her daughter's sexuality is something she might *own* herself rather than simply *give* to the man she marries.

Although supporters of the Purity movement say that it is also important for young boys to remain chaste until marriage, there are few if any such ceremonies for boys, evidence that the classical double standard is still very much in play. According to Randy and Lisa Wilson, their son will not attend the ball but will rather have a private "manhood celebration" at their home that will include some mention of purity.[24] So, while the daughters are making a grand public statement promising to entrust their sexuality to their fathers, the sons are usually not expected to make the same commitment, and certainly do not make it publicly. Those involved say that it is more important for girls to remain virgins until marriage than boys because premarital sex is more destructive to girls' "more emotional" natures.[25] This argument, of course, does not hold up under scrutiny, despite the fact that it has been used for centuries as a justification for curtailing the freedom of girls and women. And, here it is being rolled out once again under the guise of bringing fathers and daughters together, with the added suggestions that mothers cannot be trusted to protect their daughters' interests. The Purity Balls, then, are more than a vehicle for strengthening father/daughter relationships; like the "Disney Princess," they also serve to sidestep mothers, along with any disturbing ideas they may have picked up in that pesky Women's Movement. Indeed, it is difficult to predict what mothers might do if given the chance to voice an opinion about Purity Balls, or what they might do if given a chance to survive a Disney film and actually interact with their daughters. What kind of revolutionary ideas might they impart?

It would be fair to ask why, if I object so strenuously to the Disney Princesses, I allow my daughter to see the films, wear the nightgowns, and eat the fruit snacks emblazoned with their images. My partner and I have grappled and continue to grapple with this issue every day. It is impossible to shield her completely from the princesses: her friends have the merchandise, sing the songs, and play Princess incessantly. So we ask ourselves: do we allow her to choose her own role models, her own clothes and toys, granting her important autonomy, even if her choices sometimes make us cringe? Or do we withhold the things she wants that we find distasteful and dangerous to her self-esteem, knowing that by withholding them we may make her want them even more, thereby negating any feminist ideals we hope to instill? In response, we adopted a middle-of-the-road approach, allowing her to have some of the stuff, within reason, and talking to her about the limitations of the princesses' view of life and her own much broader options. And we try always to expand her horizons by encouraging her to learn, try, and do and to push herself beyond the safety of the princess plot. It is an uphill battle any parent of daughters must fight, and Disney is a formidable adversary.

NOTES

This chapter was inspired by my daughter, a princess and so much more.

1. Rebecca-Anne C. Do Rozario, "The Princess and the Magic Kingdom: Beyond Nostalgia, the Function of the Disney Princess," *Women's Studies in Communication* 27.1 (Spring 2004): 35.

2. At this very moment, however, Disney is rolling out a brand new marketing ploy: Disney Fairies. Headed by Tinkerbell, who will be given a voice for the

very first time, these characters will have the same marketing emphasis as Disney Princess and will be designed to appeal to girls aged six to nine (Disney Princess is aimed at girls three to six).

3. The striking exception to this is *Pocahontas*, who refuses to accompany John Smith to England saying that she must remain to lead her people, but this ending seems rather forced (Pocahontas has not shown any interest in leading her people up to now) and was probably merely a cursory nod to the actual historical figure of Pocahontas who did not marry John Smith. Indeed, there is very little chance that the historical John Smith actually had a romance with Pocahontas, who is believed to have been about 11 years old at the time. Conscious of the potential criticism of historians, Disney takes liberties with some elements of the story of Pocahontas and constructs a fictitious love relationship, but not a fictitious marriage, between the two characters.

4. Brenda Ayres, "The Poisonous Apple in *Snow White*: Disney's Kingdom of Gender," in *The Emperor's Old Groove: Decolonizing Disney's Magic Kingdom*, ed. Brenda Ayres (New York: Peter Lang, 2003), 40.

5. Jack Zipes, "Breaking the Disney Spell," in *From Mouse to Mermaid: The Politics of Film, Gender, and Culture*, ed. Elizabeth Bell, Linda Haas, and Laura Sells (Bloomington: Indiana University Press, 1995), 37.

6. Laura Sells, " 'Where Do the Mermaids Stand?': Voice and Body in *The Little Mermaid*," in *From Mouse to Mermaid: The Politics of Film, Gender, and Culture,* ed. Elizabeth Bell, Lynda Haas, and Laura Sells (Bloomington: Indiana University Press, 1995), 179.

7. Do Rozario "The Princess and the Magic Kingdom," 41.

8. Elizabeth Bell, "Somatexts at the Disney Shop: Constructing the Pentimentos of Women's Animated Bodies," in *From Mouse to Mermaid: The Politics of Film, Gender, and Culture*, ed. Elizabeth Bell, Lynda Haas, and Laura Sells (Bloomington: Indiana University Press, 1995), 108.

9. Karen Brooks, *Consuming Innocence: Popular Culture and Our Children* (Queensland, Australia: University of Queensland Press, 2008), 187.

10. Ariel's mother does appear briefly in a 2008 prequel to the feature film entitled *The Little Mermaid: Ariel's Beginning*. True to Disney form, however, she dies at the very beginning of the film.

11. For example, Mark Axelrod points out: "What is curious about the Disney phenomenon of motherless children (primarily daughters) is that the same storyline has continued for over fifty years. From *Snow White* (1937) to *Beauty and the Beast* (1991), it is as if Walt Disney's predilection for commodifying virtue by selling products that either ignore or dehumanize the role of woman and/or mother has become a kind of Disney trademark, if not company policy, which has been carefully nurtured" (32). Mark Axelrod, "Beauties and Their Beasts and Other Motherless Tales from the Wonderful World of Disney."

The Emperor's Old Groove: Decolonizing Disney's Magic Kingdom, ed. Brenda Ayres (New York: Peter Lang, 2003), 29–38. See also Bell, Brooks, Haas, Ornstein, and Shearer among many others. A brief but not exhaustive list of other Disney films in which the mothers are killed or erased includes *Bambi*, *Dumbo*, *Peter Pan*, *Pinocchio*, *A Goofy Movie*, and *Finding Nemo*.

12. Geoff Shearer, "Mothers Get the Flick," *Courier and Mail*, March 7, 2008, 31.

13. Sharon Lamb and Lyn Mikel Brown, *Packaging Girlhood: Rescuing Our Daughters from Marketers' Schemes* (New York: St. Martin's Press, 2006), 68.

14. Peggy Orenstein, "What's Wrong with Cinderella?" *New York Times*, December 24, 2006, Sect. 6, 34.

15. "Disney Princesses Wear Merchandising Crown," *USA Today*, September 17, 2003, 02D.

16. Brown as quoted in Ornstein.

17. Merissa Marr, "Disney Reaches to the Crib to Extend Princess Magic," *Wall Street Journal*, November 19, 2007, B1.

18. Disney, "Disney Princess—The Official Website," http://disney.go.com/princess/html/main_iframe.html.

19. Lynda Haas, " 'Eighty-Six the Mother': Murder, Matricide, and Good Mothers," in *From Mouse to Mermaid: The Politics of Film, Gender, and Culture*, ed. Elizabeth Bell, Lynda Haas, and Laura Sells (Bloomington: Indiana University Press, 1995), 195.

20. Ibid., 195

21. Mary Zeiss Stange, "A Dance for Chastity," *USA Today*, March 19, 2007, 15A.

22. Mary Vallis, "Impure Results; New Study Says Bush-Funded Chastity Movement Has Not Prevented Teens from Having Sex," *National Post*, April 28, 2007, A3.

23. Stange, "A Dance for Chastity," 15A.

24. "In Praise of Chastity; Purity Balls," *The Economist*, November 8, 2006.

25. Neela Bannerjee, "The Purity Ball: It's Not Just about Daughters; A Vow by Fathers to Set an Example," *The International Herald Tribune*, May 20, 2008, 2.

CHAPTER 3

Motherhood, Memory, and Mambo: The Case of the Missing Cuban American Mother in Contemporary American Popular Culture

Manuel Martínez

Al combate, corred, Bayameses,
Que la Patria os contempla orgullosa;
No temáis una muerte gloriosa,
Que morir por la Patria es vivir.

—La Bayamesa

To combat, run, people of Bayamo
Because the Motherland looks upon you with pride;
Do not fear a glorious death,
Because to die for the Motherland is to live.

—The Cuban National Anthem
(My translation)

The preceding quote from the Cuban national anthem exemplifies an ambivalence and tension that motherhood has historically had for Cuban and, now, Cuban American culture. It is ironic that although motherhood has come to embody the homeland, it has come to do so as a result of a reality that has been constructed and defined by masculine values.

The Latin word for father is "pater." It is from this root that the Spanish word "patria" is derived. Interestingly, however, the modern Spanish word "patria" is feminine. It refers to "la madre patria" translated as "motherland." Although this is the way that all Latin American countries refer to the nation, it serves as a useful metaphor for the case of Cuba in particular. This etymological inversion is suggestive of the ambivalence with which women and motherhood have historically been portrayed in Cuban popular culture. From the very beginning, in novels such as *Sab*[1] and *Cecilia Valdés*,[2] women have figured as part of the Cuban popular imaginary. And yet, they have been mostly displaced from a central role. There has been a tendency to represent men as the central protagonists with women being relegated to the background.

Now, patria, having both feminine and masculine elements, would seem, on the surface, to reconcile the two genders. It strikes a balance that would seem to recognize both. However, the Latin root tends to inflect the word's meaning with a masculine characteristic. Is it any wonder that the word is oftentimes translated as fatherland? Viewed in this way, the feminine fades into the background.

Despite the focus on the motherland and the identification of the maternal with the Cuban homeland, Cuban popular culture marginalizes the maternal, a tendency that suggests motherhood's importance but stops short of putting it on par with the masculine. Heterosexuality and nationality have supported each other in the development of national projects; therefore it is not surprising that we can identify the dialectical tension between the maternal component of "homeland" and the masculine component of "patria."[3] This tension can be seen in a chain from the earliest days of Cuban national consciousness, in the aforementioned novels when Cuba was still a colony of Spain, through the revolution and on to today both in Cuba and in the Diaspora. When the revolution came to power, the Cuban national anthem remained unchanged, for example. Further, although the revolution sought gender equality as a stated goal, it still emphasized the development of a "New Man" at the symbolic expense of women.

Anthropologist Ruth Behar refers to these contradictions in the ideology of the Cuban revolution in these terms:

> Cuban revolutionary ideology has always been deeply contradictory about the erotics of power. The revolution was scripted in male homosocial terms, but homosexuality was anathema. Where women are concerned, the contradictions are even more knotted .... [With the revolution] the national desire to transform gender relations was serious, radical and wide-ranging. But "feminism" as a term and concept remained unacceptable in a society where the women's movement was subordinate to the revolution.[4]

As this quote suggests, when women were portrayed in Cuban postrevolutionary popular culture, it was in their role as members of the revolutionary vanguard first and as a woman second. Their role as mother was pushed even farther into the background.

This same sort of continuity, as well as its contradictions, can be seen in Cuban American cultural production even before 1959. In his book *Life on the Hyphen: The Cuban American Way*, Gustavo Pérez Firmat discusses the origins of Cuban American culture. He traces its beginning to Desi Arnaz and especially to his role as Ricky Ricardo in the *I Love Lucy*[5] television series. He calls the cultural tradition that he spawned the "Desi Chain"[6] since he was "its initial link."[7] It was after Desi Arnaz, and during the 50-year period that followed, that Cuban American culture "evolved into a recognizable and coherent cluster of attitudes and achievements."[8]

It is in this beginning that I would argue that we see the roots of a male-centric Cuban American culture that displaces women from center stage and their roles as mother even farther into the background. Recall the basic premise of the show. Ricky ran a nightclub in whose shows Lucy would always try to insinuate herself. It is telling that when Lucille Ball became pregnant in real life, her pregnancy was written into the show only to have "Little Ricky" treated tangentially after his birth. Even after Lucy gave birth, the focus remained, not on her role as a mother, but on her attempts to become a part of the show business world to which her Cuban husband belonged. Ricky always symbolically remained in the spotlight that Lucy wanted to gain permanent access to.

Given these two currents, one flowing from Cuba and another born here in the United States, the question to be asked is if this dynamic continues within the popular cultural production of Cuban Americans or if there have been modifications that have resulted from an extended exchange with the host culture? I would argue that in the case of Cuban Americans, although they also characterize their native land as maternal, the mother figure in Cuban American pop culture is as equally invisible as it is in insular Cuban popular culture; once again demonstrating that the mother as a symbol is much more powerful than its realistic representations in novels, television shows, and printed matter.

Despite this relative symbolic absence, the figure of women in general and the mother in particular is a recurring theme in Cuban American popular culture. It is just this ambivalence that Adriana Méndez Rodenas identifies in her article "Engendering the Nation: The Mother/Daughter Plot in Cuban-American Fiction." She begins by asserting that "By far the most pressing question in Cuban studies is: How has the nation been imagined across the gender divide?" [9] She points to the silence of "cultural 'spokesmen' " [10] of the Diaspora on the role of Cuban women. She gives special mention to memoirs authored by men such as Gustavo Pérez Firmat,[11] Pablo Medina,[12] and Carlos Eire[13] as upholding "the dominant gender as [the] emblematic subject of exile." [14]

In her essay "Tierra sin nosotras" (Land without us), Lourdes Gil writes about the play between "nosotros" (us/we masculine) and "nosotras" (us/we feminine). She makes a reference to the Spanish language that could just as well be directed toward the word "patria." She states that:

> No pretendo modificar una lengua de singular plasticidad y riqueza, sedimentada por los siglos; una lengua que, lamentablemente, no nos representa con justeza. Pero sí creo que el examinar la compleja red de ambivalencias y equívocos que yacen ocultos tras esquemas diseñados por otros (los esquemas en que hemos sido educadas) puede también socavar el orden patriarcal que constriñe nuestro pensamiento. ¿De qué modo asisitimos al festejo innombrable? ¿Cómo participamos de la cacería sangrienta de la historia y del quehacer humano?[15]

> I do not pretend to modify a language of singular plasticity and richness, with centuries of layers; a language that, regrettably, does not represent us justly. But I do think that the examination of the complex web of ambivalences and errors that lie hidden behind systems designed by others (systems under which we, as women, have been educated) can also undermine the patriarchal order that constrains our thinking. In what way do we attend the unnameable feast? How do we participate in the bloody hunt of history and humanity's work? (My translation)

In this quote, she eloquently brings attention to how Cuban women have been systematically absented, in a symbolic way, from the nation.

What I intend to do in this essay is just what Gil suggests. I will examine some of the ambivalences present in the cultural production of four Cuban Americans in order to try and expand the debate on the representation of women in Cuban American popular culture. I will do so by comparing Cristina García's *Dreaming in Cuban*[16] and Ana Menéndez's *Loving Che*[17] with Andy García's movie *The Lost City*[18] and Cynthia Cidre's *Cane*,[19] the CBS television series. I have chosen these four works because they are a representative sample of contemporary Cuban American popular cultural production. In addition, the two novels will serve as a comparison for images that have been introduced into the wider popular culture through television and movie theaters.

I will begin by examining the two novels, *Dreaming in Cuban* and *Loving Che*. The former work, published in 1993, is significant for two reasons principally. First, it was the first novel by a Cuban American woman to be written and published in English by a major American publisher. Second, it became a best seller that was nominated for a National Book Award. As such, it marked, arguably, another step taken by Cuban American literature away from Cuban literature and toward the American literary tradition. *Loving Che*, published in 2003, is also significant in that it is one of the most recent additions to this new body of Cuban American literary production written in English. In addition, because of its sympathetic portrayal of Ernesto Guevara, it was widely commented on in the Cuban American community and, like *Dreaming in Cuban*, has managed to make the leap from a purely literary context to become a part of contemporary Cuban American popular culture.

Beyond their importance as examples of Cuban American popular culture, both novels deal with issues that are germane to the thesis of this essay. They both deal with personal and national identity as mediated through the lens of female identity. In doing so, both novels also speak to the mother-father dialectic. At the same time, they allude to a dialectic that runs parallel to the dialectic already mentioned between nation and gender. In the case of Cuban culture, the experience of massive migrations of Cuban citizens to the United States creates another layer of complexity to issues of cultural and national identity. Besides the tensions and ambiguities with regards to the mother as a symbol rooted in a national project based on masculinity and heterosexuality, Cubans have had to deal with the construction of a hyphenated identity once in the United States. In Adriana Méndez Rodenas's article, she argues that both Cristina García and Ana Menéndez

> center on that most pivotal of narrative plots—the story of female development and identity—"engendering the nation" by means of individual characters whose coming to womanhood coincides with the crucial turning-points in the island's history.[20]

While I agree with Méndez Rodenas that "García and Menéndez seem to urge their readers to renegotiate the terms of Cuban identity by reverting their invisibility." [21] I question the limits of this restoration. Further, when she states that, "As feminist critics, it is our task to gather these stories into the texture of a yet-to-be-born Nation." [22] I would ask, which "Nation" are we to refer to. Are we to think of this debate as being centered on Cuba with the cultural production of the Diaspora as an appendix? Or are we to consider the cultural production of Cuban Americans in the United States as an independent cultural phenomenon that increasingly responds to the influence of American popular culture?

In *Dreaming in Cuban*, Cristina García presents three generations of a Cuban family both in Cuba and in the United States. The family's story is told through flashbacks and letters that the grandmother Celia had written to a lover who had abandoned her. Celia, the matriarch, eventually marries Jorge del Pino and has three children, Lourdes, Felicia, and Javier. After marrying and giving birth to Pilar, Lourdes and her family flee the revolution in Cuba. They settle in New York where Pilar grows up. It is Pilar's trip back to Cuba with Lourdes that brings the novel full circle.

In this novel, all who could be described as main characters are women. Indeed, the protagonist is Pilar. That is how the family's lineage is implicitly presented—as being matriarchal. Although the men in the lives of these women are mentioned, they serve more as backdrop than as characters who are fully fleshed out. Considerable time is spent on the character development of not only Pilar, but of Lourdes, Celia, and Felicia as well. Here we have female characters who are placed center stage.

In this coming of age novel, García represents Pilar's development as seen through the prism of her mother and grandmother as well as tied to events on the island. It is not coincidental that García places Pilar's birthday in 1959, the year that also saw the birth of the revolution. In a sense, the author appropriates the birthday of the revolution, a project that has arguably been represented as being male-centric, and views it through a female lens.

If one were to leave it at that, it would appear that the author had successfully reverted, at least in this novel, the invisibility of women. Still, upon further analysis, I would argue that the foregrounding is symbolically incomplete. In the case of all of the main female characters in the novel, their actions and lives are overshadowed by the influence of men.

Celia's life is centered around first her failed love affair with the Spaniard Gustavo, later her husband, and finally her devotion to the Revolution as personified by Fidel Castro. Her daughter Lourdes is similarly influenced. Once in exile, Lourdes pushes her family as far away from Cuba as possible, both symbolically and geographically. Her family settles in New York, driven, in part, by Lourdes's memories of her rape at the hands of Cuban revolutionaries as well as the Cuban revolution represented by Fidel Castro. Likewise, Pilar's defining moment of independence, helping her cousin Ivanito escape during the Mariel Boatlift, has her taking a man's side against her grandmother.

This same dynamic can be seen in Ana Menéndez's *Loving Che*. The novel deals with the unnamed protagonist's search for information about the life of the mother she never knew. She was sent to Miami as an infant to be raised by her grandfather. Growing up, her grandfather said little about her mother. When she confronts him about this lack of information, he reveals that it was her mother who had asked him to take her away from Cuba. After arriving in Miami, the grandfather lost contact with his daughter. Although she now has more information about her mother, the protagonist is no closer to finding her. After her grandfather's death, she returns to Cuba where she is unable to locate her. She returns to Miami and tries to get on with her life.

Her search takes a surprising turn when a package arrives with photographs and letters suggesting that her mother had had an affair with Ernesto "Che" Guevara. Her quest to find out more about her mother suddenly changes to include the question of whether Che was her father or not. With this new information she returns to Cuba where she again tries to find out about her mother and to verify if she is indeed the daughter of Che Guevara. Although by the end of this second trip, the protagonist is no closer to finding answers to her questions or her mother, she does achieve a measure of self-awareness and self-acceptance. The novel presents the displacement of the mother to the background while the father takes on a protagonist role. Ironically, while she searches for her mother, she instead ends up searching for her father.

Still, as the presence of a man in the title *Loving Che* suggests, the spotlight is shared by the female protagonist. In fact, even before one begins to read the novel, that symbolic presence makes itself felt. What this means then is that the female characters, although foregrounded, cannot escape the overpowering presence of the male figure.

While this sharing of the spotlight by the female protagonist is an improvement over being relegated to the shadows, what is most telling in these two novels are the symbolic absences. In both cases the "matriarch" is missing, as in *Loving Che*, or commits suicide at the end as in *Dreaming in Cuban*. This symbolic erasure seems to suggest that the female character's hold on the spotlight is tenuous at best. This is even more striking when one considers that the "father figure" in both novels symbolically stays firmly in place at the end of each novel. At the end of *Loving Che*, the anonymous daughter is no closer to finding her mother, who chooses to deny her the contact that she craves. In contrast, the novel ends with her finding a photograph of Ernesto Guevara in an antiques shop. It is as if the father figure cannot be avoided. In a like manner, at the end of

Dreaming in Cuban, Fidel Castro makes an appearance in front of the Peruvian embassy.[23]

This presence of the masculine is something that Lourdes Gil identifies as a part of Cuban culture, a vestige of which is carried out into the wider Diaspora. According to her, it is

> una de las estructuras raigales del pensamiento cubano, otra dimensión más profunda de su autoritarismo patriarcal, más allá de las ideologías políticas. Ratificaron una semejanza en el seno de la comunidad cubana global (intra y extramuros), que padece del mismo síndrome anacrónico: el espectro masculinizante que rige la jerarquización social de su dividida realidad.[24]

> one of the root structures of Cuban thought, another deeper dimension of its patriarchal authoritarianism, beyond political ideologies. They ratified something similar in the heart of the Cuban global community (inside or outside the city walls), that suffers from the same anachronic syndrome: the masculinizing specter that governs the social hierarchization of its divided reality. (My translation)

Despite this, the inversion suggested by these two novels reverses the old formula of having the protagonists be men and relegating the women to supporting roles. Here we have the women up front and the men looming in the background, albeit in a large way. What we have here is "la matria" (the mother motherland) instead of "la patria" (the father motherland). But it begs the question, "Which motherland?"

A partial answer can be gleaned from the now famous line in *Dreaming in Cuban* where Pilar seems to resolve part of her issues of identity. Shortly before her return from Cuba she affirms that "sooner or later I'd have to return to New York. I know now it's where I belong—not *instead* of here, but *more* than here." [25] By having Pilar come to this point, García emphasizes her Americanness over her Cubanness. She seems to be telling us that Pilar is American Cuban, more than she is Cuban American and certainly more than she is Cuban alone.

Pilar's sentiment is certainly one that could have been expressed by the anonymous daughter at the end of *Loving Che*. The novel ends with her in a hotel room in Paris, alone except for the photograph of Ernesto Guevara that she had purchased. She is no closer to finding her mother than at the beginning of the novel. Like Pilar, at the end, she is symbolically facing away from Cuba and toward her life in the United States.

Given that these female characters, who represent the future, are symbolically set on a trajectory away from Cuba, can we really speak of this literature as contributing to the reverting of the invisibility of women in Cuban literature? Can we say this about novels written in English? Has the representation of motherhood changed once these authors decide to write in English, once the "madres" have become "mothers"? Are these second generation Cuban American authors "Cuban" or are they, as Isabel Alvarez Borland suggests, *"Cuban-American ethnic writers."*[26] In her book, Alvarez Borland identifies this group of writers as sharing certain characteristics that set them apart from other Cuban exiles. In general, these writers either were born in the United States or were brought here at a very young age. They received their formal education in English and as a general rule have moved away from the use of Spanish, especially in their work. In this sense, these writers are very much like Pilar and the unnamed protagonist in *Loving Che*.

If Alvarez Borland is correct, then these authors are writing toward the United States and not toward Cuba, to use Pérez Firmat's formulation. In his book *Life on the Hyphen*, Gustavo Pérez Firmat asserts that Cuban American authors can either write "towards" Cuba or "towards" the United States. This speaks directly to the writing subject taking a subjective position toward a particular space, be it Cuba or the United States. The perspective of the writer and his or her style and focus are either more American or more Cuban depending on which direction he or she is writing toward and how far along that spectrum he or she is. In the work of these writers, he finds an Anglocentrism that he sees reflected both in the language of the texts as well as in the distance that is established with regards to Cuban culture. Pérez Firmat believes that, unlike other Cuban American authors who write in English, those who have moved farther away from Cuba produce works where *both* the language and the underlying rhythm and accent are in English. It would follow then that we would need to take into account factors not tied strictly to a purely Cuban context.

For an indication of this, we can turn to Guillermo Cabrera Infante's[27] and Andy García's 2006 movie *The Lost City* as a point of departure. The script was written by Cabrera Infante and the film was directed by Andy García. The film has some points in common with Cabrera Infante's *Tres tristes tigres*,[28] his iconic 1967 novel. Both works are a form of elegy for a Havana that disappeared with the triumph of Castro's revolution. However, they do have some differences that are of interest for this analysis.

The protagonists of Cabrera Infante's novel are the tigers, principally Arsenio Cue, Silvestre, and Bustrófedon. Although the protagonists are male, the novel has female characters who have lives of their own. That is to say, although the "tigres" are mostly center stage, they do cede the spotlight to characters such as Cuba Venegas, Vivian Smith Corona, and, especially, La Estrella (The Star). La Estrella, in particular, is a strong presence whose character is developed through the novel. So important were the scenes dedicated to La Estrella that they were later compiled and published in a book titled *Ella cantaba boleros*.[29]

One of the reasons that *Tres tristes tigres* has female characters who can take and hold center stage is because they are fully developed in the chapters dedicated to them. It is the novel's structure that aids in the development of these characters in their own right. The novel is not linear, but rather jumps from one point of view to another. When taken as a whole, they give a panoramic view of Havana on the eve of the Cuban revolution.

The Lost City, by comparison, is a much more conventional work. Although based on the novel, it shares little of its structure or point of view. The novel includes many characters in its attempt to present a slice of Havana nightlife.

This is in stark contrast to the relative absence of women in *The Lost City*. The only female character of note in the film is Aurora, Fico's widowed sister-in-law and the love of his life. Fico, Andy García's character and the oldest of the three Fellove brothers, spends time with Aurora after her husband's death at the hands of the Batista[30] regime. More than fleshing Aurora out as a character in her own right, the romance is used as an excuse to have them tour Havana night life, a bit like the "tigres" do in the novel. There is a scene where Fico takes Aurora to see Beny Moré,[31] for example. The matriarch of the family, Fico's mother makes even fewer on-screen appearances. She is little more than part of the scenery.

It is telling that when Fico goes into exile, he does so alone. He leaves both his mother and Aurora behind. We may hear in this an echo of the voice of Méndez Rodenas's "cultural spokesmen" and their "dominant gender as [the] emblematic subject of exile." [32] In New York, where Fico settles, he recreates his life in Havana, down to the founding of a club just like the Tropicana-esque[33] one that he left in Cuba. He picks up where he left off.

If we read his new life as a continuation of his old life, then we would have to comment on the total absence of a female presence, unlike what he experienced in Havana. If we read it as the beginning of a new life in exile, then we would have to agree with Méndez Rodenas that this script and movie fall into the category of male-centric diasporic cultural production.

Certainly, given that the two driving forces behind *The Lost City* were Cuban men, it would be understandable to find here "el espectro masculinizante que rige la jerarquización social." [34] However, what are we to make of the series *Cane* produced by Cynthia Cidre? She is a Cuban American screenwriter who has been working in Hollywood since the 1980s and wrote the script for *The Mambo Kings*.[35]

Cane has been described as a Cuban *Godfather*, although Cynthia Cidre has been quoted as saying that she likes to think of it more along the lines of *King Lear*[36] and suspects that Mario Puzo was thinking more or less along the same lines when he wrote his novel. As in *The Lost City*, the protagonists are the men of the family. While the daughter Isabel does have her own plotline, her story does not drive the drama the way the interplay among the family's brothers and patriarch do. The mother, Amalia, portrayed by Rita Moreno, does play a somewhat more prominent role than does the mother in *The Lost City*, but here again, the matriarch is even further in the background than Isabel is.

In an interview, Cidre was asked about the participation of "Hector Elizondo's character, and by extension Rita Moreno's character"[37] in the series. She replied that

> They've been in every episode so far. We originally would say maybe they were meant to be more seven out of the 13, 10 out of 13, because it was such a huge ensemble cast. But the truth is they work so well and they're so pleasant and they're so much fun to watch. They're such good actors that sometimes we just can't use them because there's too much story, but we've been using them so far.[38]

In this question and answer we may have another piece of the puzzle as to why women in general, and matriarchs in particular, are even more in the background here than in the two novels mentioned, *Dreaming in Cuban* and *Loving Che*. First, the question implies that Amalia would, by definition, only appear as part of the story line as an extension of her husband and not in her own right. Second, Cidre's answer hints at the economic exigencies of TV and movie production. Unlike movies or TV shows, novels do not carry as much of an economic burden. The "market," it seems to me, intrudes more into the creative writing decisions of the former than they do the latter. It should surprise no one that young actresses would tend to receive more air time than actresses with more experience. With this in mind, it seems apparent to me that tendencies toward the diminution of the role of women in Cuban American cultural production may be emphasized as these works become progressively a part of the American popular cultural mainstream.

If this is true, then we would have a convergence of two influences that tend to work against the portrayal of strong Cuban American women in their own right. On the one hand, we have the traditional Cuban discourse on gender, which has not been significantly modified by the revolution. It is a narrative which, by and large, concedes a central role to men. It is this discourse that, despite their differences with the revolution, émigrés have carried with them out into the Diaspora. On the other hand, we also have American popular culture that, although arguably more progressive in its representation of women, still presents challenges to that portrayal. Even if economic considerations could be obviated, we would still be faced with the problematic portrayal of Hispanic women in general, ugly Betty[39] notwithstanding.

We can see just how far this discourse has been internalized both inside and outside of Cuba in the following quote from Ruth Behar's article, which I cited earlier. In it, she quotes Vilma Espín[40] as being aggresively opposed to the American feminist movement. Behar writes that,

> The national desire to transform gender relations was serious, radical, and wide-ranging. But "feminism" as a term and concept remained unaccept-able in a society where the women's movement was subordinate to the rev-olution . . . Espín's horror that the North American women's movement includes lesbians, as well as her disdain for the idea of gender egalitarian-ism, suggests that some women may have found it in their interest to collude in institutionalizing male heterosexual state power.[41]

It is this collusion, at times not obvious, that we can see at play in Cuban American popular cultural production from the very beginning to the present day. Whether it be Lucille Ball agreeing to give the show the title *"I" Love Lucy* (emphasis mine), where the "I" is Ricky Ricardo/Desi Arnaz, or the long list of symbolic effacements presented in this chapter; it is obvious that the case of the missing Cuban American mother is not one that will soon be solved.

What is left to us is what Adriana Méndez Rodenas exhorts in her article. She would have us work toward the modification of patriarchal discourses through the writing and championing of stories such as *Dreaming in Cuban* and *Loving Che*. She reminds us "to gather these stories into the texture of a yet-to-be-born Nation." [42] And I would add, be that Nation either here or on the other side of the straits of Florida. In the meantime, Cuban and Cuban American women will continue to be hidden, like the mother in the "madre patria," in plain sight.

NOTES

1. Gertrudis Gómez de Avellaneda, *Sab* (Madrid: Cátedra, 1997). *Sab* was first published in 1841. It is considered to be the first Cuban antislavery novel. Sab is a slave who falls in love with Carlota, the white daughter of his master. She is forced to marry a white suitor who is only interested in her family's money. Carlota's family, however, is bankrupt and Sab, after having come into some money, attempts to keep the suitor from abandoning Carlota when he finds out that she has no money.

2. Cirilo Villaverde, *Cecilia Valdés* (México: Editorial Porrúa, 1972). *Cecilia Valdés* was first published in 1839. It is considered to be the Cuban foundational novel. Cecilia Valdés is a mulatta who unknowingly falls in love with her half-brother Leonardo, the son of a wealthy Spanish slave trader. They have a daughter together but Leonardo abandons her in order to marry a wealthy white woman. Leonardo is murdered and Cecilia is convicted of the crime.

3. Doris Sommer, *Foundational Fictions: The National Romances of Latin America* (Berkeley: University of California Press, 1991). She proposes that Latin American national projects in general were allegorized in nineteenth-century novels in which the nation is represented by the image of bourgeois heterosexual families. As Emilio Bejel states in "Cuban CondemNation of Queer Bodies," which appears in *Cuba, the Elusive Nation. Interpretations of National Identity*, "to allegorize the project of the building of the modern Latin American nation: The citizen-father marries the earth-mother, impregnates her, and protects her from "internal" and "external" queer bodies. The earth-mother (the nation) is the object of desire that the citizen must possess and impregnate in order to achieve harmony and legitimacy. Not only the project but also the process of bourgeois consolidation had to be based on marriage, both literal and figurative. Production implied reproduction," 157.

4. Ruth Behar, "Post Utopia: The Erotics of Power and Cuba's Revolutionary Children," in *Cuba, The Elusive Nation*, ed. Damián J. Fernández and Madeline Cámara Betancourt (Gainesville: University Press of Florida, 2000), 140–141.

5. *I Love Lucy*, CBS, 1951–1957.

6. Gustavo Pérez Firmat, *Life on the Hyphen* (Cambridge: Cambridge University Press, 1989), 3.

7. Ibid.

8. Ibid.

9. Adriana Méndez Rodenas, "Engendering the Nation: The Mother/Daughter Plot in Cuban-American Fiction," in *Cuban-American Literature and Art: Negotiating Identities*, ed. Isabel Alvarez Borland (New York: State University of New York Press, forthcoming).

10. Ibid.

11. Gustavo Pérez Firmat has written poetry and fiction, as well as works of literary and cultural criticism. His books *The Cuban Condition* (Cambridge:

Cambridge University Press, 1989), *My Own Private Cuba* (Colorado: Society of Spanish and Spanish-American Studies, 1999), and *Next Year in Cuba* (Houston: Scrivenery Press, 2000), are commentaries on Cuban American culture. He is currently the David Fenison Professor of Humanities at Columbia University.

12. Pablo Medina is a poet and novelist. His books include *Arching into the Afterlife* (Tempe, AZ: Bilingual Press/Editorial Bilingüe, 1991) and *The Return of Felix Nogara: A Novel* (New York: Persea Books, 2000). He teaches at the New School University in New York.

13. Carlos Eire, *Waiting for Snow* (New York: Free Press, 2003). The memoir recounts his childhood in prerevolutionary Havana. It won the 2003 National Book Award for Nonfiction. He currently teaches religion and history at Yale.

14. Méndez Rodenas, "Engendering the Nation" (forthcoming).

15. Lourdes Gil, "Tierra sin nosotras," *Encuentro de la cultura cubana primavera/verano* (1998): 170.

16. Cristina García, *Dreaming in Cuban* (New York: Ballantine Books, 1993).

17. Ana Menéndez, *Loving Che* (New York: Atlantic Monthly Press, 2003).

18. *The Lost City*, dir. Andy García, Lions Gate Films, 2005.

19. *Cane*, prod. Cynthia Cidre, 2007.

20. Méndez Rodenas, "Engendering the Nation" (forthcoming).

21. Ibid.

22. Ibid.

23. Richard Gott, *Cuba: A New History* (New Haven, CT: Yale University Press, 2004). It was the breaching and occupying of the Peruvian embassy in Havana on April 1, 1980, by five Cubans seeking to leave Cuba that began the chain of events that eventually led to the Mariel Boatlift. The Cuban government requested that the Peruvian government return the five asylum seekers. When the Peruvian government refused, the Cuban government withdrew the embassy's police protection on Friday, April 4. By Sunday, April 6, the embassy compound had been occupied by approximately 10,000 Cubans seeking asylum. The standoff culminated in Fidel Castro's declaration that any Cuban who wanted to leave Cuba could do so. He then opened the port of Mariel to ships from the United States to pick up refugees. The exodus lasted from April until September. Eventually, nearly 125,000 people made it out of Cuba.

24. Gil, "Tierra sin nosotras," 171.

25. García, *Dreaming in Cuban*, 236.

26. Isabel Alvarez Borland, *Cuban-American Literature of Exile* (Charlottesville: University Press of Virginia, 1998), 7.

27. Guillermo Cabrera Infante (1929–2005) was a critic, novelist, essayist, and translator. An early supporter of the Cuban Revolution who grew disenchanted with it and was eventually exiled in London.

28. Guillermo Cabrera Infante, *Tres tristes tigres* (Barcelona: Biblioteca de Bolsillo, 1988). Cabrera Infante's novel (originally published in 1967, Barcelona: Editorial Seix Barral) has been translated into English. The title of the English version is *Three Trapped Tigers* (New York: Harper & Row, 1978). The novel's title refers to a tongue twister and alludes to the word games that fill the book. The novel is composed of vignettes that are told from the perspective of the characters. Taken in total, they tell the story of a Havana, especially its night-life, that was swept away by the coming of the Cuban revolution.

29. Guillermo Cabrera Infante, *Ella cantaba boleros* (Madrid: Santillana, 1996).

30. Fulgencio Batista was the president of Cuba before the triumph of Fidel Castro's 1959 revolution.

31. Beny Moré (1919–1963) is considered by many Cubans both on and off the island as the greatest singer that Cuba has ever produced.

32. Méndez Rodenas, "Engendering the Nation" (forthcoming).

33. The Tropicana Club in Havana opened in 1939 and featured lavish stage shows and musical acts. Its shows helped define the popular image of Havana nightlife in the 1950s.

34. Gil, "Tierra sin nosotras," 171.

35. *The Mambo Kings*, dir. Arne Glimcher, Warner Home Video, 1992.

36. William Shakespeare, *King Lear* (New York: Cambridge University Press, 2000).

37. Cynthia Cidre, "Exclusive Interview," http://buddytv.com/articles/cane/exclusive-interview-cane-creat-10561.aspx.

38. Ibid.

39. *Ugly Betty*, ABC, 2006. This television series premiered on ABC in 2006 and is based on a Colombian soap opera "Yo soy Betty, la fea" (I am Betty, the ugly one). Betty, the plain-looking heroine, rose from being a secretary to an executive position in a fashion design company based on her intelligence. It appeared on Colombian television between 1999 and 2001. Latin American soap operas, as opposed to American soap operas, run for a limited amount of time and have a definitive ending.

40. Vilma Espín (1930–2007) was the former wife of Raúl Castro, the current president of Cuba. She led the Federation of Cuban women from its founding in 1960 until her death. She was also a member of the Cuban Communist Party's Central Committee and its Politburo.

41. Behar, "Post Utopia," 141.

42. Méndez Rodenas, "Engendering the Nation" (forthcoming).

CHAPTER 4

Of Mamothers and Behemothers-in-Law: Toward a Twenty-First-Century Bestiary

Craig N. Owens

It is . . . a space of multiple dissentions.
—Michel Foucault, *The Archaeology of Knowledge*[1]

The European Middle Ages is widely understood as a period of turmoil, a thousand-year stretch of cultural backsliding, lubricated by a peculiar and, in contemporary depictions of the period,[2] alarmingly ubiquitous mixture of mud, feces, blood, sweat, and tears, and accelerated by the dominance of fact-proof superstition and Churchy paranoia. But, the questionable accuracy of these representations aside, in at least one way, the denizens of those times and climes had it pretty good: namely, when it came to the taxonomy of monsters. Of course, an alewife may have had no reliable way to ensure the cleanliness or consistency of her brew. But if her customers took ill after a few flagons-full of her newly tuned quaff, she would at least be able to duck the blame and spare her guests the aspersion of excess by having it given out that her stock in trade had been infested by a colony of Seps, a serpent whose venom causes pernicious necrosis. And if a farmer found his well gone dry, he could have done worse than to seek out and exterminate the likely invasion of Sea-Pigs, fishlike creatures given to draining aquifers.[3] In short, faced with any calamity of any magnitude, the Middle Ager could always rely on one of several bestiaries in circulation to identify the monster responsible for his misfortune.

Not so we moderns. Gone are the halcyon days of monstrous certainties; no longer have we at our fingertips so convenient a compendium of the causes of our woes. We find ourselves without a taxonomy for the monsters—the beasts and inner demons—with whom we daily contend: certainly nothing so straightforward as an illustrated guide that with placid good sense could remind us to beware the Palandrus, a "beast that can conceal itself by changing its appearance." [4] And, while reality television and situational comedy, the latest advertising or political campaign, and today's sex or drug or wardrobe scandal can occasionally bring to the light of day a savage beast or breast as yet undocumented, we must rely on the piecemeal sources of Internet and news media to parcel out in disorganized dribs and drabs the information formerly so navigably bound in one handsome volume.

And so our modern bestiary, diffuse and articulated as it is, and brimming with such fiends and foes as vassal and serf could not have imagined—retrovirus, pornography, avian flu, and terrorist—finds itself spread out among institutions and databases, ensconced in lore and law, and housed in laboratories and training camps. At the risk of encouraging the geometric, rhizomatous proliferation of beasts without a bestiary, I am proposing a new entry, though not a new monster, to be inserted between the *monosaurus* and the *muscaliet*: the Mother-in-Law.

The mother's monstrous nature has for some decades been considered and reconsidered, critiqued, deconstructed, represented, and dismissed. Roman Polanski's film *Rosemary's Baby* (1968)[5] remains among the most sophisticated filmic depictions of maternal monstrosity, and it emerged at the beginning of the decade that would see the production of *The Exorcist*[6] and the publication of Christina Crawford's memoir *Mommie Dearest*.[7] As if to correct George Romero's original *Dawn of the Dead* (1978), which ends with the revelation of the apparently insufficiently monstrous principal female character's pregnancy as she and the presumptive father of her child escape against the backdrop of a hopeful sunset,[8] Zack Snyder's remake (2004) of the film prominently features a pregnant woman who, in the process of becoming zombified, gives birth to a child who is also a zombie.[9]

It was also during this decade that Julia Kristeva began to formulate the foundational notions upon which her readings of maternity and its manifestations in language and literature would be founded. I want to take a few minutes to dwell on Kristeva's discussion of motherhood, partly as a way to demonstrate the degree to which maternal monstrosity has already been theorized, and partly to begin framing the questions that will sustain this inquiry into the beastliness of the mother-in-law.

Kristeva devoted much of her writing to exploring the way maternal attributes and maternal identity threatened the stability of rationalist, ordered systems of information and regulation, both psychologically and in terms of the material practices of Western, patriarchal social structures. If masculine, and indeed paternal, institutions of power and reason are understood as the unmarked, as the default, as the neutral mechanisms by which steady-state society maintains its equilibrium, poise, and balance, then maternal attributes make themselves felt as disruptions, unbalancings, even perversions, in Kristeva's view. Particularly inasmuch as the mother, according to classical psychoanalysis, is the first, most salient, and most forbidden love object of the son, she symbolizes both life-source and taboo. Conventions of language and communication, of social and symbolic order, have as their goal first to relegate whatever is "questionable" to the "archaic, instinctual, maternal territory";[10] maternity associates itself with deviance, with the derailment of proper aims and attachments. Then, by means of that association, the mother becomes not a fully self-willed agent, a subject, but rather an "object." But, she is not "like any other object"; she is "forbidden."[11]

Kristeva opens her volume *Powers of Horror: An Essay on Abjection*—the term she uses to name the sense of revulsion, perversion, and disruption associated with maternity—with a more visceral evocation of what she will later term "maternal anguish":[12]

Loathing an item of food, a piece of filth, waste, or dung. The spasms and vomiting that protect me. The repugnance, the retching that thrusts me to the side and turns me away from defilement, sewage, and muck. [. . .] When the eyes see or the lips touch that skin on the surface of milk—harmless, thin as a sheet of cigarette paper, pitiful as a nail paring—I experience a gagging sensation and, still farther down, spasms in the stomach, the belly; and all the organs shrivel up the body, provoke tears and bile, increase heartbeat, cause forehead and hands to perspire. Along with sight-clouding dizziness, nausea makes me balk at that milk cream [. . .].[13]

In this passage, Kristeva dwells at length on the physical manifestations of the revulsion inspired by food-"loathing"; but the food in question is not just any food: It is milk, the food with which the mother feeds the child, the nutriment that connects the infant to his *alma mater*. The "repugnance," "dizziness," "nausea," "spasms," and "shrivel[ing]" brought on by the encounter with the mother, symbolically mediated by milk, is, for Kristeva, the same kind of reaction elicited by an encounter with "a piece of filth, waste, or dung." Thus, the disruptive power of the maternal, and everything to do with it, classes the mother with the "abject" waste products of daily life: "filth" and "dung."

But the monstrous nature of maternity does not transfer easily or without transformation to the character of the mother-in-law. As a cultural concept, constructed through centuries of discourse, the mother-in-law has developed her own distinct bestialities, thanks to a fraught and highly mediated relationship to motherhood proper. Fortunately, a recent film has gone a good deal of the way toward addressing this problem by exploring, somewhat circuitously, the question of how the monstrous nature of the mother-in-law compares to that of the mother.

Robert Luketic's film *Monster-in-Law* (2005) is an apparently simplistic film with a simple premise.[14] Kevin Fields (Michael Vartan), an inexplicably single neurosurgeon, meets Charlotte (Jennifer Lopez), a latte bohemian living in what appears to be Venice, California, and who prefers to go by the more tomboyish "Charlie." She makes her living as a temp at a medical clinic, as a dog walker, as a sometime yoga instructor, and as a sometime clothing designer. Her unstructured life and easygoing outlook, we are given to understand in about three minutes of perfunctory dialogue during which Kevin waxes eloquent in praise of her eyes, are precisely what Kevin's high-pressure, highly educated, highly eligible, and high-income life has lacked all these years. The complication in this improbable but otherwise unremarkable romance is Kevin's mother, Viola (Jane Fonda). Widowed by Kevin's father, and now out of two subsequent unhappy marriages, Viola has made Kevin the center of her world, a world considerably less time-consuming, if also less rewarding, now that she has been replaced by a tiny blonde woman of barely 20 as the host of her own talk show, *Viola!*

Having established Viola's jealous devotion, the movie then follows Viola's increasingly outrageous but equally futile attempts to undermine her son's impending marriage to Charlie. Her unsuccessful derailments begin simply enough, as a kind of overbearing insistence on helping Charlie plan and execute the wedding ceremony; soon enough, however, she decides to move in with the already cohabiting pair after a faked anxiety attack "diagnosed" by an actor playing the role of psychiatrist. In between, Viola interviews Charlie, apparently in preparation for naming her in her will, but in reality as an attempt to find out personal information about her regarding STDs and her citizenship status. And, in one of the sillier moments of the film—quite an honor indeed, given the relentless silliness of the whole thing—Viola "mistakes" an air horn for an air freshener, further alienating Charlie in the hopes of inspiring second

thoughts about the family into which she is about to marry. Utterly predictably, Charlie eventually turns the tables on Viola, getting her own
back in a series of increasingly less passive passive-aggressive maneuvers
leading up to the wedding itself, during the immediate preparations for
which the two finally come to terms: Viola will respect the boundaries
of Kevin's new relationship. So much for plot.

Viola's relationship to her son and her behavior toward Charlie certainly seem monstrous in the colloquial sense of the word: outrageous
and deeply ill intentioned. But to understand the way the film contributes
to the as-yet-undeveloped contemporary lexicon of maternal bestiality, it
might be useful to consider a somewhat more carefully defined notion of
the monstrous. "The monster," according to Michel Foucault's 1974 and
1975 lectures to the College de France, compiled in the volume *Abnormal*, is "a mixture." While he suggests that the elements of which the
monster is composed may vary, including "two species," "two realms,"
"two sexes," "two individuals," and even "life and death," the fact that
one being represents a blending of two usually distinct elements is the
essence of the monster for Foucault. He even offers examples of these
monstrous "mixture[s]" from eighteenth-century sources, as if to horrify
as much as to inform his readers: "[T]he pig with the sheep's head"
may seem bizarre, but not compared to the "person who has two heads
and one body" or "the fetus born with a morphology that means it will
not be able to live" more than a short time.[15]

Viola seems to fit Foucault's formulation of the monster, an unnatural
"mixture" of traits and behaviors typically associated with motherliness
and those seemingly antithetical to it. She fills the maternal role partly
by having simply given birth to Kevin. Her interest in his new girlfriend
and in her fitness as a potential lifelong partner for Kevin is understand-
ably maternal as well. Kevin's attitude about his mother helps to characterize their mother-son relationship: For his part, he is concerned that his
mother should approve of Charlie, and that Charlie and she should
become friends. But if Viola is a mother, she is a potentially monstrous
one. Her excessive devotion to her son, and his to her, borders on the
erotic; in an early scene, she kisses Kevin with such ardor that he leaves
her embrace with her lipstick emblazoned across his mouth; in another,
when his mother phones while he and Charlie are involved in some very
preliminary foreplay on his couch, Kevin actually answers the phone [!]
and carries on a conversation with Viola that sounds more like pillow talk
than a filial chat. While Kevin certainly enables this behavior, refusing for
whatever reason to declare to his mother that her behavior is grotesque, he

is not always the catalyst for it. Ruby (Wanda Sykes), Viola's personal assistant, informs Viola that Kevin is a "fine piece of ass," by way of explaining why women find him attractive. Ruby's evaluation of Kevin only fuels the already simmering jealousy Viola has begun to feel since learning of his new relationship. So, if Foucault is right—that the monster is a mixture of seemingly antithetical elements—and if the movie is right —that Viola is some kind of monster—it is tempting to think of her as a monstrous mother, a mother whose relationship with her son is improperly contaminated by the erotic tension between them.

The problem, however, is that Viola's monstrosity seems, in this respect, confined to her maternal role. That is, as a mother, she appears monstrous, but in a Foucaultian, not Kristevan, way. After all, it appears that Kristeva is concerned with the way maternity, as a category of existence, is always monstrous already; Foucault, by contrast, concerns himself with the way the monstrous is culturally defined. In either case, though, while maternity and monstrosity find themselves linked, neither seems at first glance to offer us a way to understand the mother-in-law as engaging a monstrous identity distinct from that of the mother proper. In other words, the question remains whether the *monster*-in-law is just the monstrous mother of one's spouse, or if, in her relation to her child's partner, a distinct change in the nature of her monstrosity is to be observed.

Before returning to the film's special contribution to this field of inquiry, I want to take some time to piece out the question of the concept of the *mother-in-law* as we have inherited it, in the hopes of both focusing and complicating this inquiry into the way this iconic figure has found herself represented in *Monster-in-Law*. As a way of using language to formulate a relationship, the term *mother-in-law* tries to legitimate the mother-in-law's maternal status by statute. The elaboration "in-law" attached to "mother" wants to institute her maternity by contract, to guarantee her integration into a legally binding conception of motherhood. And yet, it also suggests a kind of double identity: However much she is to be understood as occupying full motherhood, with all the rights and privileges appertaining thereto, she is *not quite* a mother, and her maternal status must be qualified by a supplemental phrase that *only seems* to reinforce the legitimacy of the mother-in-law's maternity, but in fact calls attention to its merely contractual quality. Thus, the mother-in-law is both mother *and* not-mother at the same time. In saying this, I am aware that I am not making a new observation, but rather that I am simply putting into a convenient formulation the contradictory and often seemingly irresolvable tensions and contradictions that constitute mother-in-law-ness, in general, and our vexed relationships to our own mothers-in-law, more particularly.

Again, Foucault's insights may offer us a way of making sense of this apparent duality. His historiographic revision *The Archaeology of Knowledge* (1969) considers precisely the way the contradictory natures of such a cultural position as the mother-in-law gets negotiated in discourse. He remarks that "[f]ar from being an [...] accident of discourse"[16]—the system of meaning making within which mother-in-law-ness makes sense, in our case—such internal contradictions constitute "the very law" of the discourse itself.[17] That is, the fact that the mother-in-law is both legally constituted as a kind of mother, but as *only* a *kind of* mother, does not disrupt the discourse of family relationships: it reinforces and, in part, enables it. But, Foucault explains, the contradictions inherent in such systems and the ideas they enable are rarely explicit, rarely obvious in the language of the system itself; instead, the way a culture speaks about and represents phenomena, especially touchy ones, attempts to "translate and overcome"[18] any sense of contradiction, to erase or deny or rationalize it. And yet, because any attempt to construct a system both comprehensive in its scope and noncontradictory in the relationship among its various elements, according to Kurt Gödel's theory of radical incompleteness, is doomed to failure, such a rationalization is only rationalization.

That is why it is always so formal, so forced, and awkward when, in the cinematic nuptial scene, after the toasts and speeches, the bride's mother embraces the groom and insists, "Call me mother"—or worse, *mom*. The ceremony, for all its ritual unifications, nevertheless preserves the distance between the principals and their mothers-in-law that makes the contemporary American stereotype possible in the first place—caricatures ranging from *Bewitched*'s crafty Endora[19] to *Everybody Loves Raymond*'s Marie.[20] They barge into the American televisual or cinematic home, unannounced and uninvited, but inevitable, with advice and impunity.

And is that not precisely what vexes one's relationship with one's mother-in-law? Not that she is too close, always there, hovering, and intervening, but that her legal status keeps her too distant: guaranteed not by the years of familiarity, preceded in most cases by some months of physical connectedness, but rather by a contract, by proxy, by accident. No, our relationships are not too close for comfort, but too far away. It is as if her in-law-ness were a de facto restraining order against those who would do her violence. She is out of reach of the *lex talionis* that would satisfy our bloodlust, would keep down the gorge that rises at the slightest affront, the unsolicited commentary, the backhanded compliment, the passive-aggressive advice. And, if the suffix *in-law* in the English formulation belies the need to qualify or second-guess the mother-in-law's actual maternal status, its counterpart in the French, *belle-mere*, overstates the family fondness for her. She is more than mere *mere* [mother]; she is *belle* [beautiful]. But, in this *belle*, do we not sense an ironic smirk, the tongue-in-cheek, a kind of "if-you-can't-say-something-nice" restraint?

And while we are on the etymology behind this affect—because what you call something helps determine what it is—the Italian has *suocera* and the Spanish *suegra*, words related to each other, but entirely unconnected etymologically to mother [*madre*] in either language. Instead, they derive from the Latin *socrus*, a very ancient feminine fourth-declension noun that, in its own etymological past, was also—maybe even primarily—gendered masculine: it meant both *mother-* and *father-in-law*. I point this out not as an amusing or edifying tangent through the European Romance languages, but to make a point about the way Western culture conceives of the mother-in-law's social and family position. Whereas English (like German) displaces the mother-in-law's maternity onto the legalistic discourse, French prefers the winkingly ironic, mocking alternative: *la belle-mere*. These two languages build the mother-in-law's distance from her child's partner into the term itself: and, while the modifiers *in-law* and *belle* may be tonally ambiguous, their presence, as appendages to *mother*, mark the fact that the mother-in-law's maternity is at a distance: motherliness once removed. By contrast, the Italian and Spanish emphasize this maternal remove by leaving *madre* out of the formulation altogether, taking their provenance from a transgendered etymological past. The essential shared characteristic among these four formulations is that they express themselves in such a way as to highlight the distance that constitutes the very special kind of maternity motherliness-in-law is. She is a figure, as figured in language, just out of reach, unstranglable, unslappable, untouchable.

Or as Kristeva might have her, "forbidden." [21] This, at least, is the status of the mother as her son relates to her: the incest taboo, constraining and channeling filial desires away from the mother and toward more appropriate objects, also constrains language, at its most basic levels, to the conventional laws of diction, syntax, and grammar. For Kristeva, the paternal Law, the Law that intervenes in the mother-son relationship and institutes taboos, is precisely the same Law that, in language, prevents slippages in meaning, the force that binds the signifier to the signified, the definition to the word. Kristeva insists on this link between the laws of language and the laws of sexual desire in order to enable a complex and compelling understanding of "poetic" language: namely, that the play of meaning and sound, the *double entendre* and figures of speech, in short, in those unconventional uses of language we classify as privileges guaranteed by poetic license, are manifestations of a kind of female protest against both cultural and lexical constraint. And, with poetic license comes a kind of licentiousness, the hint of outlawed desires. To put this another way, the mother and the mother-in-law are to be kept at a distance, not so much from one another—though I would recommend that, too—but the one from her son, and the other from her child's spouse. One notable difference, however, is that while that distance prevents the mother-son relationship from being destabilized by an excess of desire, it prevents the mother-in-law's relationship to her child's partner from becoming destabilized by an excess of venom.

If the formulation *mother-in-law* suggests a particular and exceptional case of motherhood, then *Monster-in-Law* would, by the analogy suggested by its near homophony, seem to specify a particular kind of monster. But that is not quite the sense of monster-in-law as it first appears: it is not as if the monster-son relationship were the norm and the monster-in-law relationship were a special and primarily legally constructed version of this relationship. The witticism suggested by the film's title seems to fail precisely here: it is not as if *monster* and *mother* were, by themselves, as nearly synonymous as they are nearly homophonous: They do not mean the same thing so much as they sound somewhat similar. Rather, the mother-in-law is only monstrous because of her in-law-ness, not because of her maternity.

The wit that makes the slight slippage from *mother* to *monster* in the film's title, however, is more complex than it first appears. For instead of relying on only one element of play—the convenient homophony of *monster* with *mother*—it depends on two simultaneous elements of play, of instability. One is its economy of expression: it compresses, in a neat and immediately decipherable phrase, the sense of monstrosity that is maternity-in-law. But if the only thing the film were trying to suggest is that a mother-in-law is a kind of monster, it could have just called itself *Monster*. To put this a different way, if the mother-in-law is already a monster, then the monster-in-law would be something like the mother-in-law-in-law. But, the fact that *monster-in-law* retains the *in-law* at the end only *appears* excessive. In fact, it suggests the second element of play at work in the title: specifically, that as it compresses the notion of monstrosity and mother-in-law-ness, it also suggests the mother proper is a monster in her own right. After all, the word that gets most obviously replaced with *monster* is not the whole formulation *mother-in-law*, but simply *mother*. This second, simultaneous sense of the title suggests that Kevin's mother, in the film, is already a monster, whether or not Kevin ever marries.

This kind of doubled *double entendre* is precisely what happens to language inflected through the feminine in general and through the maternal in particular, according to Kristeva. She considers at length how constraints on language, such as rules, conventions, and established discourses, make using language a matter of control and of gatekeeping. She explains that the conception of the way language works in the twentieth century and contemporary culture, particularly outside of the academy, tends to compartmentalize and rationalize language into discrete and namable functions: " 'signifier,' 'primary processes,' displacement and condensation, metaphor and metonymy, rhetorical figures," all of which, despite the potential to erupt out of their defined functions, nevertheless remain "subordinate [...] to the principal function of naming [...] ."[22] Thinking of language in this way, as purely rational and functional, for Kristeva, allows language to "constitute itself" as a complete and unself-contradictory system, but only "at the cost of repressing instinctual drive and continuous relation to the mother." The antidote to this repression, she continues, is "poetic language," whose deployment is always "unsettled and questionable," and which therefore "maintains itself" by "reactivating this repressed instinctual, maternal element." That maternal element in language, then, emerges at the moment that conventional usages break down or get displaced by more playful, poetic expression.

To the extent, then, that the formulation *Monster-in-Law* relies on a complex linguistic compression and doubling that, in the end, do not conform to a formalist analytical attempt unproblematically to make coherent and uncontradictory sense of the term is testimony to the Kristevan maternal "drive" that allows the film's title to make immediate sense without seeming to stand up under scrutiny. And that maternal drive, the instinctual wit that animates the title's wordplay, also suggests what I take to be the underlying question of the film itself: What is monstrous about the monster-in-law? Her ersatz maternity or her statutory in-law-ness? Or is it both, making her doubly and differently monstrous at the same time?

But there is something else to be said about the homophonic shift from *mother* to *monster*: the near homophony, the wit it evinces, suggests a poetic, rather than conventionally stable, orientation to language. If the wordplay is sensible or striking or funny or witty in any way, it has to do with the fact that we are likely to recognize the verbal relationship *monster/mother* as analogous to the conceptual relationship of *monster* to *mother-in-law*. For when the mother-in-law becomes the *monster*-in-law, then the law that governs the strict conventions of language, that would forbid wordplay and puns and slippage, fails, and a kind of forbidden relationship, a forbidden maternity, makes itself felt in language. The wordplay of *monster-in-law* rends the fabric of literal meaning and calls attention to the way an out-of-reach femaleness attempts to cross that minimal distance just as Viola, the mother-in-law herself, transgresses the minimal filial distance that would have stabilized her relationship with Charlie.

As we have seen, Viola as a mother certainly seems monstrous, whether we understand her monstrosity in Foucaultian terms—as "a mixture" of maternity and *eros* in her relationship to Kevin—or in Kristevan terms—as a woman whose excessive show of power, wealth, and devotion evokes "nausea" and "dizziness." But if we read the Foucaultian formulation through the Kristevan, we see that the mixture that is Viola's maternity precisely constitutes a conventional, if exaggerated, maternal type: the Oedipal mother. When Kristeva links poetic uses of language to liberated expression of maternity, she concludes that "*poetic language would be* [. . .] *the equivalent of incest.*" [23] In other words, because poetics breeches the usual boundary that has for so long divided the rationalist-formal elements of language and meaning making from the irrational, instinctual, drives that underlie it, poetic language commits a crime against the paternal repressive law of language exactly analogous to the crime of incest, a crime committed against the father and involving the breech of boundaries. What Kristeva is suggesting, then, is that the incest taboo is not what constitutes an appropriate maternal relation to the son; it is the possibility of incest itself. The excessive and explicit incestuous familiarity Viola shows toward Kevin may make her a monster in a colloquial and social way; but, in the terms of this discussion, it simply makes her too much a mother, what we might call the *obscene mother*.

Obscenity and monstrosity, it is important to note, are not the same. The difference can be characterized like this: Obscenity is too much of something; monstrosity is the *wrong thing* altogether. So, while gratuitous sexual content in film and photography is considered obscene, a film or photograph showing explicit sex acts between an adult and a child or an animal is monstrous. It is not that it shows too much, but that it shows a combination of elements (adult/child or human/animal) that makes it unthinkable, unable to be accounted for within an order rationalized as "natural." Mother-son incest, particularly when it is framed as an excess of maternal devotion to her son, and not as a preliminary to sexual relations— Viola and Kevin never consummate their relationship, of course—is obscene in these terms, because it is gratuitously maternal. But it is not monstrous if we accept the Freudian line that mother-son incest, even if only expressed or felt as a desire, remains accounted for in a rationalized—in this case psycho-analyzed—notion of the natural, the normal, the thinkable.

And it is clear that we understand it as obscene, and not as monstrous, because it has become possible for maternal incestuous desires and behaviors to serve as the central conflict of a romantic comedy.[24] But even in such thrillers as *Psycho* (1960)[25] and its remake (1998),[26] the now-dead mother, however overbearing and jealous she may have been during her life, is not the site of monstrosity: Norman is, with his need to internalize his mother's desires and, before he kills the young women he finds tempting, to embody his mother by dressing in her clothes. Norman is the mixture, the monstrous figure in the movie, even if the final scene suggests that his monstrosity is a symptom of his mother's obscene maternity.

In short, films like *Psycho* and *Monster-in-Law* are part of the very mechanism by which American film culture has made maternal incest thinkable as obscene—horrifying or comic in its inflection—rather than as monstrous; and thereby we have come to understand the incestuous mother as one kind of mother, not a transgression of motherliness altogether. So, if there is something monstrous about Viola, we might want to consider not her maternity by itself, but rather the way it is constituted, as a statutory category, in relation to Charlie. If it is not the *mother* that is monstrous, maybe it is the *in-law*.

It may be helpful here to recall an earlier moment in this essay, when it posited that

> [t]he elaboration "in-law" attached to "mother" wants to institute, statutorily, her maternity, to guarantee her integration into a legally binding conception of motherhood [. . .]

Whereas motherhood is, essentially, a biological fact (though it is becoming less and less so), mother-in-law-ness is only secondarily or coincidentally biological, inasmuch as it presumes a biological relationship to the other spouse in a marriage.[27] Primarily, it is a culturally or legally constructed category, and as such is a relative category of existence.

Once a mother, always a mother; but a mother-in-law is only a mother-in-law during visits.

When Viola comes to the house Kevin and Charlie share, however, it is not on a visit: she is there to stay for the long haul, while she recovers from her so-called "anxiety." It is here that Viola's name suggests her essential behavior: to *viola*te the demilitarized zone that separates her from Charlie and would stabilize their relationship. And, lest there be any question whether Viola arrives as a monstrous mother or as a monstrous mother-in-law, Kevin is conveniently called away on some kind of doctor business for a few days. So, Viola gets the chance to remain mother-in-law for some time, while temporarily abdicating her role as mother. She essentially reverses the categories of mother and mother-in-law. Her maternity becomes dispensable, contingent; her mother-in-law-ness is here to stay.

And during her stay—the permanence of which is signaled by the bags, cases, and portmanteaux she brings with her—she manages to encroach on Charlie's space even more than she already has by taking over her wedding planning and by moving in: on the first night, for instance, Viola pretends to suffer from nightmares and anxiety, and insists that Charlie sleep with her to soothe her. Then, apparently in the throes of horrible dreams, she embraces Charlie, effectively depriving her of a night's sleep and physically enacting her inappropriate invasion of Charlie's space. This kind of behavior, finally, establishes her monstrosity as mother-in-law: she refuses to maintain the mere-most minimum distance that, earlier in the essay, I suggested constitutes the appropriate mother-in-law/daughter-in-law relationship. The fact is, then, that for a mother to sleep with her daughter-in-law is worse than sleeping with her son: the one is monstrous, the other merely Oedipal.

If Charlie is to reestablish their relationship within the boundaries of the "law" that constitutes it, then she must put some personal distance between the two of them. And she does so, at last, by insisting that Viola wear the most frumpy, frilly, maternal mother-of-the-groom gown imaginable. This strategy is enforced by Viola's own mother-in-law (Elaine Stritch)—dyked out in pantsuit and necktie, with her hair cut short and her voice pitched deep—who browbeats Viola into submission. The fact that this strategy works, containment, both figuratively and literally, in a dress so unlike the youthful couture she prefers, reveals what is truly monstrous about Viola as a mother-in-law: her refusal to play the role of mother simultaneously. Her excessive, obscene maternity, leading up to Kevin's announcement that he and Charlie are engaged, becomes a complete renunciation of the maternal. Her role as mother-in-law, into which she throws herself entirely, becomes her primary identity. And that is the monstrosity: For she has confused her primary role, as Kevin's mother, with her secondary one, and has thus mixed the antagonistic behavior that characterizes in-law-ness with the perverse, obscene closeness and permanence that characterize maternity.

But we have left something hanging, something unaddressed. This essay posited, earlier, that the Kristevan wit of the film's title seemed to depend on a double wordplay: on the one hand, it suggests that Viola is a particularly monstrous mother-in-law; on the other, it suggests that she is a particularly monstrous mother. She is two monsters at once, it appeared. But, since then, in establishing her monstrosity-in-law, this essay has also neutralized her maternal monstrosity, demonstrating that what first appeared as monstrous maternity is, in fact, merely obscene.

We are left, then, with two possible ways of accounting for this loose end. The first is to conclude that Viola bears only a single, not a double, monstrousness. In that case, the seemingly double wordplay we observed in the title plays one time too many, and the film's thematic simplicity belies the title's apparent complexity. The other possibility, however, is that Viola's second monstrosity emerges not from her maternity, but from something else, that her apparent but neutralized monstrosity as a mother is a red herring for another kind of female monstrosity.

If that is so, we need not look very far into the film to find it: we meet Viola first not as a mother or as a mother-in-law, but as a talk-show host fired from the show that bears her name because she no longer connects to younger audiences. She proves herself completely unable to interview a shallow, celebrity-addled Britney Spears–like pop idol, preferring instead the familiar company of the heads of state, diplomats, and laureates who attend her parties. To this extent, she is like a combination of Hillary Rodham Clinton and Barbara Walters. But Viola's age and her connections, which would give any man immense influence, only get her fired. The fact that Jane Fonda plays the role of Viola is impossible to overlook or dismiss in this regard. A symbol of youthful, radical indignation over the Vietnam war, Hanoi Jane transformed herself into the symbol of the "Me" generation's youth and body obsession in the 1980s. Without question, Fonda's public persona contributed to the American resistance to superannuation over the past three decades. That is why, in returning to film after a 15-year hiatus for *Monster-in-Law*, and playing the role of an obsolete professional woman desperately clinging to a youth long gone, Fonda brings with her almost as much cultural baggage as Viola brings literal baggage for her stay with Kevin and Charlie.

The film's barely veiled concern with the anxiety women of a certain age are expected to feel in contemporary America points toward Viola's second site of monstrosity. The formulation "monster-in-law" uses "monster" as a wry synonym not for "mother," but for "old woman," particularly one who insists on maintaining her looks and influence, one who refuses to accept her cultural obsolescence. Botoxed and bleached perhaps, maybe lifted and liposuctioned, tucked, trim, toned, intelligent and outspoken, well-connected and powerful, she is the second monster with which the film invites us to contend. Wedged between Basilisk and Bittern is the *Beldame*. From the Old French for *grandmother*, we see in *beldame* the kind of contradiction, the incongruity that marks Foucault's monsters. Etymologically, it suggests "beautiful lady" [*bel[le] dame*]. But, in colloquial Old French, from which English has adopted the word, the *bel-* prefix would have been understood not as a literal sign of beauty, but rather of respect. In English, the term actually suggests ugliness and old age. Three facts about *beldame* strike me salient in regard to this film: first, it shares its *bel-* with *belle-mere*, the French mother-in-law; second, it names the grandmother, the title Viola rejects, insisting that her future grandchildren call her the generationally ambiguous "Aunt Viola"; and last, the word, like the woman it names, is obsolete.

This essay began by promising a new entry into our contemporary bestiary: the *Mother-in-Law*. It ends having delivered two. In doing so, it has shown the alarming fact that, for the contemporary American mother, maternity always verges on monstrosity—in more ways than one. It has also evinced a monstrosity of its own, primarily Foucaultian in its inflection. Samuel Johnson famously dismissed John Donne's poetry by claiming that in it metaphorical elements were "yoked by violence together," and that therefore it was monstrous. Has not this essay "yoked" high theory "by violence" to unapologetically popular culture, *viola*ting the film's right to speak for itself, and for everyday audiences unencumbered by French philosophies of language to experience their own culture and to make sense of it without academic interference? Is this not interference, this scholarly "mixture," [28] mixing in other people's business? Even in a Kristevan sense, does it not "dizzy" and "nausea[te]" [29] with its self-satisfied flippancy. Is it not possible that, when it comes to monsters, it takes one to know one? If so, then the film I have characterized as "simplistic" and "silly" may have revealed something serious about the status of cultural and film studies, of a scholarly undertaking that lays claim to an objective position on the edge of culture, elevated above the ray of everyday life: that it is excessive, out-of-bounds, its objects of inquiry "forbidden."[30] In short, it is monstrous. And so, to *mother-in-law* and *beldame*, we may as well add *academic*, both as an honest accounting for the kind of cultural monstrosity an essay such as this may in fact be and as a warning against becoming all the more monstrous.

NOTES

1. Michel Foucault, *The Archaeology of Knowledge and the Discourse on Language*, trans. A. M. Sheridan Smith (New York: Pantheon, 1972), 155.

2. I am thinking particularly of such films as *Monty Python and the Holy Grail* (1975) or Leslie Megahey's *The Advocate* (1993).

3. David Badke, "Beasts," *The Medieval Bestiary*, ed. David Badke, http://bestiary.ca/index.html (accessed October 22, 2008).

4. Ibid.

5. Cf. Roman Polanski, dir., *Rosemary's Baby* (Paramount Pictures, 1968).

6. Cf. William Friedkin, dir., *The Exorcist* (Warner Brothers, 1973).

7. Cf. Christina Crawford, *Mommie Dearest: A True Story* (New York: William Morrow and Co., 1978).

8. George Romero, dir., *Dawn of the Dead* (United Film Distribution Co., 1979).

9. Zack Snyder, dir., *Dawn of the Dead* (Universal Studios, 2004).

10. Julia Kristeva, "From One Identity to Another," trans. Thomas Gora, Alice Jardine, and Leon Roudiez, *The Kristeva Reader*, ed. Kelly Oliver (New York: Columbia University Press, 1997), 104.

11. Ibid.

12. Julia Kristeva, *Powers of Horror: An Essay in Abjection*, trans. Leon Roudiez (New York: Columbia University Press, 1982), 12.

13. Ibid., 2–3.

14. Robert Luketic, dir., *Monster-in-Law* (New Line Cinema, 2005).

15. Michel Foucault, *The Abnormal: Lectures at the College de France 1974–1975*, trans. Graham Burchell (New York: Picador-St. Martin's Press, 1999), 63.

16. Foucault, *The Archaeology of Knowledge and the Discourse on Language*, 151.

17. Ibid.

18. Ibid.

19. Cf. Agnes Moorehead, perf., *Bewitched* (American Broadcasting Company, 1964–1972).

20. Cf. Doris Roberts, perf., *Everybody Loves Raymond* (Columbia Broadcasting System, 1996–2005).

21. Kristeva, "From One Identity to Another," 104.

22. Ibid.

23. Ibid. Italics in original.

24. This contrasts with the morbid situational conflict (sit-con) of morbid tragedy as it was performed in Classical Athens at the debut of Sophocles's *Oedipus Rex*.

25. Cf. Alfred Hitchcock, dir. *Psycho* (Universal Studios, 1960).

26. Cf. Gus Van Sant, dir., *Psycho* (Universal Pictures, 1998).

27. Is the mother of a partner in a common-law marriage the *mother-in-common-law*?

28. Foucault, *The Abnormal: Lectures at the College de France 1974–1975*, 63.

29. Kristeva, *Powers of Horror: An Essay in Abjection*, 3.

30. Kristeva, "From One Identity to Another," 104.

CHAPTER 5

Killer Instincts: Motherhood and Violence in *The Long Kiss Goodnight* and *Kill Bill*

Angela Dancey

In *The Long Kiss Goodnight* (1996), an amnesiac small-town mom named Samantha Caine (Geena Davis) makes an astonishing discovery: she is actually a highly trained and ruthless CIA agent named Charly Baltimore. As her violent personality reemerges along with her old enemies, Charly must choose between her dangerous career and her daughter Caitlin. In *Kill Bill: Vol. 2* (2004), skilled assassin Beatrix Kiddo (Uma Thurman), also known as The Bride or Black Mamba, describes herself as "the deadliest woman in the world." When Beatrix discovers she is pregnant by her boss and lover Bill (David Carradine), her attempt to quit the elite Deadly Viper Assassination Squad in favor of motherhood triggers a frenzy of betrayal, bloodshed, and revenge that spans both volumes of Quentin Tarantino's epic film. As violent professional killers who are also mothers, these warrior moms incorporate social roles that are culturally and ideologically incompatible. Through this exaggerated incongruity, each film attempts to negotiate the cultural anxiety surrounding motherhood and career through the typically masculinized framework of the action genre.

While their campy dialogue, scenes of extreme violence and spectacular special effects mark them both as action films, *Kill Bill* and *The Long Kiss Goodnight* also employ narrative patterns typical of the maternal melodrama—what Mary Ann Doane describes as "scenarios of separation, separation and return, or of threatened separation." [1] Thus, even as Beatrix and Charly behave like male action heroes, their respective films repeatedly return to the favored emotional themes of the woman's film: maternity, self-sacrifice, female friendship, domesticity, and choice (between love and children, love and career, career and children). My argument here is that when examined together, these two films represent a kind of intersection between the woman's film and the action film, a generic space where family and violence converge within the context of women's work.

"GET AWAY FROM HER, YOU BITCH": WARRIOR MOMS PAST AND PRESENT

Sigourney Weaver's Ellen Ripley in the *Alien* series and Linda Hamilton's muscular mom Sarah Connor in the *Terminator* series serve as archetypes of the kick-ass mother who battles her enemies (and shows off her toned muscles) in a skimpy tank top. In *Super Bitches and Action Babes*, Rikke Schubart points to Ripley as the original ferocious cinematic mother:

> She is the prototype after which later mother heroes—Sarah in *Terminator 2: Judgment Day*, Charly in *The Long Kiss Goodnight* . . . and Beatrix in *Kill Bill*—are fashioned. A unique combination of masculine and maternal qualities made Ripley the first female hero to initiate a film series and reach mythic proportions.[2]

I would agree with Schubart's observation that Charly and Beatrix are obviously modeled after the violent mothers who came before them, women Yvonne Tasker describes as "female heroes acting to protect their children, whether biological or adoptive." [3] However, I would argue that the more recent warrior moms in *The Long Kiss Goodnight* and *Kill Bill* share a much more complex relationship with violence, one that reflects our current cultural confusion about motherhood.

In the *Terminator* series, Sarah's fierceness arises directly from the maternal instinct to protect her son. However, in both *Kill Bill* and *The Long Kiss Goodnight*, maternal instinct functions only as partial motivation for each woman's violent behavior. Unlike Ripley and Sarah, Charly and Beatrix are trained killers who are motivated by a need for revenge as much as maternal instinct. Beatrix's systematic execution of her former colleagues is vengeful retribution for their part in her betrayal at the hands of Bill, while Charly's initial search for the truth of her identity is one that actually takes her further away from her role as a mother. Thus, while each character's violent quest is *personal*, it is not necessarily *maternal*, at least not right away. It is only near the conclusion of each film that each heroine fully becomes a mother, as Beatrix unexpectedly discovers her daughter is still alive, and Charly reluctantly embraces her own maternal responsibility. This shared ambivalence surrounding motherhood, I would argue, reflects a profound confusion about its meaning in our contemporary, postfeminist culture.

I also want to point out that what Beatrix and Charly *do for a living* also threatens their families, a hyperbolic articulation of the current social debate about working motherhood. In other words, both characters function as dramatic examples of how working motherhood potentially places children at risk. In *The Long Kiss Goodnight* and *Kill Bill* the mother herself—her choices and her occupation—is represented as a prospective menace to the family. Charly and Beatrix (as well as other female assassins in *Kill Bill*) invite violence into the home through their own behavior and the possible retribution of their enemies. This idea is represented in *The Long Kiss Goodnight* in a fight scene where one of Charly's enemies breaks into her house in bucolic Homedale and attacks her. While Charly has not fully recovered her memory, she nonetheless draws on her latent skills and violent instincts to fight off her male attacker and protect her daughter and boyfriend, turning the domestic setting into a battleground.

Finally, while Charly and Beatrix might differ from Ripley, Sarah, and other kick-ass movie moms of the 1970s and 1980s, they are also similar to them in one very significant way—their shared whiteness. While the past few decades have produced at least a few nonwhite action heroines, such as blaxploitation star Pam Grier, Angela Bassett, Michelle Rodriguez, and Michelle Yeoh, it is difficult to find *any* examples of nonwhite action babes who are also mothers. While Tarantino borrows heavily from blaxploitation in all of his films, his heroine in *Kill Bill* is nonetheless blonde, blue-eyed, and fair-skinned, while actresses of color (Lucy Liu, Vivica Fox) are relegated to supporting roles. It seems clear that Hollywood finds the possibility of white maternal violence acceptable, whereas nonwhite maternal violence is not. I would argue that this reveals some very complicated cultural ideas about motherhood, race, and female agency.

THE FAMILY THAT SLAYS TOGETHER, STAYS TOGETHER

In *The Long Kiss Goodnight* and *Kill Bill*, mothers are contradictory figures: they produce and support the family even as they represent the source of its destruction. Similarly, while violence is portrayed as a threat to the family, it is also the means by which the family unit is repaired. This paradox, according to Karen Schneider, is a common one in the contemporary action film:

> Quite consistently in the action-thrillers of the 1990s, fractured families are rearticulated within a context of extreme violence of one sort or another. . . . This . . . not only confirms the irrational depth of our anxiety about the state of the family but also clearly illustrates our culture's profound ambivalence toward violence.[4]

This paradoxical relationship, argues Schneider, reveals a willingness to tolerate violence—despite our supposed cultural outrage regarding media images of violence—as long as the family unit is preserved. In other words, the fractured family is a much greater threat to our cultural well-being than that posed by violent imagery and behavior.

Both *Kill Bill* and *The Long Kiss Goodnight* participate in this paradox. When Charly sets out to rescue Caitlin from the clutches of her kidnappers, she puts into motion a chain of violent events—apocalyptic explosions, car chases, gunfights—that nearly kill her and her sidekick Mitch. Beatrix's vengeful rampage is even more violent, particularly the extended fight scene at the House of Blue Leaves, where Beatrix lops off people's limbs left and right with her samurai sword, producing geysers of blood and piles of writhing bodies. However, the end result of all this violence: both women are reunited with their daughters, and this most basic family unit is restored.

Both films repair the mother-child unit through the elimination of the father. Fathers and father figures are rampant in *The Long Kiss Goodnight*, including bad fathers (Mitch, Charly's former mentor Leland Perkins, and Timothy, Caitlin's biological father) and good though ineffectual ones (Charly's boyfriend Hal and her family friend Dr. Waldman). An important element of Caitlin's rescue involves the killing of her kidnapper and biological father, Timothy, a secret agent turned terrorist. Charly's revelation to Timothy that Caitlin is his daughter and her subsequent appeal to him to spare Caitlin's life are both ignored—Timothy is the ultimate bad father, who finds the prospect of murdering his own offspring amusing rather than horrifying. Throughout the explosions and gunfire of the film's climactic action sequence, Timothy manages to hang on until the very end, grimly determined to destroy both Caitlin and Charly. Thus, Timothy represents the final obstacle Charly must overcome in order to save her daughter and herself.

The destruction of the father is a key element in *Kill Bill* as well, and as in *The Last Kiss Goodnight*, there is no shortage of fathers and father figures. Bill functions as both a paternal figure for Beatrix (she introduces him as her father at her wedding rehearsal) and the father of her child. Bill himself has accumulated several father figures, including sword maker Hattori Hanzo, kung fu master Pai Mei, and pimp Esteban Vihaio, who raised Bill from childhood. Interestingly, these father figures provide similar guidance for Beatrix during her quest for revenge, offering training, weapons, and even information about where to find Bill, perhaps suggesting that Beatrix is in some way *becoming* Bill, rendering him obsolete as her mentor and a parent to their daughter, B. B. Beatrix's brutal quest for revenge culminates in the killing of Bill, though his death is treated less as a vindictive slaying than a necessary, almost tender act of violence required for the reunion of Beatrix and her daughter. In this way, both *The Long Kiss Goodnight* and *Kill Bill* see the family reduced to its most basic unit—mother and child—and the violence that helps to achieve this is represented as necessary and natural. As Lisa Coulthard writes about the conclusion of *Kill Bill: Vol. 2*:

> The end of the film offers a family devoid of its patriarch, but the emotive and narrational force of the film transforms this absence into positive presence. The absence of patriarchy is an absence of violence and threat, and the female violence of the film is configured retroactively as temporary, aberrant, obligatory, and curative.[5]

Both *The Long Kiss Goodnight* and *Kill Bill* transform the single mother—typically portrayed as powerless, tragic, and even pathetic, particularly in the woman's film—into a violent and destructive force to be reckoned with. However, this potentially liberating activity does little to actually challenge traditional cultural notions about parenting and gender—in fact, through their melodramatic vilification of the paternal and their emphasis on the reunion between mother and child as narrative resolution, both films reinforce the idea that a child "naturally" belongs with the mother as primary caregiver. Thus, while Beatrix and Charly are subversively violent and self-sufficient single mothers, their actions actually serve to reinforce retrograde, sexist ideas about the nuclear family.

THE LONG KISS GOODNIGHT: GOOD MOTHER VERSUS BAD MOTHER

The opening montage in *The Long Kiss Goodnight* simultaneously conveys a contrast and a connection between violence and family. We see a hand with a knife, followed by a slow pan across a collection of family portraits in ornate frames, reminiscent of the opening credits for a daytime soap opera. Spy-thriller icons such as reel-to-reel tapes, a CIA personnel form, and bullets being loaded into a gun are countered with images of a feminine charm bracelet, wrapped Christmas presents, and the sounds of Christmas music. While this imagery is clearly meant to represent an ideological contrast between violence and traditional family values, the fact that they are aesthetically woven together also signals their proximity in the film.

The Long Kiss Goodnight articulates the binary of domesticity and violence in another important way: through the narrative device of dual or split identity, where the good mother battles the bad mother for dominance. As Hilary Neroni writes, "*The Long Kiss Goodnight* offers us an example of a woman who actually has two distinct identities—an actual, rather than a theoretical, split between her violent half and her feminine half." [6] After a blow to the head in a car accident, Samantha, the good, somewhat frumpy mother and schoolteacher (clearly reminiscent of Davis's portrayal of the eccentric single mother Muriel in 1988's *The Accidental Tourist*), begins to remember her previous, forgotten identity as Charly, a sexy, tough assassin. At first, Samantha is confused but also delighted by her newfound physical abilities, imagining that her skill with knives means she was once a chef. However, it soon becomes clear these skills represent a much darker occupation.

The film portrays Samantha as a quirky but loving single mom and an "exemplar of white bourgeois femininity" [7]—a good mother and productive member of the community. However, as Charly begins to reemerge, she manifests some distinctly unmotherly behavior toward her daughter Caitlin, best represented by a scene where mother and daughter are ice skating on a frozen pond. When Caitlin falls, whining that she cannot skate, her mother reacts harshly: "Stop being a little baby and get up. Life is pain. Get used to it. You will skate all the way to the shore, princess. And you will not fall again. Am I understood?" In the ice skating scene, as in several others where Charly begins to overpower Samantha, Charly seems to inhabit Samantha's body like an evil spirit—her voice changes its pitch and tone, and her language becomes more like what we would expect from a male action hero like Bruce Willis or Nicholas Cage. In this way, her character embodies the parallel binaries of femininity/masculinity and woman's film/action film.

Charly's final victory over Samantha—the triumph of the bad mother over the good mother—is confirmed by a makeover sequence that takes place in an Atlantic City hotel room. As Santana's "She's Not There" plays on the soundtrack, the makeover montage begins with multiple shots of Charly's naked body as she showers, indicating that the bad mother is an object of desire in a way the good mother is not, even though they are played by the same attractive actress. Next we see fragmented images of Charly cutting and coloring her hair, then applying dark eye makeup and red lipstick. The final reveal indicates that any traces of the frumpy Samantha have been completely erased, replaced by a glamorous and tough bleached blonde dressed in tight black clothing, looking more like a sexy video game heroine than a mom. However, while Charly is clearly an object of male desire, she is also marked as masculine, particularly in comparison with Samantha's motherly behavior and feminine appearance. Tasker notes that Samantha's transformation into Charly "constructs a tension between femininity and masculinity which is expressed through costume and behavior."[8] These masculine activities include swigging hard liquor, swearing like a truck driver, and aggressively propositioning her companion Mitch, the black private detective who has agreed to help her uncover her past. Mitch is clearly horrified by the emergence of this tough and sexually assertive woman, and reminds Charly that she is, after all, a mother. "I didn't ask for the kid," Charly snarls in response. "Samantha had the kid, not me."

These characteristics of the bad mother are systematically erased during the course of the film, beginning with a scene where Charly tears apart her daughter's bedroom looking for the key to a safe deposit box that contains a fake passport and enough money to help her escape to a new life. Charly pauses to observe Caitlin through the sights of a rifle as she participates in a nativity scene. The apparatus of the rifle helps to construct an obvious binary: a violent, sexualized woman confronted by a sentimental image of communal and religious harmony. Tasker also detects a stylistic connection to the maternal melodrama in her analysis of this scene:

> If the image of Charly looking at her family through the gun suggests that she is divided between killing and caring, the soft music signals the return of maternal feelings. Moreover the camera first closes in on Charly's face and then pulls back into an image of loss and yearning familiar from the woman's picture—a woman framed in a medium shot looking out through the bars created by the window.[9]

Charly's shift in attitude toward her daughter, and thus her identity as a mother, represents the film's attempt to naturalize maternal impulses. This activity is strengthened by Charly's response to her daughter's kidnapping. Rather than dismiss her daughter as "the kid" who Samantha had, not her, she quickly employs her skills as a former government agent to locate the girl and come to her rescue. Thus, Charly's initial rejection of her daughter is revealed simply as posturing, and the maternal reemerges to dictate Charly's behavior, much as her "real" identity resurfaces after her memory loss.

The Long Kiss Goodnight concludes not only with an idealistic reunion of mother and daughter, but the redemption of Mitch in the eyes of his estranged family. Violence has restored not just one but several families— it has even restored Charly's relationship with the ultimate paternal figure, the president of the United States. Charly herself is able to repair the schism in her own identity, incorporating elements of her good mother identity with those of her sexy, violent identity. Like her transformation from good mother to bad mother, this blending of traits is represented primarily through her appearance. As Neroni explains, "In the last scene, Sam (the new combination of Samantha and Charly) has long blond hair, a little bit of makeup, and wears a loose but sexy . . . dress. In this way, the film combines not only her attributes but also her appearances." [10] Therefore, the film attempts to soften or blur the severity of the sexualized binary of good mother/bad mother it had previously worked so hard to establish. Charly's hybrid appearance at the conclusion of *The Long Kiss Goodnight* reflects a careful mix of both personalities, so that the socially acceptable traits (maternal instinct, femininity, modesty) are emphasized, while the negative traits (aggressive sexuality, heavy makeup, masculine behaviors) are brought under control.

KILL BILL AND THE POLITICS OF CHOICE

Compared to the relatively linear action narrative of *The Long Kiss Goodnight*, *Kill Bill* is an exercise in stylized chaos, jumping backward and forward in time and borrowing heavily from multiple B-movie genres: spaghetti westerns, Hong Kong martial arts films, blaxploitation, rape-revenge movies, and animé. The key moments of the film in terms of motherhood, I would argue, are the out-of-sequence fight with Vernita Green at the beginning of *Kill Bill: Volume 1*, the final confrontation with Bill, and the film's conclusion, where Beatrix is reunited with her daughter. Each of these scenes relates important information about the construction of motherhood in the film.

Beatrix's ultraviolent confrontation with Vernita Green (Vivica Fox) takes place in Vernita's suburban home, where the former member of the

Deadly Viper Assassination Squad has built a new life for herself as Jeannie Bell, doctor's wife, mom, and softball coach. What makes this fight particularly symbolic is that Vernita has achieved the life Beatrix wanted but was forcefully denied, and Vernita herself was one of the agents of this betrayal. It speaks to the film's interest in violence and family that the first extended fight sequence of the film is a face-off between two warrior moms. However, Beatrix is still behaving under the assumption that her daughter is dead, and this belief precludes any empathy for Vernita's own status as a mother. Beatrix makes it clear that her need for revenge is stronger than her compassion when she says to Vernita,

> Just because I have no wish to murder you before the eyes of your daughter does not mean parading her around in front of me is going to inspire sympathy. You and I have unfinished business. And not a goddamn fuckin' thing you've done in the subsequent four years, including getting knocked up, is going to change that.

The fight sequence between Vernita and Beatrix juxtaposes sunny, heteronormative domesticity with subversive, masculinized violence as the women punch, kick, and beat each other without mercy. As they fight, they literally destroy the home around them, using glass-topped coffee tables and other mundane objects as deadly weapons. The extreme contrast between the women's all-out violence and the visual markers of contemporary middle-class family life (toys in the yard, a yellow school bus, Vernita's velour sweat suit) are typical of Tarantino's postmodern, hipster irony. However, it is difficult to tell whether this scene and others like it are intended to mock conventional family life by revealing the violence simmering beneath the surface or to celebrate it as a worthy goal for women, particularly in light of *Kill Bill*'s idealistic conclusion.

While Beatrix initially refuses to kill Vernita in her own home and in front of her daughter, she is forced to react quickly and violently when Vernita attempts to shoot her with a gun hidden in a cereal box (yet another clever juxtaposition of the everyday and the violent). Just as Beatrix kills Vernita, her daughter Nikki comes into the room and witnesses her mother's death. Beatrix tells her, "It was not my intention to do this in front of you. For that I'm sorry. But you can take my word for it, your mother had it comin'. When you grow up, if you still feel raw about it, I'll be waiting." In this way, the film conveys the idea early on that killing (and revenge) is the work of mothers and daughters, a kind of maternal legacy passed from one generation to the next. The relatively large number of female fighters in the film (Beatrix, Vernita, O-Ren Ishii, Elle Driver, Sofie Fatale,

Gogo Yubari) as well as extended fight sequences between them reinforces this sense of violence as female work. However, Beatrix's choice between her daughter and her violent occupation—"I had to choose," she says. "I chose her"—actually contradicts this association.

During her final confrontation with Bill, Beatrix explains her initial reaction to the results of her pregnancy test: "...once that strip turned blue, I could no longer do any of those things. Not anymore. Because I was going to be a mother." By "those things," Beatrix refers to the violent behaviors associated with her job as a paid assassin. Because Beatrix sacrifices her career in her attempt to be a good mother, she is essentially making the same choice that conservative society would like all mothers to make: giving up work in favor of child rearing. Of course, Beatrix's decision is more ideologically complex than the average woman's, since she recognizes the incongruity of her chosen occupation with her reproductive status. Thus, her rejection of her work is simultaneously a rejection of violence.

This repudiation of violence, however, is negated by the wedding massacre and the events that follow. While Beatrix engages in over-the-top violence throughout both volumes of *Kill Bill*, she does so with the belief that she is no longer a mother, and that her baby died as a result of the wedding massacre. Once Beatrix discovers that she is, in fact, still a mom, everything changes. After bonding instantly with her daughter, the first instance in the film that she has had the opportunity to actually be a mother, she turns her attention toward the final name on her list of enemies, Bill. Consistent with the revelation of B. B.'s existence, Beatrix makes her final kill in the most deliberate and bloodless way possible, using the "Five-Point Palm Exploding Heart Technique" taught to her by Pai Mei. Her use of this symbolic and relatively merciful technique, where the victim takes a few steps and simply falls down dead, implies that Beatrix cannot kill in the same way that she could when she believed herself to be childless. The gratuitous bloodshed and vindictive anger are gone, replaced by an almost loving and tearful execution of her former lover, boss, and father figure.

In this way, the film is able to have it both ways in terms of Beatrix's character—she can be the good mother and the bad mother *simultaneously*. Throughout the majority of *Kill Bill*, Beatrix behaves violently and unmotherly ("It's mercy, compassion, and forgiveness I lack," she says to Vernita during their confrontation) because she is unaware that she actually *is* a mom. The audience, however, has been aware of her daughter's survival since the conclusion of *Kill Bill: Vol. 1*, and therefore can enjoy Beatrix as both a straightforward action babe and a subversive combination of the maternal and the violent. At the same time that Beatrix is portrayed as a violent mom, the film uses her character's choices to convey the idea that motherhood and violence are fundamentally incompatible. Thus, the representation of motherhood in *Kill Bill* is at once transgressive and conservative.

The film ends with mother and daughter reunited, their future uncertain. An intertitle indicates it is the morning after Beatrix has reclaimed B. B. from Bill. As Beatrix lies on the bathroom floor, holding a stuffed lion and crying, B. B. watches TV in the other room. Beatrix's tears turn to laughter as she whispers, "Thank you, thank you." A shot of mother and daughter beaming is accompanied by upbeat music, and an intertitle states: THE LIONESS HAS REJOINED HER CUB AND ALL IS RIGHT IN THE JUNGLE. The comparison of Beatrix to a lioness evokes an image of ferocious maternal protectiveness, while her "cub" B. B. will most likely follow in her mother's fierce footsteps—they are, after all, the same type of animal. Perhaps a confrontation with Vernita's daughter, Nikki, is in the future.

The larger implication is that mother and child belong together—this is the natural and "right" place for them to be. And while it is presented as a happy ending, I find this conclusion both contradictory and deeply unsatisfying. It assumes that this reunion was Beatrix's goal all along, when in fact she had not even been aware of her daughter's continued existence until just the night before. As Coulthard writes, "The violence of revenge is merely shifted with the discovery of the child, as the Bride's motivation becomes one of maternal recovery." [11] Thus, the film recasts her previous acts of violent revenge as a necessary means to this melodramatic and sentimental conclusion.

Ultimately, it is difficult to know what we are supposed to think of Beatrix and Charly as both mothers and action heroes. Beatrix functions as a "warrior mom," but, according to her own character's logic, these roles are mutually exclusive. Unlike Charly, Beatrix fully embraces motherhood, doing everything in her power to end her violent career, and it is only the intervention of Bill and her extended killer "family" that prevents this. Thus, despite *Kill Bill*'s excessive violence and postmodern irony, it actually presents a more traditional conception of motherhood. In contrast, Charly's initial rejection of Caitlin in favor of her own career reflects a much more subversive attitude to career and motherhood. However, this transgression is only temporary, as Charly's "natural" motherly impulses kick in, resulting in an idealized mother/daughter reunion similar to that in *Kill Bill*. As characters, both Beatrix and Charly are fraught with contradiction and ambiguity, reflecting our culture's continued anxiety regarding contemporary motherhood.

NOTES

1. Mary Ann Doane, *The Desire to Desire: The Woman's Film of the 1940s* (Bloomington; Indianapolis: Indiana University Press, 1987), 73.

2. Rikke Schubart, *Super Bitches and Action Babes: The Female Hero in Popular Cinema, 1970–2006* (Jefferson, NC: McFarland & Co., 2007), 169.

3. Yvonne Tasker, *Working Girls: Gender and Sexuality in Popular Cinema* (London; New York: Routledge, 1998), 69.

4. Karen Schneider, "With Violence if Necessary," *Journal of Popular Film & Television* 27, no. 1 (1999): 11.

5. Lisa Coulthard, "Killing Bill: Rethinking Feminism and Film Violence," in *Interrogating Postfeminism: Gender and the Politics of Popular Culture*, ed. Yvonne Tasker and Diane Negra (Durham, NC; London: Duke University Press, 2007), 170.

6. Hilary Neroni, *The Violent Woman: Femininity, Narrative and Violence in Contemporary American Cinema* (Albany: State University of New York Press, 2005), 156.

7. Ibid., 150.

8. Tasker, *Working Girls*, 68.

9. Yvonne Tasker, "The Family in Action," in *Action and Adventure Cinema*, ed. Yvonne Tasker (London; New York: Routledge, 2004), 262.

10. Neroni, *The Violent Woman*, 158.

11. Coulthard, "Killing Bill," 167.

CHAPTER 6

Hip Mamas: *Gilmore Girls* and Ariel Gore

Robin Silbergleid

When *Gilmore Girls* premiered in the fall 2000 lineup of the WB—a network known for its youth- and family-oriented shows such as *Seventh Heaven* and *Dawson's Creek*—it had the distinction of being the first program financed by the Family Friendly Programming Forum (FFPF), an organization charged with "supporting and promoting the development of family friendly content" (Association of National Advertisers).[1] While the organization's Web site claims that "the definition of family friendly is deliberately broad," the FFPF endorses programs that are "appropriate in theme, content, and language" and, significantly, those that portray "a responsible resolution of issues." Undeniably, the show takes the family as its central focus, with the mother-daughter relationship of Lorelai and Rory serving as its emotional and thematic core. Yet what is particularly striking, in the post–Dan Quayle, post–Murphy Brown[2] television of the new millennium, is that Lorelai gave birth to Rory at age 16. What has happened in the past decade to allow the teenage mother to become the symbol of family values on television? Dare I believe that the success of award-winning *Gilmore Girls* marks a legitimate win for feminism and for the valuation of nontraditional families?

Lorelai, as any viewer of the show quickly realizes, is no ordinary single mother. The pilot episode sets up a financial and emotional arrangement that underwrites much of the action for the rest of the series: the Gilmores are rich, enabling them to shell out thousands of dollars for Rory's tuition at an elite private school. In exchange, Lorelai and Rory only need to show up for dinners Friday nights at the Gilmore family mansion. While her relationship with her overbearing parents functions as a major conflict of the series, Lorelai literally buys into her family's values of education and good breeding, doing whatever it takes to ensure that Rory will be able to get an Ivy League education, a dream they have shared since Rory was a preschooler. That is to say, in a culture that generally presumes single mothers to be African American and poor, Lorelai is a rich white woman whose ancestors came over on the Mayflower and whose mother is a proud member of the Daughters of the American Revolution. More importantly, this breeding is not extraneous character detail but a fundamental aspect of the show's ideology and popularity. Lorelai's upper-crust background and desire for upward mobility allow her to function as both a culturally adored "hip mama" and an exemplar of "family values"; in this way, *Gilmore Girls* is a visible space wherein the dominant ideology of the American dream recuperates the potentially radical nature of the teen mother by choice. Much as I agree with Jane Juffer, who argues that the influx of single mothers on television is important because "TV has the potential to either make what's going on at home seem weird and different or to seem everyday and 'normal,' " I argue that *Gilmore Girls* presents a unique opportunity to think about the nature of motherhood and family in the popular sphere, suggesting that television representation and political representation do not always go hand in hand.[3] Instead, in depicting Lorelai as a self-sufficient heroine, the show obfuscates any meaningful discussion about the controversies surrounding teen pregnancy, single motherhood, and the welfare state in the contemporary United States. And at a historical moment when the pregnancies of celebrity teens such as Bristol Palin and Jamie Lynn Spears take center stage on the news, such analysis becomes more urgent than ever.

Set against the quaint backdrop of sleepy Stars Hollow, Connecticut, Lorelai's relationship with her precocious teenage daughter, Rory, is established as idyllic, if not utopic.[4] The series opens not with the hardships of unplanned teen pregnancy but 16 years later, well after Lorelai left home to make it on her own with her infant daughter. Now manager of the allegorically named Independence Inn that provided her first job as a maid, Lorelai reads as an exemplar of a young woman's triumph over formidable obstacles. To put it bluntly, she is not the culturally deplored "welfare mom"—widely, if incorrectly, assumed to be young, African American, and lazy—but an illustration that desire and hard work bring happiness and success, arguably, the very principles that undergird the so-called American dream. Ruth Sidel, describing Lorelai's real-life counterparts, declares that "these single mothers epitomize the finest American values—or, as some might say, family values." [5] Indeed, with its fictional history dating back to the Revolutionary War, Stars Hollow itself is synecdochic for American ideals more broadly, setting up a symbolic equation between Lorelai's flight from the Gilmores and the colonization of the "New World." If Rory and Lorelai thus serve as the "normal," desirable protagonists in a space populated with dysfunctional families and cartoonish secondary characters, Lorelai in particular is positioned as the ideal mother of the series. Lorelai is strikingly juxtaposed against her own mother, Emily, who is critical and unforgiving, and Mrs. Kim, mother to Rory's best friend Lane, who is likewise distant and hyper-religious, leaving Lane to hide CDs under her floorboards and sneak to the Gilmore home for pizza and Pop Tarts. Reacting to her own stifling childhood, Lorelai is happy to oblige, provided she does not need to "break the code" and lie to Mrs. Kim about Lane's whereabouts. [6] In this symbolic economy, Lorelai is the mother to be. She and Rory appear to be best friends, rather than mother and daughter, drinking coffee together at a local diner, chatting about their days, and indulging in the latest bit of gossip. They have regular pizza and movie nights, attend every town function together, and seem to communicate well about everything, from current events and popular culture to dating and romance. Their relationship is the opposite of what Lorelai had with her own mother, and what Lane has with Mrs. Kim. Lorelai goes so far as to suggest, in a conversation with Mrs. Kim, that such overprotectiveness results in the very rebellious behavior it attempts to prevent; for Lane, it involves listening to rock music and consorting with boys in her band, while for Lorelai it was stealing drinks from her parents' well-stocked liquor cabinet and having sex instead of preparing to become a debutante.

Considering this characterization of Lorelai, *Gilmore Girls* would seem to suggest not only the acceptance but also the desirability of teenage motherhood; if Rory's unplanned birth serves as the catalyst for Lorelai's entrance into adulthood and emancipation from her parents—who, she takes every opportunity to remind Rory and the viewing audience, stifled her—then her "youthful" mode of parenting results in an endearing child who graduates from the Ivy League and charms herself into a job as a journalist for Barack Obama's presidential campaign. [7] Lest there be any doubt about Lorelai's contribution to her daughter's success, the series finale underscores that point, as Rory publicly declares to her mother, teary-eyed, at a bon voyage party thrown by the town, "You've given me everything I need." [8] While these closing scenes might be read as the kind of "responsible resolution" that the FFPF wants to see achieved—signaling a legitimate cultural recognition of the multiple ways that families can thrive—in what follows I want to suggest that such an idealized relationship closes off sustained discussion of the complexities of teen motherhood and the harsh economic realities faced by most single mothers in contemporary American culture. As such, it might also be understood as contributing to the phenomenon that Susan Douglas and Meredith Michaels characterize as the "new momism." [9]

The cultural and political landscape in which *Gilmore Girls* first aired, at the dawn of the twenty-first century, was a highly contentious space when it came to issues of motherhood and family. On the one hand, there was an unquestionable rise of single mothers, both in the population and in popular culture. Celebrity moms including Jodie Foster, Camryn Manheim, Angelina Jolie, and Diane Keaton took center stage as single mothers by choice, gracing the covers of *Us* and *People* magazines. Notable characters, Rachel from *Friends* and Miranda from *Sex and the City*, also became mothers outside of marriage, joining the ranks of other single moms on prime-time television, such as Amy Gray from *Judging Amy*.[10] The apparent acceptability of the single mother on television went hand in hand with a real rise of single parenting; whether by divorce, widowhood, or choice, most children were not being raised in a "traditional" nuclear family with a male breadwinner and female caregiver.[11] In fact, Judith Stacey, describing postmodern family forms, boldly claims that "the family of woman" has now replaced the patriarchal family associated with the 1950s.[12]

Given this boom of single mothers, the success of *Gilmore Girls* is not that surprising, nor is it surprising that the show aired in the midst of a significant backlash against such trends. Taking the "family values" crisis to its logical conclusion, the Clinton era witnessed the Defense of Marriage Act and welfare reform, while the Bush administration and its conservative followers continued its attacks on women's reproductive rights. In a cultural climate some wrote off as "post-feminist," writers such as Sylvia Ann Hewlett bemoaned professional women's choice to put their careers first and delay childbearing at the expense of their fertility; her book *Creating a Life* was published on the heels of a controversial advertising campaign sponsored by the American Society for Reproductive Medicine in the fall of 2001.[13] Such political moves work hard to resist changing family forms, attempting to return the United States to life before *Roe v. Wade* and the interventions of second-wave feminism. Social science research, of course, does not bear out what Stacey refers to as the "sitcom sociology" that demonizes unwed mothers, suggesting that their children are at significant risk.[14] Moreover, contrary to popular perception, Kristin Luker reports, "older women and white women" statistically replaced "African Americans and teens as the largest groups within the population of unwed mothers";[15] indeed, birth rates to teen mothers declined to an all-time low by the turn of the twenty-first century.[16] The real "epidemic" and threat to American families, then, is not rampant teen pregnancy but the effects of poverty and a government that fails to provide social and economic support. "There seems to be nearly an inverse relationship between a nation's rhetorical concern over the plight of children in declining families and its willingness to implement policies to erase their suffering."[17] Taken together, these trends suggest that the "crisis" of the family infamously raised by Dan Quayle serves as a discourse used to frame the ideological threat of financially independent women—like infamous sitcom character Murphy Brown—who *choose* to become mothers outside the context of marriage, even as it ends up punishing those women who most need assistance. Given this political climate, in ignoring the economic realities of most single/teen mothers, who often live below the national poverty level, *Gilmore Girls*— while ostensibly providing a positive portrayal and success story—is a potentially problematic representation.

Over the course of the series, Lorelai's pregnancy is both the cause and the symbol of the problem between her and her family, as well as the catalyst for her independence and move to Stars Hollow. On the one hand, the stuffy Gilmores seem to represent mainstream social values; when Lorelai becomes pregnant at age 16, the impending birth of Rory is a "problem" that must be dealt with, as evidenced by a dramatic scene from the pilot episode. Here, Lorelai and Emily discuss the choice Lorelai made to raise Rory outside the confines of marriage:

Lorelai: Isn't that interesting? Because, as I remember, when Christopher got me pregnant, Dad didn't like him so much.

Emily: Oh, well, please, you were sixteen. What were we supposed to do—throw you a party? We were disappointed. The two of you had such bright futures.

Lorelai: Yes. And by not getting married we got to keep those futures.

Emily: When you get pregnant, you get married. A child needs a mother and a father.

Lorelai: Oh, Mom. Do you think Christopher would have his own company right now if we'd gotten married? Do you think he would be anything at all?

Emily: Yes, I do. Your father would have put him in the insurance business and you'd be living a lovely life right now.

Lorelai: He didn't want to be in the insurance business and I am living a lovely life right now.

Lorelai understands that while an unplanned pregnancy is not the end of the world, getting married at 16 would be. Rejecting her family's plan for her, a few months after Rory's birth, Lorelai leaves the security of the Hartford mansion to strike out on her own, becoming a maid at the Independence Inn, where the owner, Mia, acts as a surrogate mother and provides a home. Though only 30 miles away, Lorelai remains distant from her family, only visiting on holidays and major occasions, until she needs money for Rory's schooling, the moment when the series opens. If Emily understands such an act as taking her granddaughter away and breaking up the family, Lorelai views Rory's birth and the choices she made as necessary acts of independence: "I worked my way up. I run the place now. I built a life on my own with no help from anyone." [18] As this scene indicates, even after this reconciliation and her obvious success in raising Rory on her own, Lorelai's pregnancy is marked as the crisis— both the problem and the turning point—in the Gilmore family history.

It does not take much to figure out that Lorelai's story is unlikely, even fantastical and utopic. How does a teenage mom manage to work her way up from a maid living in a shed to running the inn, owning her home, and sending her child to private school? Hard work, the show tells us, ignoring the real economics of life as a minimum wage domestic worker, which Barbara Ehrenreich's work makes stunningly clear. Household workers, she reports, earned a median income of $223/week for full-time employment in 1998, a figure below the poverty level for a family of three.[19] Given these economic conditions, Sidel explains, "one of the most damaging aspects of single motherhood is downward mobility." [20] Against such findings, *Gilmore Girls*, like recent "welfare reform," presents a world in which the rhetoric of self-sufficiency overcomes simple math. Thus, while the show gives lip service to the difficulty of Lorelai's early years with Rory, it presents us with characters who are upwardly mobile—Lorelai dreams of owning an inn like the one she manages, Rory works toward admission to the Ivy League, both of which come true—and who have significant disposable income for take-out, movies, magazines, and other modes of consumer entertainment. Exaggerated as these qualities might be, they arguably work to mold the Gilmore girls into "family friendly" television characters. To borrow Juffer's description of the new single mother,

Lorelai's character is "palatable because she constantly demonstrates her self-sufficiency, distancing herself from the welfare mom." [21] Indeed, the show is the ultimate presentation of the American dream, single mom style, even as it elides the class and race realities that make Lorelai's success possible in the first place. The final scenes of the series underscore Lorelai's heroism, as the usually cool Richard Gilmore tears up to sing his daughter's praises at the going-away party thrown for Rory; he says, "I think this party is a testament to you, Lorelai, and the home you've created here," noting the community of Stars Hollow and the friends who have served as family since Rory's infancy. "It takes a remarkable person," Richard continues, "to inspire all this." [22]

As I have suggested, Lorelai's "remarkability" comes, in large part, from the combination of her die-hard Protestant work ethic and her best-friends-first parenting philosophy. In the absence of Rory's father, Lorelai takes on a multitude of roles in a parodic rewriting of traditional television mothers. Far from the clichéd stay-at-home mom who bakes cookies to share with her child after school, Lorelai mocks anyone who tries to cook in her kitchen and serves up Pop Tart appetizers plated like fine cuisine; in fact, one episode in the first season uses the occasion of watching an episode of the Donna Reed show to comment on the changing nature of gender and family, making it clear that Lorelai's version of mothering is also part of her feminist practice.[23] She chooses not to cook (and we never see her clean), even as she is a skilled seamstress who makes Rory's gowns for school dances, provides costumes for town functions, and designs Lane's wedding dress. By the time Rory is a teen, Lorelai is a savvy working woman who goes to business school and seizes the opportunity to open the Dragonfly Inn when it becomes available, and yet she prioritizes spending time with her daughter. In this way, Lorelai serves as a striking example of the ways that it is possible to be a "good mother" outside the confines of a female homemaker, male breadwinner family. In the end, even her biggest critics—her parents—can find little fault in her methods given how well Rory turns out.

Yet, if Lorelai demonstrates that it is entirely possible for a young woman to be successful, both personally and professionally, despite (because of?) teen pregnancy, the show also implies that the reasons for such success, and Lorelai's social acceptance, are largely based on socio-economic status and race. Rickie Solinger, in an important analysis of reproductive politics after *Roe v. Wade*, notably claims,

In the minds of many Americans, legitimate pregnancy now has less to do with having a husband and more to do with having "enough money." In

the minds of many people, legitimate pregnancy has now become a class
privilege reserved for women with resources. Other women—those without
resources—who get pregnant and stay pregnant are often regarded as making bad choices.[24]

One only needs to consider Bristol Palin, daughter of the 2008 vice presidential nominee Sarah Palin, whose unplanned pregnancy served as an
occasion to champion family values over reproductive rights, to see that
the legitimization of teen motherhood as a viable "choice" is only
afforded those with financial (or political) power. Throughout the presidential campaign, Bristol's story has functioned for the Republicans not
as a cautionary tale of what happens to teenage girls when they have
unprotected sex but, ironically, as a narrative of responsible reproductive
and familial choice. Undoubtedly, had her skin color been different—
and her mother not running for political office—she would have been
treated as just another statistic.[25]

Thus, with money as grounds for cultural legitimacy, the upper-class teen
mom appears not much different from a 30- or 40-something single mother
by choice (SMC), a conflation that Lorelai's character makes abundantly
clear. Indeed, in every way other than age, Lorelai fits the description of
an SMC given by Jane Mattes, the group's founder: An SMC is "a woman
who decided to have or adopt a child, knowing she would be her child's sole
parent, at least from the outset." [26] According to the organization's Web
site, "Single motherhood is ideally for the woman who feels she has much
to give a child and who has adequate emotional and financial resources to
support herself and her child." Knowing that she and Christopher were not
right, or ready for, marriage, and seemingly ignoring the options that many
of her real-life counterparts would have chosen (abortion or adoption), she
chose instead to raise Rory on her own, having the financial wherewithal
to do so. As Mattes says, "a mature [16-year-old?] mother can do at least
as well as, if not better than, someone who was unexpectedly left with the
task [of single motherhood] at the end of a bad marriage and an upsetting,
life-disrupting divorce." [27] In both the rhetoric of SMC and the narrative
of *Gilmore Girls*, Lorelai makes the "right" choice, a choice retroactively
validated by her success in raising Rory and reproducing middle- to
upper-class values; born out of wedlock, Rory is thus marked "legitimate"
by socioeconomic standards. Money, it seems, trumps age and experience in
this narrative of responsibility and choice.

Thus, while the show's most dramatic plot turns have to do with the
complications of Lorelai or Rory benefiting from the Gilmore wealth,

the characters' class aspirations and deep entrenchment into consumerism are more than merely flavor but a central ideology of the series. If Emily's spending habits verge on ridiculous—buying a plane because she is mad at Rory, for example—Lorelai and Rory themselves use money to signal their financial and familial well-being. They can buy $40 worth of candy (and spend an additional $15 for pizza) on a seemingly typical Friday night, subscribe to voluminous periodicals, and eat out for almost every meal. Lorelai can spontaneously redecorate the living room and "make Asia" when Rory's trip falls through.[28] When Rory is worried that Lorelai does not have enough money to open the inn, she comments on the absence of some of these class markers, and the presence of "real" food in the refrigerator. What the show does not self-consciously reflect on is that they can afford these luxuries because there is always the Gilmore fortune to fall back on as a safety net: for Chilton, for Yale, for Lorelai's inn, for urgent and expensive home repair. Instead, the dialogue highlights a discourse of self-reliance and choice, ignoring the ways that such choices are only available to those of a certain class and skin color.

Along these lines, the episode "Secrets and Loans" illuminates the connection between fiscal and familial well-being on the one hand, and the rhetoric of self-reliance and reality of economic interdependence on the other.[29] Outwardly, the episode uses Lorelai's dialogue to assert her self-sufficiency; even after she is turned down by several local banks for a loan to finance repairs to the foundation of her home, Lorelai refuses to go to her wealthy parents for money. Rory presses her on the issue, saying that there is an "obvious" solution to their problem; in response, Lorelai remarks on the important distinction between asking for money for Rory's tuition and for herself (though presumably fixing their home would also benefit Rory). After Rory betrays her mother and discloses their "exterminatoritis" to Emily, the younger Gilmores have what Rory views as their most significant fight to date. In the end, a compromise is reached as Lorelai accepts her mother's willingness to cosign on a loan from a bank run by a family friend, allowing her simultaneously to get the money she needs and save face. The episode concludes with a critical conversation between Lorelai and Rory in which Lorelai asserts that she has earned the right to make decisions—or "mistakes"—because she has always been able to support their family, reinforcing the correlation between their emotional bonds and material goods, even as it ignores *where* their money comes from:

Lorelai: Rory, have you ever been without food or clothes or books, or book covers for that matter, or anything else you needed?

Rory: No.

Lorelai: No and see, the reason for that is me. I have a pretty good track record for keeping you alive.

Rory: Yeah, you do.

Lorelai: So when I tell you I can handle something, you need to respect that, especially since you have no evidence proving I won't. Understand?

Rory: Yeah, I understand. I'm sorry.

Here, Lorelai suggests that she is a fit parent because she has always been able to provide for her daughter, even as the multiple banks she contacts contend that she is not a good candidate for a loan, and, once again, Lorelai accepts help from her own parents' "old world" money. As this episode makes abundantly clear, there is a fundamental distinction between the rhetoric of self-reliance and actual economic independence. Of course, in the "real" world a financial adviser would do well to point out that Lorelai might have money in her savings account if they ate at Luke's Diner once a week instead of several times per day. But in the world in which these characters live, consumerism serves as a vital means of buying Lorelai's suitability as a mother. It seems her years working as a maid during Rory's childhood were merely a fiscal detour from her real path to business ownership and disposable income. The ability to mother and the ability to consume go hand-in-well-manicured-hand.

Yet, within the dialogue and narratives of the show, Lorelai's maternal success is attributed not only to her "adult" (even masculine) capacity to provide for offspring but also her youthful attributes; Lorelai's a good mom because she does not act like a mom (she often plays the "kid" to Rory's "grown-up"). Indeed, one might read Lorelai as the ultimate exemplar of the "hip mama" lauded by former teen mom Ariel Gore. This real life Lorelai Gilmore has become a celebrity in the parenting world, putting out a popular zine and book *The Hip Mama Survival Guide*, telling a generation of Martha Stewart wannabes to get over themselves.[30] As the self-proclaimed spokesperson for the "new generation" of mothers, she shows us that you can rent an apartment and still be a great mom. You can feed your kid cereal for dinner and be a great mom. You can get pregnant at 18 and not only be a great mom but make money off it, as Gore herself has used single, teen motherhood to launch her career. At first glance, then, Gore's work seems to be a much-needed departure from the standard discourse of parenting books and popular images of motherhood. Gore's books offer a version of motherhood where it is a celebrated choice, not an expectation, where even the most disenfranchised moms can find a voice of welcome and support. The words of *Hip Mama* are fiery and down-to-earth, usefully complicating the one-dimensional images of mothers presented in magazines and mainstream television and film. As Gore writes in the introduction to *Breeder*: "We aren't the neo-June Cleaver corporate beauties you see in mainstream parenting magazines, and we aren't the purer-than-thou organic earth mamas you see in the alternative glossies." [31] Instead, Gore acknowledges that there are as many ways to be a good mother as there are mothers: "If there's one thing I've learned about mothering, it's that there are a million ways to raise good kids, and none of them is perfect." [32] *Hip Mama*, which began as Gore's senior thesis, sets out to define a new version of motherhood, one that is politically grounded in Gore's anti-Republican, pro-feminist stance, one that directly engages the "family values" controversy of the 1990s. As Gore says in the introduction, she has been described as "conservative America's worst nightmare." And the "Family Values" chapter features a hilarious flow chart, for which the only possible outcome to the scenario "Are you pregnant?" is "go to hell." Alongside fairly standard discussions of pregnancy, birth, and new motherhood, Gore devotes sections of the book to dealing with poverty, family breakups, and parenting alongside work and school. She supplements her own personal anecdotes and opinions with interviews and stories by other parents and only a few renowned experts, in the hopes that they "will come in handy as [readers] invent motherhood all over again." [33] In short, Gore's work is about as inclusive in its understandings of mothering as it possibly can be.

Yet, despite this pro-mom, pro-feminist veneer, a more careful analysis indicates that Gore, like Lorelai, is a more ambiguous cultural figure. Though her early work in *Hip Mama* poses a clear challenge to conservative approaches to parenting—and the writing of parenting manuals—later texts, such as the anthology *Breeder* and her own Web site, seem much more devoted to conflating "hip mama" with "unwed teen mama." In the most curious moments in these texts, Gore champions unplanned pregnancy by turning it into a "choice" and by reading youth as an asset to good parenting. As she puts it in the introduction to *Breeder*:

In a culture where women often delay childbearing as long as nature and science will allow, we chose to have our kids *while*, not *instead of*, following our other dreams. [...] As the daughters of the 1970s feminist movement, we cherish our reproductive freedom. And as willing breeders, we refuse to be oppressed by the institution of motherhood.[34]

In Gore's own language, chosen teen motherhood, then, is pitted against late-life professional moms, in a move not unlike the rhetoric of antifeminist writer Sylvia Ann Hewlett. And while a multivalent look at the lives of teen parents is unquestionably necessary—as is the recognition that teen moms can be great moms—I have to wonder about the implications of this redefinition of the "hip," progressive mom. Is teen pregnancy really hip?

In *Gilmore Girls* it is likewise Lorelai's status as a teenage mother—and therefore a young 30-something mother of a teen—that makes her a desirable character. As early as the pilot episode, Rory and Lorelai are figured not so much as mother and daughter but as sisters or best friends, an idea that recurs through the series' seven season run. The first scene of the series introduces Lorelai as she is being hit on by a man, who unknowingly proceeds to flirt with teenage Rory as well; as the embarrassed young man confesses, "You do not look old enough to have a daughter. No, I mean it. And you do not look like a daughter." In "Double Date," Lorelai is likewise described by a teenaged boy as a "babe," which she takes to be the highlight of her evening.[35] As Rory begins to socialize with her Chilton schoolmates, they comment on how "fascinating" Lorelai is.[36] When one observes, "it's almost more like having a big sister," Rory concurs: "She's my best friend." And, indeed, in a second season episode featuring Lorelai and mother Emily visiting a spa together, Lorelai remarks that she and Rory are "best friends first and mother and daughter second, and you and I are mother and daughter always."[37] In the logic of the series, then, Lorelai's mothering by friendship is presented as the desirable method of parenting. This is possible because Lorelai and Rory seem to grow up side by side, Lorelai reliving the adolescence cut short by Rory's birth as her daughter is now a teenager herself. If Lorelai is "hip" both in the context of the series and also among viewers because she is youthful—Lauren Graham won a Teen Choice Best TV Mom Award—I am not convinced that such desirability translates into a legitimate valuation of teen mothers or motherhood more generally.

To the contrary, we might understand the very figure of the "hip mama" and, by extension, Lorelai's character, to contribute to the "new momism" explored in the astute critique *The Mommy Myth*. The ideological descendant of Friedan's "feminine mystique," the new momism, Douglas and Michaels explain, "is a set of ideals, norms, and practices, most frequently and powerfully represented in the media, that seem on the surface to celebrate motherhood, but which in reality promulgate standards of perfection that are beyond your reach."[38] A type of cultural backlash designed to make real mothers feel inadequate, regardless of whatever choices they make, the new momism takes hold at the cultural moment when women have gone back to work in greater numbers, when they do not need to be wives/mothers in order to be financially independent. While today's mothers are bombarded with media images and parenting advice wherever they turn, profiles of celebrity mothers, Douglas and Michaels contend, are "probably the most influential media form to sell the new momism." [39] Whereas Gore's "hip mama" might outwardly protest such normative figures of motherhood, a closer analysis reveals its deep imbrication in the new momism backlash. The hip mama is the mother of the new generation, and this type is arguably no less oppressive—and no less real—than Donna Reed or June Cleaver or Martha Stewart. The hip mama is in 2000 what the super mom was in 1980. In a momist culture already saturated with advice books to mothers, Gore provides an "alternative," yet it is an alternative predicated on the very same logic: That certain qualities make desirable mothers. That maternal desirability should be disseminated in magazines, books, Web sites, and so forth. For Gore, such desirability is, in large part, youth. Unplanned teen pregnancy here is rewritten as not merely choice but desirable outcome, juxtaposing "youthful" mothers against "older" mothers, who often battle infertility and high-risk pregnancy, just to become mothers. Rejecting the models of maternity she has been handed, Gore chronicles her own story in order to "transform the energy our culture has taught us to use to scrutinize and blame ourselves, and turn it inward, into something revolutionary." [40]

Gore's own narrative, chronicled in her memoir *Atlas of the Human Heart*, recounts a story similar to Lorelai's, in which unplanned pregnancy and motherhood grounds her and provides raison d'être; after years of wandering Europe and Asia, Gore gives birth and moves back home, eventually launching her career as a writer with the production of *Hip Mama*.[41] Gore is, no doubt, an American success story. She raised a daughter who ended up being captain of her cheerleading squad and graduated from high school in a mere three years. At present, Gore is the author of multiple parenting manuals—notably including *Whatever, Mom*, which offers advice on how to parent a teenager—a memoir, a novel, and an instructional guide for aspiring writers.[42] In her late thirties, when her daughter Maia headed off to college, Gore gave birth to a second child, Maximilian, whom she is raising with a partner. For those of us hungry for alternate images of mothers, different from our own, different from what Hollywood tells us we should be, she is an inspiring figure, to be sure. But I cannot help but wonder what it means when the rhetoric of feminism and choice becomes mobilized to not only support—as it should—but privilege teenage motherhood. Gore's discussion of Bristol Palin on her Web site does much to shed light on her feelings about teen pregnancy in general. Offering hearty congratulations, Gore says, "It's great to have babies when you're young enough to stay up all night and still be able to pay attention to your college lectures in the morning. [...] *Unwed teenage mama power!*" [43] Here, Gore aligns with young Palin, Barack Obama's mother (also only 18 at the time of his birth), and other well-known teen moms, turning the difficulties of parenting and going to school into the strength of the youthful mom. Ultimately, as the character of Lorelai and Gore's own narrative make clear, the figure of the hip mama can put a glamorous spin on a life that, for most teen mothers, presents significant challenges.

Considering the story arcs of the entire series, the treatment of teen pregnancy in *Gilmore Girls* is slightly more complicated. Even if Lorelai's youth is given as one of the qualities that make her a good parent to Rory and an interesting counterpart to the majority of television mothers, the show's treatment of teen motherhood as a social issue is, at best, conflicted. This is best seen in the episode "The Big One" in which Rory and her friend Paris discuss the possibility of sexual intimacy with their boyfriends. [44] Eavesdropping on the girls, Lorelai boasts, "I have the good kid," when she learns that her daughter is the one who is not sexually active. And her reward, this episode would have us believe, is getting into Harvard; Paris has sex and gets a rejection letter, connecting the two events causally in an embarrassing speech to her schoolmates and camera crews at a major school event, the same day virginal Rory receives acceptances from three Ivy League schools. Even for Lorelai, teen pregnancy is not a desired outcome for her daughter; as she confides in strict mom Mrs. Kim, "Now I got lucky, because having Rory—totally the best thing that could have happened. But let's be honest, I certainly don't want Rory to turn out like me." [45] Therefore, when Rory falls asleep with her boyfriend and does not come home one night after a school dance, Lorelai panics and declares that Rory is going on the pill. [46] As these moments suggest, although Rory is much beloved—by her mother, her grandparents, and the entire town of Stars Hollow—single motherhood is presented, at best, as an obstacle that must be overcome, not a desirable choice. One only needs to consider Luke's sister Liz—a stereotype of the "bad" single mom, with a teenage son who is disrespectful and ultimately fails to graduate from high school—to see that the show displays very particular notions of family values, tied up with choice, socioeconomic status, and race. In this respect, the stories *Gilmore Girls* tells about single mothers are ultimately very much in line with mainstream beliefs.

However compelling the project of *Gilmore Girls* might be, its characterization of Lorelai is not in itself a marker of significant social change and respect for single mothers and teen pregnancy. Ironically, its very representation has the potential to obfuscate the real conditions of single/teen mothers in the political sphere, at a moment teens like Bristol Palin become figureheads for reproductive choice, even as her mother and Republican presidential candidate John McCain argue, at most, for "abstinence only" models of sex education and work to undo *Roe v. Wade*. Teen mom Amy Pace, quoted on Gore's Web site, provides a much-needed reminder about the cultural and economic situation of many young mothers:

> I am not Jamie Spears. I am not a millionaire fake celeb. I am not Bristol Palin. Do you think either of these girls will walk into their local welfare office and wait hours, just for that extra $100 a month in foodstamps? Will they ever spend week after week on the phone with operators hired by a privatized Medicaid system, trying to find a doctor who will actually see their asthmatic child? Will they spend years fighting the Attorney General's office for child support, waiting a year just to get to court? Will they ever try to pay for their generic can of beans with WIC coupons and be treated like a leper? Have someone roll their eyes as they buy food with food stamps after they just got off an eight-hour shift standing on thier [*sic*] feet, cutting nasty hair?[47]

As Pace's description of teenage motherhood makes strikingly clear, Lorelai Gilmore and Ariel Gore might be cultural icons, but only because they fit the model of the American success story, rather than the stereotype of the welfare mom. On this point, Juffer's critique of the single mother by choice is an apt warning about the work that television representation and a rhetoric of choice can do: "In its insistence on autonomy and distance from obligations to other kinds of mothers, SMC may contribute to the conditions in which some single mothers are rendered more vulnerable, less able to fulfill their obligations to their children." [48] It would be naive to suggest that all television needs to be realistic—Teen Motherhood, The Reality Show—or that it should overtly grapple with social and political problems. It is, after all, fiction. But, at the other extreme, reading *Gilmore Girls* as the bastion of family values and the American dream, as its financial backers clearly did, is precisely to forget its utopic, even satiric, mode. If we understand utopias as speculative, as visions their creators would like to see achieved, then I take *Gilmore Girls* world as a space I can fantasize about, a space where single motherhood is legitimately hip, where children are raised as part of a larger community, where hard work and desire really do pay off, where the single mom can be the heroine rather than the woman scorned. Oh, if only I were living in Stars Hollow.

NOTES

1. Other programs which received the FFPF Script Development Fund include *Brothers and Sisters*, *Friday Night Lights*, *Notes from the Underbelly*, *American Dreams*, *High School Musical*, and, surprisingly, *Ugly Betty*. While this sampling of shows does suggest the range of what the Forum deems "family friendly," most seem to be fairly conservative in their portrayals of American families. The FFPF also sponsors the Annual Family Television Awards, which, in many cases, end up recognizing the same programs the organization funds. See Association of National Advertisers, "Family Friendly Programming Forum," http://ana.net/ffpf (accessed January 14, 2008).

2. I refer here to Dan Quayle's infamous attack on fictional Murphy Brown, who became a single mother. For more on this attack, the family values campaign, and the changes to welfare it inspired, see Judith Stacey, *In the Name of the Family: Rethinking Family Values in the Postmodern Age* (Boston: Beacon, 1996).

3. Jane Juffer, *Single Mother: The Emergence of the Domestic Intellectual* (New York: New York University Press, 2006), 65.

4. As Carol Cooper puts it, "this is the most idealized mother-daughter relationship on earth. Men come and go—but these two hang tough. They are so seamlessly bonded that suddenly you know where Lorelai poured the energy she might otherwise have invested in college life, high society, or in conforming to her own parents' expectations." See Carol Cooper, "Mama Don't Preach," *Coffee at Luke's: An Unauthorized Gilmore Girls Gabfest*, ed. Jennifer Crusie with Leah Wilson (Dallas: Benbella Books, 2007), 175.

5. Ruth Sidel, *Unsung Heroines: Single Mothers and the American Dream* (Berkeley: University of California Press, 2006), 58.

6. *Gilmore Girls*, dir. Amy Sherman-Palladino, perf. Alexis Bledel and Lauren Graham, dist. Warner Home Video, 2000, episode 1.12.

7. *Gilmore Girls*, episode 7.22.

8. *Gilmore Girls*, episode 7.22.

9. Susan J. Douglas and Meredith W. Michaels, *The Mommy Myth: The Idealization of Motherhood and How It Has Undermined Women* (New York: Free Press, 2004).

10. The April 23, 2001, issue of *Us Weekly*, for example, bears the headline "The New Single Moms and How They Do It." The magazine spotlights Camryn Manheim's "new life as a single mother" shortly following the birth of her son, and also provides brief bios on Jodie Foster, Calista Flockhart, Diane Keaton, Rosie O'Donnell, Katie Couric, and Nicole Kidman. As the article proclaims, quoting Aretha Franklin, in Hollywood, "sisters are doing it for themselves." See Monica Rizzo, "And Baby Makes Two," *Us Weekly*, April 23, 2001, 31–36.

11. Stacey, *In the Name of the Family*, 45.

12. Stacey, *In the Name of the Family*, 51.

13. The campaign, composed of bus posters and short radio messages, ostensibly provided women with information about age-related infertility; it was seen by NOW and many feminist thinkers as a scare tactic designed to push women back into the home. According to Dr. Michael Soules, past president of the ASRM, its publicity came in large part from the August 13, 2001, *Newsweek* cover story "The Truth About Infertility: Why More Doctors Are Warning That Science Can't Beat the Biological Clock," as well as Sylvia Ann Hewlett's *Creating a Life: What Every Woman Needs to Know about Having a Baby and a Career* (New York: Hyperion, 2002). For an analysis of the campaign, see Michael R. Soules, "The Story Behind the American Society of Reproductive Medicine's Prevention of Infertility Campaign," *Fertility and Sterility* 80, no. 2 (2002): 295–299.

14. Stacey, *In the Name of the Family*, 99

15. Kristin Luker, *Dubious Conceptions: The Politics of Teenage Pregnancy* (Cambridge, MA: Harvard University Press, 1996), 85.

16. According to Nancy Shields and Lois Pierce, based on National Center for Health Statistics, childbearing among teens 15–19 peaked in 1957 and "declined to an all-time low in 2003." Yet arguably due to acceptance of sex outside marriage and the widening of reproductive choice, the pregnancy rate of *unmarried* teens increased. Even so, "most babies born outside marriage are actually born to older women, rather than teenagers." Framing these conflicting statistics, they explain, "The relationship between the social construction of teen pregnancy as a social problem and the actual number of teen births is an interesting one." See Nancy Shields and Lois Pearce, "Controversial Issues Surrounding Teen Pregnancy: A Feminist Perspective," *Teenage Pregnancy and Parenthood: Global Perspectives, Issues, and Interventions*, ed. Helen S. Holgate, Roy Evans, and Francis K. O. Yuen (Routledge: London, 2006), 129–130.

17. Stacey, *In the Name of the Family*, 48.

18. *Gilmore Girls*, episode 1.1.

19. Barbara Ehrenreich, "Maid to Order," *Global Woman: Nannies, Maids, and Sex Workers in the New Economy*, ed. Barbara Ehrenreich and Arlie Russell Hochschild (New York: Henry Holt, 2002), 92.

20. Sidel, *Unsung Heroines*, 150.

21. Juffer, *Single Mother*, 47.

22. *Gilmore Girls*, episode 7.22.

23. *Gilmore Girls*, episode 1.14.

24. Rickie Solinger, *Pregnancy and Power: A Short History of Reproductive Politics in America* (New York: New York University Press, 2005), 217.

25. For an astute analysis of this situation, see Rebecca Traister, "Palin, Pregnancy, and the Presidency," http://www.salon.com/mtwt/broadsheet/2008/09/01/palin_baby (accessed November 11, 2008).

26. Single Mothers by Choice, organization Web site, http://singlemothersbychoice.com (accessed January 16, 2008).

27. Jane Mattes, *Single Mothers by Choice* (New York: Three Rivers, 1994), 13.

28. *Gilmore Girls*, episodes 1.7, 7.2.

29. *Gilmore Girls*, episode 2.11.

30. Ariel Gore, *The Hip Mama Survival Guide: Advice From the Trenches* (New York: Hyperion, 1998).

31. Ariel Gore, "Introduction," *Breeder: Real-Life Stories: from the New Generation of Mothers*, ed. Ariel Gore and Bee Lavender (Seattle, WA: Seal Press, 2001), xiii.

32. Gore, *Hip Mama*, 247.

33. Gore, *Hip Mama*, 7.

34. Gore, "Introduction," xiii.

35. *Gilmore Girls*, episode 1.12.

36. *Gilmore Girls*, episode 1.13.

37. *Gilmore Girls*, episode 2.16. For an analysis of the "best friends" nature of the Rory-Lorelai relationship, see Stephanie Lehman, "The Best Friend Mom," *Coffee at Luke's: An Unauthorized Gilmore Girls Gabfest*, ed. Jennifer Crusie with Leah Wilson (Dallas: Benbella Books, 2007), 53.

38. Douglas and Michaels, *Mommy Myth*, 5.

39. Douglas and Michaels, *Mommy Myth*, 113.

40. Ariel Gore, *The Mother Trip: Hip Mama's Guide to Staying Sane in the Chaos of Motherhood* (Seattle, WA: Seal Press, 2000), 8.

41. Ariel Gore, *Atlas of the Human Heart* (New York: Seal Press, 2003).

42. Ariel Gore, with Maia Swift, *Whatever, Mom: Hip Mama's Guide to Raising a Teenager* (Emeryville, CA: Seal Press, 2004).

43. Ariel Gore, "Congratulations, Bristol Palin," http://arielgore.com/archives/2008_09_01_archive.html (accessed November 17, 2008).

44. *Gilmore Girls*, episode 3.16.

45. *Gilmore Girls*, episode 1.12.

46. *Gilmore Girls*, episode 1.9.

47. Amy Pace, "An open letter from teen mama Amy Pace," quoted by Ariel Gore, http://arielgore.com/archives/2008_10_01_archive.html (accessed November 13, 2008).

48. Juffer, *Single Mother*, 214.

CHAPTER 7

Running the Home, House, and Senate: Political Moms Pelosi, Clinton, and Palin

Ann C. Hall

Though motherhood is still treated as a "dirty little secret" in many American workplaces, in the past several years, mothers have come out of the closet in American politics in a big way.[1] The moniker is no longer a scarlet letter but a red badge of courage.[2] Tracing Nancy Pelosi's rise to power in the House, Hillary Clinton's presidential run, and Sarah Palin's vice-presidential nomination, it is clear that "moms" are on the move to higher office and greater public relations. Times are changing for American mothers, but as many commentators are quick to note, are they changing enough? Proclaiming transferable motherhood skills is tricky business, much like balancing the needs of unruly children, and there are only a few mothers who have successfully navigated the Scylla and Charybdis of American motherhood and American politics.

Women who use their motherhood credentials must do so very carefully, since Americans still have unresolved feelings over the role of mothers in the workplace, in the home, and in politics. As Celinda Lake, a Democratic pollster notes, "For male candidates, people think having young children is a total plus—people think, 'Oh, this is great, he's going to be concerned about family issues, he'll be more future-oriented. . . . A male with young kids, everyone likes it."[3] As we all know, for women, this interpretation is not the case. For good or ill, mothers, are still held responsible for the outcome of their children, much more than fathers. Americans expect their mothers to be nurturing and their politicians

tough, so in addition to the usual unreasonable expectations hoisted upon
our political leaders, mothers have the added burden of appearing nurturing and tough, as well as committed to their family and country in ways
that men are not. By examining the images of Pelosi, Clinton, and Palin,
it is clear that motherhood is now an important part of the political process, with each of these three women reflecting a variation on the motherhood theme, but it is also clear that placing motherhood on a political
resume does not ensure voter support. As the 2008 presidential election
illustrated, the Republican party underestimated what most working
mothers know—you are damned if you do, and you are damned if you
don't. Motherhood can assist a candidate or it can break a candidate, so
elected officials must invoke the maternal cautiously.

Perhaps one of the most successful mothers in politics today is House
Speaker Nancy Pelosi. A self-proclaimed liberal who manages to work
with both parties and who manages to get things done, her image may
be one of the more palatable ones in politics—the "grandma with the
gavel." [4] During her swearing in, for example, children, her own and
those of other House members, surrounded her. As Ruth Marcus of the
Washington Post notes, her own response to the image was contradictory:
"my first thought was: This is so choreographed. My second thought was:
Awwwww." [5] And given Pelosi's appearance prior to the swearing in, but
following her victory, she needed some toning down. During her first
appearance, for example, she wore a vibrant, unapologetic red, while her
colleagues donned the usual gray suits. The choice may have been too
much—like hubris. During her swearing in, then, Pelosi "humanizes her
image as shrill San Francisco Democrat." [6] But she does so in a very interesting way, one that demonstrates her abilities to work both sides of the
aisle, both sides of the motherhood mystique in American culture, and
both sides of just about anything that comes her way. By bringing her
daughters, especially, on stage, there is something more than the usual
American "mom and apple pie" representation of femininity and motherhood. Instead, with her daughters and children beside her, she communi-
cates the old ad campaign, "We've come a long way, baby." As Marcus
points out, " 'powerful' and 'mommy' are not concepts we're used to
holding simultaneously. . . . Pelosi is playing it differently: motherhood
as preparation for public office." [7]

And this choice appears to have supporters for a number of reasons.
This strategy works because we are living longer, and the idea of having numerous careers, vocations, and roles in life is becoming more
common and acceptable in the American workplace and political arena.

Further, women are actually gaining more respect for the work they do, both in and outside the domestic realm. Further still, Pelosi's "grandma" image is not as threatening as other, more feminist images. Pelosi, for example, enjoys her work in Congress, but that choice is not her vocation: "Nothing in life will ever, ever compare to being a mom. Not being a member of Congress, not being speaker of the House. I wish I could do it all over again, but my children won't give me my grandchildren." [8] In this way, Pelosi's image highlights maternal, nurturing images, and her support for social programs highlights this "softer" side of female leadership, as well. Such a tactic soothes and reassures: leadership and maternal qualities are complementary, not at odds. Women are mothers and sympathetic leaders. Running Congress is secondary to her true calling. She is really not as ambitious as she seems, and she is certainly humble by associating herself with the most common of roles.

Pelosi, however, also highlights her maternal managerial skills. Rather than only representing motherhood as a nurturing, compromising, service-oriented role, Pelosi demonstrates that her motherhood skills prepare her for tough challenges, too. Running the House is such a challenge. While, "the House looks a lot more like the complicated diverse country its members are supposed to represent," [9] the job of House Speaker requires "the ability to know when to bury bills or send them out to the floor for a vote . . . If passing laws is like making sausage, then the speaker is the butcher-in-chief." [10] It is about making tough decisions, making deals, and working with others. And though the ability to compromise and remain flexible are skills frequently associated with women, Pelosi highlights her decisive, tough-mother side when she threatens rowdy house or press members with her infamous, do not make me use my "mother-of-five" voice.[11] Everyone, from one-child to multiple-child families, understands what this means. Mothers are in charge, and they will use their arsenal of emotional weaponry, persuasive tactics, and other characteristics to establish order. And Pelosi has a remarkably steady hand. Her Web site, admittedly biased, reflects a good deal of the legislation she has shepherded through, and her work regarding the current economic crisis has been admirable. For good or ill, bailouts were necessary, and she was at the helm to make sure it happened.[12]

Even her use of compromise has been decidedly determined. Despite her liberal stance, for example, she has been able to work with Republicans, and her ability to compromise is laudatory. Her mantra has been "partnerships . . . not partisanship." [13] In somewhat Machiavellian fashion, her flexibility and willingness to work with the other side has taught her a few tricks from the conservative side of the House floor: "If Pelosi has stolen anything from the Republicans, it is total devotion to the discipline of message control." [14] In this way, Pelosi uses compromise and flexibility to gain strategic advantages.

In addition to managing her dealings with the members of the Republican party, Pelosi has had to work with her own Democratic party, one characterized by some as a party "perpetually at war with itself." Friend and fellow legislator Jim McDermott says she is successful because "she's very realistic." She will not use the "hammer" Tom Delay style to keep her party in line. Instead, she will say, " 'You are free to do what you want.' But you can be sure she'll remember if you don't do the right thing." [15] And who, among us, has not heard our own matriarchs use the same line? It is not quite a threat, but there is something very effective and devious about the statement. Pelosi's ability to balance the conflicting views in the House and her own party, then, might stem from motherhood itself, a role that, for many women, requires a great deal of balancing, compromise, and flexibility.

And though Ann Coulter snidely commented that the *New York Times* coverage of Pelosi's swearing in as Speaker was on par with the invention of cold fusion, Pelosi is very judicious when it comes to media coverage.[16] In fact, it may be the key to her success. Like female leaders before her who guarded their public appearances vigilantly, Pelosi's media appearances are few and far between. She admits, "Two thirds of the public have absolutely no idea who I am. . . . I see that as a strength. This isn't about me. It's about Democrats." [17] The self-effacing tone only enhances the effect of her low visibility. She is a humble, public servant. The country, her kin. That strategy has been successful. As Republican lobbyist Ed Rogers says, "We were hoping that she would be more loud and abrasive than she turned out to be . . . But she's played it smart and kept her knee-jerk, left-wing tendencies pretty well in check." [18] This comment, of course, speaks volumes about conservative Republicans' expectations of this new, female, Democratic leader. The subtext suggests that they were expecting some combination of the Anti-Christ and Cruella De Vil, the embodiment of a liberal and a feminist. The characterization is consistent with some of the difficulties women in the media face. If they are tough, hard-hitting politicians, they are seen as hysterical, knee-jerk lunatics. Pelosi's care with her image reaps benefits here because this Republican, at least, is able to see her for what she is, not a cartoon created by antifeminist propaganda.

Of course, Pelosi is not immune to criticism. In 2007, for example, she was "maligned for not reaching political benchmarks—the implication being that she fell short because she's a woman," but as the *Advocate* editorial continued, "doing things constitutionally in the bright light of day takes longer than doing them unconstitutionally in the dark of night." [19] Pelosi's integrity may cost her some accomplishments, but in the long run, it is what most Americans expect from a mother and politician—plain speaking and honest dealing. It is also the platform she ran on, with her campaign slogan, "It'll take a woman to clean House." [20] Her "New Direction" initiative in Congress, for example, led to greater collegiality and ethics reforms.[21]

Pelosi's pedigree buttresses her self-effacing, common-good profile, as well. As Breslau notes, Pelosi comes by politics and its deal making and haggling naturally through her childhood in an Italian immigrant neighborhood and through her dealings with her mayor father, Thomas D'Alesandro Jr.: "She has learned her way around Washington in her two decades in the House, but her real political education began in her own house when she was a young girl." [22] In this way, Pelosi is a renegade and dutiful daughter. She has been taught by her father to be a politician, and she has exceeded his expectations. What more could a father or every father want from a child? Pelosi has managed to make politics look like fly fishing or automotive repair, an unusual interest for a young girl, but one that may gain patriarchal and electoral approval because she learned it at her father's knee, that is, honestly. Again, Pelosi balances or tempers extremes. She is a politician, but her father made her so—she comes by it honestly, through the patriarchy, and this lineage may help calm the ire of some of her enemies. She is a mother, who nurtures and commands. She is a fierce fighter who also knows the importance of compromise. She is a good daughter, following in the footsteps of Dad. She is a mother who took care of her own home and who is now taking care of our House. All of these characteristics add up to a successful image for this mother and politician.

Senator Hillary Clinton has not managed this image quite as smoothly as Pelosi, though her rise to power, her run for president, and her appointment to the position of secretary of state under Barack Obama's administration is nothing to discount. And to a certain extent Clinton's own struggles for independence as a wife, mother, and politician have paved the way for other women, like Pelosi. But the role of mother and politician for Clinton has not been as smooth. And to a certain extent, the difference is generational. As Ruth Marcus notes in her discussion of Nancy Pelosi, Pelosi is different from many women who may have started their careers a generation or so earlier than she. It was the " 'dress for success' era, in which women were solemnly instructed to dress as much as possible like male wannabees. . . . Even more important than looking like men was acting like them—to suppress any suggestion that motherhood might compete with career. If you had to cut out of the office for the third-grade play, better plead an emergency root canal than look like a mom." [23] And to a great degree, this training and interpretation of working motherhood challenges the traditional stereotypes of motherhood held so tightly by the American populace, a group that still clings to the belief that while mothers may work, their primary duty is to their children. Pelosi herself articulates these sentiments. More importantly, the American stereotypes regarding motherhood require that while women may work, they cannot be seen to enjoy working more than mothering.

Clinton clearly enjoys her work. As Eleanor Clift mentioned during a discussion with one of my English classes, Senator Hillary represents the well-prepared female student in all of our classes, the good girl, as far as homework goes. [24] Akin to Hermione in the Harry Potter series, Hillary Clinton does all her reading, takes notes, and hands in her work early. We all value this kind of behavior, particularly if we are the teachers or the constituents on the receiving end of this perfectionism, but we all, secretly or not, hope bad things will happen to those who are so well-prepared and informed.

Add the fact that Hillary has only one child, and Americans, even though more and more families are having fewer children, look suspiciously on the one-child home—maybe she did not like being a mother. Maybe there was something wrong. And given her spouse, further imaginative and unflattering comments and images come to mind. Loving your work and your family are still not options for most women in America today. Women must choose, and if they are looking for public support, sympathy, and votes, they must choose family over career.

Hillary, however, chooses a more feminist image, and this has caused her trouble. First, she is well-educated, and if there is anything Americans distrust more than a working mother it is an intellectual. Of course, the Obama election may have proved this assumption wrong, but there is something about a well-educated and informed woman that sends the electorate on edge. This is not to imply that Pelosi or other female politicians are not well-educated, but the Pelosi story overcomes any anxiety Americans may have about intellectual competence. Her story is the Horatio Alger type, from kitchen to Congress, from working class to ruling class. As Judith Warner, author of *Perfect Madness: Motherhood in the Age of Anxiety*, humorously noted during Clinton's campaign, the problem with Clinton, again as in Clift's comments, is that she is almost too good at her job, and this causes audiences to be suspicious. Comparing Pelosi to Clinton, Warner says that Pelosi is an "Everymom" who fights back tears when talking about American troops in Iraq. Clinton, however, is not "wired" that way: "what you probably shouldn't do [but what Clinton does] is talk policy, with a passion and warmth and profound sense of purpose." [25] Women just cannot express too much enthusiasm for their work.

Warner continues reminding us of the burden that women have to bear when it comes to elections:

> Not only does she [Clinton] have to overcome the electability thing, the likability thing, and with some voters at least the Bill thing. Now she's got to live up to the whole woman thing...in other words...Hillary has to become someone every woman can relate to. She not only has to represent us, but also to mirror us, lift us up and move us, and know how we feel, what we want, and how we live. [26]

Of course, this is probably true of every candidate, but it is particularly challenging for women who historically have never served as representatives for anything. Women, mothers in particular, have frequently served as props for the main event, the male performance.

Though Warner does not mention it, the entire Hillary situation is akin to a famous story by Henry James titled "The Real Thing." The gist of the story in this context is that real people cannot represent themselves; stand-ins, frequently models from completely different classes and educational backgrounds, may actually represent wealth and class better. In Clinton's situation, she is the "real thing," a devoted wife, mother, and supporter of children's and women's rights, but her image and the expectations of the American people distort this image, frequently transforming her into something that she is not, a liberal monster, the political equivalent to Eve.

In addition to the expectations regarding femininity and motherhood, Hillary had the added burden of having served as a first lady, a role that many Americans view with an almost religious fervor. For most Americans, Laura Bush or Jackie Kennedy embodies the role of the first lady—smiling, quiet, working on children's issues, fashion, home life. Clinton, of course, took on national health care. So, Clinton's feminist, active role, combined with her role as first lady, a predominantly passive role in American politics, brought greater concerns and challenges for Clinton.

Aware of these associations, as well as the difficulties in her marriage and her husband's administration, Hillary attempted to address concerns by referring to herself by her first name. Though her spokesman Jay Carson said, Hillary works "because it reflects the warmth and familiarity people feel towards her," [27] it is clearly a break from her connection to her husband. Ironically, by referring to herself by her first name, a reference that would indicate a diminution of status, she actually established herself as an independent being, separate from her husband. It was her name, after all, and she was her own woman, her own candidate. She is married to Bill, the former president, but she is now running her own campaign. In some way, the choice worked, as Pelosi's swearing-in worked. Hillary represents familiarity and power, dependence and independence, and this combination may be one of the keys to successfully marketing motherhood in American politics.

Clearly, however, Hillary's use of motherhood is much different from Pelosi's. Her Web site, for example, has a tab, "Motherhood and Advocate." [28] There are few references to family and many more references to her work advocating for mothers and children through public policy and service. For example, the site mentions, "Hillary ran a legal aid clinic for the poor when she first got to Arkansas and handled cases of foster care and child abuse. Years later, she organized a group called Arkansas Advocates for Children and Families." [29] This is a far cry from Pelosi's Web site, which does not highlight motherhood as explicitly as Hillary's but which, in her personal history, highlights her father and her children. Such separation of the political and the personal seems antithetical to feminism, which was founded on the phrase, the "personal is political," but ultimately the strategy attempts to show that Hillary is just like other politicians—competent, successful, and, in her case, committed to the needs of women and children.

Of course, there are other explanations. By referring to her personal life, she invokes her husband, Bill, and that connection could work against her career. But in another way, the fact that she distances herself from her home life and family may, in effect, be the most motherly of all acts. Hillary is very protective of her daughter, Chelsea, and she is loath to use her daughter or her daughter's life and antics as political fodder; such restraint is admirable and certainly understandable in a one-child family home. Pelosi's larger family dynamics afford her the opportunity to use family stories because individual children are protected under the anonymous term "the kids," rather than individuals. If, for example, Hillary said, "don't make me use my mother voice," most Americans would wonder what kind of kid Chelsea was to invoke such vocals. Ironically, by distancing herself from her specific family dynamics, then,

Hillary may, in fact, be a good mother in the traditional sense: by placing her family first, however, she has been the object of some criticism for, ironically, not being a good enough mother.

In the case of Pelosi and Clinton, both women have successfully maneuvered incredible challenges, stereotypes, and difficulties. Both illustrate various ways of shuffling the motherhood card into the American political deck. Hillary's brand of motherhood may seem cooler and not appeal as completely at this time, and Pelosi may not offer a feminist enough image for others, but both offer women some models with which to model their own behavior in the workplace, models that respect individual women's personalities rather than the dictates of a patriarchal culture. That is, both Pelosi and Hillary show women that motherhood and politics can work together, and women can use their own personalities and styles to make them work together. There is no one perfect model for political mothering.

There may, of course, be an imperfect model, which brings us to the phenomenon of Sarah Palin, the governor of Alaska chosen by John McCain as his running mate during the 2008 election. As Laura Ingraham noted when she accepted an award from the Republican National Coalition for Life on behalf of Sarah Palin, "Sarah Palin represents a new feminism . . . And there is no bigger threat to the elites in this country than a woman who lives her conservative convictions." [30] Such a comment raises many questions and issues. Why, for example, does a feminist, a person committed to advancing the equality of women, making sure that an underserved population is served, constitute an elite? And why, for the first time ever, are Republicans finally using the "f-word"? But Ingraham's comments presented at least one explanation for McCain's choice in his vice-presidential candidate. Republicans needed a woman to lure the disenfranchised Hillary Clinton supporters away from the Democratic Party, a party that many felt betrayed them in their support of a male, presidential candidate, Obama, over that of a qualified female candidate, Hillary. Of course, this strategy did not work. As Gloria Steinem noted, "To vote in protest for McCain/Palin would be like saying, 'Somebody stole my shoes, so I'll amputate my legs.'" [31] *The Irish Times* reports that Dana Milbank of Philadelphia wrote that Hillary did not bring votes for Obama, "although by her count she has made more than 50 appearances for Barack Obama. Nor was it the work of Obama . . . No, the one who put the Hillary Clinton voters in Obama's column was John McCain, with his choice of running mate." The report continues, "Palin—God forbid! Where did they find her?" [32]

The Republicans got behind Palin very quickly and touted her as a new kind of feminist, in the language and spirit very similar to the Ingraham sentiment. All women are not alike, they argued, and a conservative woman is a great threat to the monolithic liberal, feminists who have been saying that they are the only ones who know what women want. Of course, using Steinem again, it was clear that Palin was a political and patriarchal pawn, not a feminist: "She opposes just about every issue that women support by a majority or plurality." [33] And for many older feminists like myself, she represented other women who opposed women, Phyllis Schlafly and Anita Bryant, for example.

What is ironic is that underlying the Republican party's great emphasis on female difference was the assumption that women are, in fact, interchangeable. The argument is as follows: if, for example, Hillary Clinton supporters were feeling betrayed and marginalized by their party, then another woman, any woman, would appeal to them and take them away from their home party. Of course, such an argument seems ludicrous, but given the alternatives for the Palin choice, it is a feasible conclusion, one which many commentators suspected immediately following the announcement. The Republican strategists for McCain assumed that women who want to vote for women will vote for any woman.

Within days of the announcement, of course, feminists protested and, ultimately, even the National Organization for Women threw their support to Obama. The most famous and succinct statement was Gloria Steinem's, which noted, "Palin shares nothing but a chromosome with Clinton." [34] In this way, the Republicans were right. This was a new brand of feminism. Palin created a new way of thinking about feminism. The Democrats and other feminists during this election asked women not to support women at all costs, but rather to support policies and politicians that support women, mothers, and children. And this is precisely what Steinem concluded in her piece on Palin—Palin has a right to be wrong, but if supporting women is the goal, then vote Obama/Biden. [35] They were, in fact, the feminist ticket, the ticket without a woman.

For some, like Camille Paglia, Palin represented a brand of "can-do, no-excuses, moose-hunting feminism—a world away from the whining, sniping, wearily ironic mode of the establishment feminism represented by Gloria Steinem." [36] And to a certain degree, there was something appealing about that kind of frontierswoman persona that Palin exuded. In addition, as Paglia noted and others thought, a pro-life feminism or option in feminism would appeal to "third-world cultures where motherhood is still honored and where the Western model of the hard-driving, self-absorbed career woman is less admired." [37] Of course, Paglia does not elaborate on how the third world countries honor motherhood by keeping them impoverished, uneducated, and pregnant, but clearly Palin's down-to-earth roots were appealing to many, and it served her well during her vice-presidential debate with Biden, who was more experienced and prepared for such public events.[38]

And there is something likeable about Palin. Even after the election, Palin critics admitted that when they thought about her, they did not find themselves hating her as much as they thought they would.[39] She embodies, after all, a good part of the heartland and its stories, a rags-to-riches tale that landed a relatively unknown, inexperienced woman in the governor's mansion. But, as the email that circulated throughout the campaign, if she were black, her story would not be so heartwarming—poorly and educated erratically, a family in a dysfunctional state, a pregnant, unwed daughter. These tales would not inspire confidence in and compassion for a black leader, and ultimately, they did not inspire confidence in this white, female governor.

Ironically, it was not the liberal feminists who undid Palin. Instead, it was her own party's inability to accept her decisions regarding motherhood and politics. Lifetime conservatives could not offer their support to a woman who apparently could not manage her own family. While Pelosi lauds her maternal managerial abilities, Palin touted her motherhood in a mundane way—she, like many other mothers, had a daughter who made a mistake. And while the decision to keep the baby was laudable, conservatives and others had a difficult time wondering how Palin could put her vulnerable daughter in a situation that would make her more vulnerable and open to criticism. In a word, Palin's house was not in order.

Rumors spread about Palin's offspring in many ways. Was the child that Palin just had her own or her daughter's? Such tabloid questions made the McCain campaign look chaotic and rudderless. Ultimately, the world discovered the truth—the child was Palin's, but then other stories began to emerge about this pro-life, new feminist mother. She hid her own pregnancy from her advisors and her constituents until the final month of her pregnancy, and she was reported to be leaking amniotic fluid when she was attending a conference. Far from being the "Everymom" that the Republicans hoped for, Palin was looking more and more like the career-driven uber-mom, who abandoned her children for the sake of her own ambition. The ultimate sin of American motherhood: placing your career above your family. As one blogger notes, "You can juggle a Black-Berry and a breast pump in a lot of jobs, but not in the vice-presidency." [40]

Like it or not, Americans are still very conflicted about the role of mothers in public life. In industry, if a hiring committee knows that a woman is a mother, she has less of a chance of getting hired. And yet, 67 percent of all mothers in America are working mothers. Women account for only 16 percent in Congress.[41] The mommy image can be used to either make or break a candidate, and in the case of Sarah Palin, she has clearly been broken by her invocation to motherhood. In a way, Palin opened the door to mommy competition. Any mother who has ever had an elementary child in a school play or been asked to host a birthday party knows it is a dirty game. Women and society have so much invested in the good mother image that it is virtually impossible to meet the high and often conflicting expectations. The bottom line—women are still the primary caregivers to children in the United States, and those who opt to leave that role are often judged harshly, not good enough, or mistaken in their priorities. Palin, with an infant at home and a pregnant teenage daughter, was told by the American people in no uncertain terms—take care of your family first. Run later. Ironically, the Republican strategists who have harped on keeping women in the home in very traditional ways underestimated the power of their own rhetoric. It is one thing to have a mother run when the children are grown; it is entirely another matter to have her run with the children still dependent.

On the darker side, Palin's ambition was equated with a beauty pageant mentality. Her desire to run and serve in public office were seen as selfish and self-serving, the ultimate downfall of any American politician, male or female. Expensive haircuts, wardrobe, and toys have all undone men, but here they served to highlight Palin's role as a bad mother, only interested in herself, buying toys to placate abandoned children.[42] Of course, men have had to justify their own haircuts, and recently Governor Bill Richardson's beard has been the subject of much discussion, so American politics can get pretty superficial; but for Palin and her party, they underestimated the deep and frequently irrational feelings about motherhood and political power. And while many may disagree with Palin's ideology, ideologies that perpetuate the oppression of women and children, it is interesting to note that her party's own ideology ultimately undid her. She needed to be home with the kids, running a state, not the country.

Mothers in American politics have come a long way, but there is still a great deal of thinking and changing to occur. Working mothers with young children are still held to impossibly high expectations, more so than working fathers with young children. Today's women can have it all, but they may not be able to have it all at the same time, as Pelosi's and Clinton's successes demonstrate. Americans still believe that youngsters need their mothers in significant and important ways, ways that cannot be substituted by childcare or even daddy care. At the same time, Americans are reluctant to offer support to these women. Women are expected to manage their offspring on their own and expected to survive the "societal schizophrenia when it comes to balancing work with domesticity." [43]

NOTES

1. Kara Jesella, "Mom's Mad and She's Organized," *New York Times*, February 22, 2007, 1. Jesella notes a study by the *American Journal of Sociology* that "employers are less likely to pursue and interview if they find out that a candidate" is a mother.

2. Caroline Kennedy, for example, while defending her credentials mentioned that she was a lawyer and mother as some of her top qualifications to lead. And during a heated discussion between Barbara Boxer and Condoleezza Rice, the motherhood issue was raised by Boxer saying that the Iraq war would have no effect on her life, since her children were grown or too young "for military service." Boxer then added that Rice would not have to pay "a particular price, as I understand it, with an immediate family." Rice fired back, "I thought you could still make good decisions on behalf of the country if you were single and didn't have children." Qtd. in Robin Toner, "Women Feeling Freer to Suggest 'Vote for Mom,'" *The New York Times*, January 29, 2007, 1. Clearly motherhood has taken on a very different life in American politics.

3. Qtd. in Lyndsey Layton, "Mom's in the House, With Kids at Home: For Congresswomen with Young Children, A Tough Balance," *Washington Post*, July 19, 2007, A01.

4. Ruth Marcus, "Grandma with a Gavel," *Washington Post*, January 10, 2007, A13.

5. Ibid.

6. Ibid.

7. Ibid.

8. Qtd. in Kathy Kiely, "Nancy Pelosi Speaks About Being a Mom: Politician Tells Younger Women: Don't Think of Motherhood as a Minus," *USA Today*, May 10, 2007, 9D.

9. Eugene Robinson, "After the 100 Hours, A War Awaits," *Washington Post*, January 5, 2007, A17.

10. Brian Kelly, "That's Madame Speaker to You, Buddy Boy," *U.S. News and World Report*, November 20, 2006, 26–27.

11. Marcus, "Grandma with a Gavel."

12. Congresswoman Nancy Pelosi. http://www.house.gov/pelosi

13. Silla Brush et al., "We Won! Now What the Heck Do We Do?" *U.S. News and World Report*, November 20, 2006, 50–53.

14. Karen Breslau et al., "Rolling with Pelosi," *Newsweek*, October 23, 2006, 44–46. *Academic Search Complete*, EBSCO *Host* (accessed November 11, 2008).

15. Qtd. in Breslau, "Rolling with Pelosi."

16. Ann Coulter, "Media Missed Mileston on Road to Pelosi," *Human Events*, November 20, 2006, 1–8. *Academic Search Complete*, EBSCO *Host* (accessed November 11, 2008).

17. Qtd. in Breslau, "Rolling with Pelosi."

18. Qtd. in Andrea Stone, "Pelosi Surprises Critics, Gives GOP Little Ammo," *USA Today* (n.d.). *Academic Search Complete*, EBSCO *Host* (accessed November 11, 2008).

19. "Women of My Year," *Advocate*, January 15, 2008, 26–27. *Academic Search Complete*, EBSCO *Host* (accessed December 22, 2008).

20. Tim Reid, "Matriarch with an Unruly Family to Keep Order," *The Times (London)*, November 18, 2006, 47.

21. Congresswoman Nancy Pelosi. http://www.house.gov/pelosi/newdirection .html. At the time of publication, however, the "collegiality" is probably debatable, given the attacks Pelosi has received regarding her comments that deny her knowledge of the interrogation techniques used on Iraqi prisoners.

22. Breslau, "Rolling with Pelosi."

23. Marcus, "Grandma with a Gavel."

24. Eleanor Clift, Class Discussion, Ohio Dominican University, Spring 2006.

25. Judith Warner, "The Really Real Hillary: Women in Power II," *New York Times*, March 15, 2007, 6.

26. Ibid.

27. Suzanne Smalley and Martha Brant, "Hillary: What's in a Name?" *Newsweek* 151.13 (March 31, 2008), 9. *Academic Search Complete*, EBSCO *Host* (accessed December 22, 2008).

28. Hillary Clinton, "Mother and Advocate," http://www.hillaryclinton.com/ about/mom/ (accessed November 11, 2008).

29. Ibid.

30. Qtd. in Robin Abcarian, "Republican National Convention: Insiders See 'New Feminism'; Outside the GOP Convention, However, Questions Are Raised about Palin's Family Responsibilities," *Los Angeles Times*, September 4, 2008, 13.

31. Gloria Steinem, "Wrong Woman, Wrong Message," *Los Angeles Times*, September 4, 2008, 29.

32. "Hockey Moms and Pitbull Politics Drive Hillary Faithful Back to the Fold," *The Irish Times*, October 15, 2008, 11.

33. Ibid.

34. Ibid.

35. Ibid.

36. Camille Paglia, "Fresh Blood for the Vampire: A Beady-Eyed McCain Gets a Boost From the Charismatic Sarah Palin," *Salon*, September 10, 2008, http://www.salon.com/opinion/paglia/2008/09/10/palin/ (accessed November 11, 2008).

37. Ibid.

38. During a discussion of Pelosi and Palin, however, GOP pollster Frank Luntz noted that he advised candidates to challenge Hillary because "it's always dangerous to attack a woman." This might have been the Biden strategy as well. Qtd. in Stone.

39. Rebecca Traister, "Sarah Palin Thanks the Young Girls at Her Rallies," *Salon.Com*, http://www.salon.com/mwt/broadsheet/2008/11/13/palin_girls/ (accessed November 13, 2008).

40. Qtd. in Judith Timson, "Unleashing the Mommy Wars Upon This Election," *The Globe and Mail*, September 3, 2008, L1.

41. "High Stakes for Candidates Using Mom Image," *Chinadaily.com.cn, Lexis Nexis*, http://www.lexisnexis.com.ezproxy.ohiodominican.edu/us/lnacademic/search/homesubmitForm.do (accessed November 13, 2008).

42. See, for example, David P. Gushee, "The Palin Predicament," *USA Today*, September 15, 2008, 12A, which outlines the challenges of conservative ideology and rhetoric regarding motherhood with the real-life Palin nomination. Timson's essay notes a number of negative comments from conservative female bloggers who ask Palin, "on being selfish: where is the line?" See, too, Jodi Kantor et al., "Fusing Politics and Motherhood in a New Way," *The New York Times*, September 8, 2008, 1. Here Palin is reported to have hidden her pregnancy from family, friends, and constituents, as well as traveling to Texas a month before her special needs child was born, with amniotic fluid "leaking." And though a doctor approved the travel, the story can clearly be used against her and her maternal instincts.

43. Dana Goldstein, "GOP Moms: Between a Rock and the Hard Right," *American Prospect*, July 27, 2007, http://www.prospect.org/cs/articles?article=gop_moms_between_a_rock_and_the_hard_right (accessed December 13, 2008).

CHAPTER 8

The Mommy Lift: Cutting Mothers Down to Size

Mardia J. Bishop

Nothing compares to the joy of motherhood, but the havoc you go through to get your body back into shape can bring tears to your eyes.
—Laurie Tarkan, *Fit Pregnancy*[1]

Those badges of motherhood have turned into badges of shame, and, if you're the one caught without a tummy tuck, then you won't get invited to the party. It peeves me no end that something as drastic as surgery, as this blatant nonacceptance of one's own body in whatever shape it happens to be in, has become so pervasive.
—Karen Murphy, StrollerDerby Blog[2]

In *Mommy Myth: The Idealization of Motherhood and How It Has Undermined Women*, Susan Douglas and Meredith Michaels argue that the climate for mothers today is hostile thanks to a cultural icon—or "myth"—of the Perfect Mom. The Perfect Mom—think Clair Huxtable from *The Cosby Show* who was a partner in a law firm, kept a beautifully decorated and clean home, and tended to her five children's needs—is the symbol of "new momism," Douglas and Michaels's term for the contemporary ideology that defines the qualities of a good mother. " 'New momism' insists that no woman is truly complete or fulfilled unless she has kids, that women remain the best primary caretakers of children, and that to be a remotely decent mother, a woman has to devote her entire physical, psychological, emotional, and intellectual being,

24/7 to her children." [3] In other words, in order to be considered a good mother today, a mother has to "sneak Echinacea" into the "freshly squeezed, organically grown orange juice" she has made, and teach her children how to "download research for their kindergarten report on 'My Family Tree—The Early Roman Years,' "[4] before she hand stitches Halloween costumes, creates window treatments, bakes ten dozen cookies for the school bake sale, and heads off to her professional career.

New momism is "a set of ideals, norms, and practices, most frequently and powerfully represented in the media, that seem on the surface to celebrate motherhood, but which in reality promulgate the standards of perfection that are beyond . . . reach." [5] As argued by Douglas and Michaels, new momism makes it seem that being a mother is valuable, but in reality, since government and industry have reduced support for mothers and the Perfect Mom creates impossible standards to meet, new momism simply works to undermine whatever power mothers supposedly have, primarily by having mothers waste time, energy, money, and sanity on trying to adhere to the Perfect Mom standards.

And yet the picture painted by Douglas and Michaels is not bleak enough. On top of the standards they present, representations in popular culture illustrate that there is another quality that needs to be added to the list that defines the Perfect Mom—she has to have the perfect body. However, just like the other standards, the perfect body is beyond reach because the perfect body does not appear to have given birth. In other words, current ideology tells women they have to be a mother, but they cannot look like one. So what is a perfect mom in training supposed to do? Fortunately, cosmetic surgeons have offered a solution in the form of the "mommy lift," a procedure that not only gives women "improved" bodies, but also serves as a cultural symbol for the role of women, particularly mothers—they are creatures that must be nipped, tucked, and snipped into submission—literally cut down to size.

Ironically, while the ideal mother's body is getting smaller, motherhood itself is getting bigger. According to Douglas and Michaels, "motherhood became one of the biggest media obsessions of the last three decades, exploding especially in the mid-1980s." [6] And the new model of motherhood positioned by the media is the "always gorgeous, always sexy, always devoted celebrity mom," who is presented "as the mother who can balance work and family and always say that it's more rewarding to be a mother than be at work." [7] The celebrity mom also provides the beauty standards for mothers, which include a thin, fit body with firm, perky, large breasts, tight, flat abs, firm skin, and cellulite-free butt and thighs. In addition, the celebrity mom as presented in various media serves as a role model on how to achieve the thin, fit body after having a baby. For example, Halle Berry lost "30 lbs. in 4 months," hitting the gym three weeks after delivering her baby; Jennifer Lopez dropped 30 pounds by walking and saying, "no oil, no butter!"; Nicole Kidman did "Yoga Days after Birth!"; Jessica Alba bought NutriFit's meal delivery service and "3-2-1 Baby Bulge Be Gone!" exercise plan;[8] Jaime Pressly "relied on daily hour-long runs and 90-minute weight-training sessions"; Mel B "hit the gym just five days after giving birth" . . . and "did twice-daily cardio- and strength-training sessions."[9] (Tori Spelling and Nicole Richie, though, did not have to do anything, as they credit their fit, thin post-baby bodies to "good genes.") Of course, not mentioned is what these celebrity moms did with their newborns during their lengthy workouts or how they physically managed to exercise strenuously when experiencing sleep deprivation caused by newborn eating schedules. That is, assuming the celebrity moms personally and consistently take care of their babies. Also not mentioned is that the celebrity mom's job is to be "beautiful" and help define beauty; consequently, the celebrity mom does not have to fit in gym time with her other responsibilities. Moreover, she has the money to hire a personal trainer and chef. Most importantly, what is not mentioned is that the post-pregnancy body is different from the pre-pregnancy body, that the celebrities' approaches to post-pregnancy fitness and weight loss might not be the healthiest, and that the post-pregnancy body will never be the same as it was before pregnancy.

That said, for those mothers who cannot "get their body back" quickly through the dieting and exercise programs as advocated by celebrity moms, the American Society of Plastic Surgeons (ASPS) offers a cure— the mommy lift. There are two types of plastic surgeons: reconstructive, who focus on repairing birth defects, such as a cleft palate, or repairing injuries, such as restructuring someone's facial structure after that person has been in an automobile accident; and, cosmetic, who focus on surgically changing the body in order to adhere to a beauty ideal. The "mommy lift" is cosmetic surgery.

A mommy lift, also called a "mommy makeover" and "mom job," is a combination of cosmetic surgery procedures, including a breast lift (mastopexy) and/or breast augmentation, a tummy tuck (abdominoplasty), and liposuction, that are performed during one long surgery. The procedures' goals are to lift loosened skin and remove pregnancy fat. Both pregnancy and breast-feeding result in a temporarily increased breast size. Sometimes, the breast skin does not fully contract after pregnancy, resulting in "excess" or loosened skin. A breast lift removes the excess skin and "tightens the surrounding tissue to reshape and support a new breast contour." [10] A breast augmentation increases the breast size using implants. During pregnancy, skin in the abdominal area is stretched and muscles are weakened. If the skin does not fully contract after pregnancy, the skin will appear loose and be considered excess skin. A "tummy tuck" removes excess skin in the abdominal area and tightens abdominal muscles. Liposuction removes fat from body areas that a pregnancy will typically cause, such as the abdomen and thighs. All of these procedures are considered major surgery with side effects and extensive recuperation time.

The number of mommy lifts has increased substantially over the past few years. According to the ASPS, in 2006, more than 325,000 mommy lifts were performed, up 11 percent from 2005.[11] These numbers only refer to the mommy lift—the package including all three procedures. Numbers of women having only a breast lift, abdominoplasty, or liposuction also have increased dramatically. In 2007, 59 percent of ASPS members indicated they had seen an increase of post-childbirth related procedures over the past three years.[12] Since 2000, the number of breast augmentations done has increased by 64 percent, breast lifts by 97 percent, and tummy tucks by 137 percent. In 2007, 347,524 breast augmentations were performed, 104,176 breast lifts, and 148,410 tummy tucks.[13] The cost of these procedures varies due to geographic locations; however, the national average surgeon fee for a breast augmentation in 2007 was $3,800, for a breast lift $4,200, for a tummy tuck $5,300, and for liposuction $3,000.[14] These are only the surgeon fees. Additional fees include anesthesia and anesthetist fees, operating room costs, medications, and others. Further, these procedures seem to be recession-proof. As recognized by the ASPS, "despite domestic concerns like inflation and a looming home lending crisis, average Americans [predominantly Caucasian women] continue to spend money on plastic surgery." [15] One of the reasons for the spending is the outstanding job cosmetic surgeons, the media, and pop culture have done to pathologize the post-pregnancy/post-breast-feeding body and market a cure.

On a simple level, what is occurring is that the media and cosmetic surgeons are playing on the fears and anxieties mothers have about their bodily changes, defining a natural process as a disease, and offering a cure. Since our culture is a consumer one, and the cosmetic industry long ago established that beauty could be bought, the media and cosmetic surgeons are merely participating as producers in our consumer culture. Although critics will argue that women are freely making the choice to have cosmetic surgery and exercising their power as consumers to do so, they are not in power when it comes to cosmetic surgery. Instead, cosmetic surgery erodes a woman's/mother's power.

In the surgeon/patient relationship, the surgeon has the power. The way that cosmetic surgery works is a surgeon looks at a patient to criticize culturally perceived flaws. The patient has to confess or admit flaws and ask the surgeon to "fix" her, thereby giving power to the surgeon. Carole Spitzack argues that the surgeon's clinical eye functions like Foucault's medical gaze: "it is a disciplinary gaze situated within apparatuses of power and knowledge that constructs the female figure as pathological, excessive, unruly, and potentially threatening of the dominant order." [16]

Indeed, cosmetic surgeons are well known for pathologizing the natural, material body. In the 1980s, it was the Asian eyelid. A popular plastic surgery among Asian populations was a type of blepharoplasty (eyelid surgery), which widens the upper eyelid in order to achieve a more "Western"-shaped eye. In several medical articles and textbooks, when discussing blepharoplasty, the Asian eyelid is pathologized. For example, one article refers to this type of surgery as a "Correction of the Oriental Eyelid." [17] Another describes the Asian eyelid as having a "poorly defined or periorbital appearance." [18] In the 1990s, the female breast was pathologized. During the silicone breast implant dispute, the American Society of Plastic and Reconstructive Surgeons diagnosed small breasts as a disease. In its petition to the Food and Drug Administration, the organization stated that for "the female breast that does not achieve normal or adequate development . . . there is a substantial and enlarging body of medical information and opinion . . . to the effect that these deformities are really a disease." [19] Currently, in our youth-oriented culture, natural aging processes are pathologized. The majority of cosmetic surgery procedures that occur are ones that attempt to counteract the effects of natural body deterioration. One such procedure is removing eye bags. Balsamo explains that eye bags occur because as the body ages, skin tissue loses its elasticity and begins to sag. As eyelids weaken, fat deposits build up around the eye and cause wrinkling and sagging. While eye bags are part of the natural aging process,

> it is quite common, in both the popular and professional literature, for a plastic surgeon to refer to eye bags as a "deformity." This is a simple example of the way in which "natural" characteristics of the aging body are redefined as "symptoms," with the consequence that cosmetic surgery is rhetorically constructed as a medical procedure with the power to "cure" or "correct" such physical deformities. [20]

Part of the pathologizing of the postpartum body stems from our culture's obsession with a youthful appearance—for women that means perky breasts and a flat stomach. A natural result of having a baby is that the female body produces effects that seem to be age-related, such as stretched, loosened skin and accumulated fat. The aesthetic effects of pregnancy on a woman's body, as well as the body's ability to "return" to its pre-pregnancy state, differ depending on genetics, age, and many other factors. But, there are several permanent effects. They are sagging breasts and stomachs, stretch marks, loose abdominal skin, a permanent weight gain of approximately five pounds, a redistribution of weight, wider hips (about one inch), scarring from a caesarean section, varicose veins. Again, these effects are natural results of being pregnant; yet, through the media and cosmetic surgeons, these effects are seen as abnormal, diseased, and/or flawed.

In looking through cosmetic surgeons' Web sites, the majority emphasize the non-normalcy of the post-pregnant body and the inability of women to control their bodies. Again, remember the cosmetic surgeon's medical gaze "constructs the female figure as pathological, unruly, and excessive...." [21] Fittingly, cosmetic surgeons' Web sites describe mothers as having difficulty controlling their bodies. Dr. Huffaker declares that "Women do have trouble getting back together [getting their body back to its pre-pregnancy shape]." [22] And Dr. Stoker comments that "Many of my patients are young moms who are doing their best to take care of themselves, but their bodies have gone through some irreversible changes that they find discouraging [and cannot control]." [23] Cosmetic surgeons reassure potential patients that they can help mothers control their bodies. Dr. Koger insists that "One of the benefits of having extra pounds and skin surgically removed is that the appetite is easier to control.... Fewer fat cells need less insulin, blood sugar is more even, and the appetite not so large." [24] And Dr. LoVerme states that "Liposuction can be performed on virtually any area of the body in order to eliminate stubborn, excess fat." He adds that "More and more women, particularly those who have had children, are taking control of their bodies" [through having the mommy lift]. Furthermore, the Web sites position women who have mommy lifts as better than those who do not. Dr. LoVerme's site declares that he "can provide deserving mothers [with cosmetic surgery]" [25] and another surgeon's Web site comments that "health-conscious women ... come to us for 'mommy makeover' procedures." [26]

In addition to finding women at fault for not controlling their bodies, cosmetic surgeon Web sites emphasize the non-normalcy of the post-pregnant body. Most Web sites mention that the mommy lift is for women who cannot get their pre-pregnancy bodies back through diet and exercise, "responsibly" positioning plastic surgery as a last resort. Yet, the reality is, it is impossible to return to the body one had before pregnancy because pregnancy permanently changes a woman's body. So instead of discussing the normalcy of what a postpartum body is and looks like, our culture ignores the new norm (post-pregnancy) and insists that the old norm (pre-pregnancy) is the only one available for "health-conscious," "deserving" women. Consequently, cosmetic surgeon Web sites and popular literature—women's magazines and Internet articles—use terms that emphasize the pre-pregnancy (and youthful) norm. Popular phrases and words include: "get your body back," "recapture," "return," and "restore." Cosmetic surgeons promise to "help you get your body back," to "reverse those effects [from pregnancy]," and to "restore your youthful shape." Some even refer to themselves as figure restoration specialists. Notice that the terminology, in the form of directives, indicates that a woman can and should control her physical body. In essence, cosmetic surgeons are describing the postpartum body as a woman's enemy and telling women that surgeons are here to help women wage war on their bodies, promoting self-hatred on a huge level.

The new post-pregnancy body is not desirable and is never described as such. Instead, it is described as being unattractive, nonyouthful, uncontrollable, and excessive. One woman on a cosmetic surgeon's Web site described her abdomen as a "pooch of overhanging fat" and her breasts as "deflated sacks." [27] Another woman, this time in *People* magazine, described her abdomen as "a disfigured stomach" with "loose skin and muscle damage." [28] One cosmetic surgeon's Web site describes the effect of pregnancy on a woman's body as creating "detrimental change," including "deflated," "droopy," "hanging," "collapsed in" breasts and "loose, redundant, and stretch-marked" abdomens.[29] And yet another cosmetic surgeon's Web site declares, "Every mother deserves to feel beautiful, and a mommy makeover can help make that ideal a reality. By combining post-pregnancy plastic surgery, cellulite removal, body and breast lift procedures, and skin therapy, you can get back the youthful appearance that you thought was gone forever." [30] The messages here indicate that having a baby makes you physically ugly and abnormal. In order to become beautiful and normal a mother has to control her body, and the only way to control it is through the help of cosmetic surgeons. Of course, the previous quote offers a tremendous contradiction—after so much surgery, how can you be sure, or a surgeon for that matter, that what you end up with is the body you had before you were pregnant.

In addition to making a woman surrender her power by "confessing" culturally perceived abnormalities, cosmetic surgery erodes a mother's power by dividing her body into parts. The surgeon's "gaze" "disciplines the unruly female body by first fragmenting it into isolated parts—face, hair, legs, breasts—and then redefining those parts as inherently flawed and pathological." [31] As for the mommy lift, the postpartum body is fragmented primarily into breasts and abdomens. And, those body parts are consistently redefined as flawed and pathological. Drpollock.com refers to these parts as "postpartum deformities." [32] Docshop.com and drteitelbaum.com define post-pregnancy breasts as "sagging" and "shrunken" due to having "excessive," "loose" skin and a "decrease in volume." The abdomen is defined as a "postpartum bulging belly" and as a stomach with "loose, redundant, and stretch-marked skin, a bad caesarean section scar, and a very lax abdominal wall." [33]

The fragmentation or dissection of a mother into parts is not just the work of cosmetic surgeons, however; it is rampant in media, especially media focusing on celebrities. For the past couple of years, celebrity media have been preoccupied with who is sporting a "baby bump." Magazine spreads are devoted to photographs of female celebrities that try to prove the celebrity has a "bump." The photos are focused on the abdominal area and often have an arrow pointing to the abdomen. A spread in a recent *Life & Style* featured seven photos of Jennifer Garner that show how "she's been hiding her bump!" Four pages later, the magazine has a photo of Uma Thurman in a bikini showing off "what looked like a small bump" and a photo of Gwyneth Paltrow featuring "a small bump spotted under her dress." [34]

The preoccupation with the abdomen does not end once celebrities have given birth either. An October 2008 issue of *Star* was dedicated to whether or not Angelina Jolie had a tummy tuck. The magazine's Web site even showed closeup photos of Jolie's abdomen and invited people to respond to whether or not they thought she had one. Within minutes the blog had numerous responses that indicated the participants had microscopically examined the Jolie abdomen photos. One blogger insisted that Jolie did not have surgery because "Anyone could see the 'Spanx' outline under her dress." [35] I could not see it, but I admit I did not use a magnifying glass. Unfortunately for most mothers, the public's preoccupation with a woman's abdomen turns from a joyful, anticipatory one when concentrating on a "baby bump" to a negative, judgmental one when examining women for a "postpartum bulging belly" or "kangaroo pouch."

The problem with dissecting a woman/mother into parts is that, not only can the parts be pathologized, but the mother is not seen as a whole human being. In photos of the postpartum mother, whether on cosmetic surgeon Web sites or in celebrity media, the photos not only do not show the whole physical woman, but the accompanying text does not comment on any other characteristics that compose the whole woman, such as intelligence or artistic talent. Instead, she is reduced to a few biological parts that have something to do with producing babies, and once those parts do their job, they need to be "fixed" or controlled. Moreover, by pathologizing a natural bodily process, such as pregnancy, women are compelled to think about themselves in terms of parts, not a whole person, and to think about those parts as diseased (remember the woman from *People* describing her postpartum abdomen as "disfigured" with "muscle damage") and needing treatment. So instead of enjoying being a mother, a woman becomes preoccupied with her body and identifies herself as a sagging breast or a cellulite-filled hip.

Cosmetic surgery also perpetuates the pursuance of a "natural" beauty ideal that is not natural. The "natural" body proposed by cosmetic surgeons is that of a body that has not been pregnant and one that can be contrived only through surgical means. In other words, it is plastic. And often looks that way, as commented on by Andrew Stephen based on his observance of the Washington elite at an "A-list" event: "A large proportion of the people not only looked unreal, but were unreal: their faces and bodies had been chiseled and moulded to the extent that some looked, literally, artificial." [36]

Using artificial means to achieve a "natural" beauty is not new nor only the tool of cosmetic surgeons. "Women had been camouflaging and transforming their natural appearances ever since Eve discovered shame. . . . [Today], American cosmetic manufacturers perpetuate the socially constructed oxymoron 'natural good looks,' with offers of makeup 'that's the foundation for beautiful skin' (Estee Lauder) . . . [and] lotion to 'give you healthy-looking color that's all your own.' " [37] Artificiality is the essence of a "natural" beauty ideal because beauty ideals are not "naturally" defined, but culturally defined. Moreover, beauty ideals change. For this reason, Balsamo argues that cosmetic surgery should be called fashion surgery. In studying plastic surgery procedures over the past several decades, Balsamo notes that "requests for cosmetic reconstructions show the waxing and waning of fashionable desires." For example, the "pert, upturned nose" of the 1940s and 1950s went out of style and the preferred nose is now "a classic" one.[38] With this in mind, the thought of having a mommy lift (at least three major surgeries at one time) that will only fulfill the current beauty standard, consequently requiring another type of lift for the next beauty standard, is even more repugnant.

As mentioned previously, beauty ideals are culturally defined and as such support dominant power structures. In contemporary America, the beauty ideal for women is still presented as a Caucasian woman. Cosmetic surgery supports this in that most textbooks describe the "ideal" or "aesthetic face" in terms of Caucasian beauty.[39] Although the number of cosmetic surgeries performed on "ethnic patients" was up 13 percent in 2007, 75 percent of those receiving cosmetic surgery are Caucasian women.[40] So, if our society defines a good mother as one who adheres to the beauty standard, women of color are once again demonized as bad mothers.[41]

All in all, the mommy lift sets women up for psychological, physical, and economic difficulties. Psychologically, research consistently shows that the majority of girls and women are dissatisfied with their bodies throughout their lives, including post-pregnancy. Unfortunately, there is only a small amount of research on postpartum body image, but it is growing, and the majority of what is available indicates that women are dissatisfied with their postpartum bodies.[42] Moreover, "[T]he combination of psychological stressors of new motherhood and body image concerns intensified by the residual bodily changes of pregnancy may predispose women to have an exacerbation in eating disordered symptoms as well as the development of postpartum mood disorders."[43] And, research has long shown that body dissatisfaction is caused in part by exposure to media that flaunt thin, perky bodies as beauty ideals. "There is no doubt that media portrayals of attractiveness, gender, and technologies of health both reflect and contribute to body dissatisfaction, unhealthy eating and weight management, and disordered eating in females. . . ."[44] The media plays on and creates hysteria about the maternal body, exacerbating mothers' feelings of insecurities regarding their bodies. So, the majority of postpartum women are feeling bad about their bodies because the current beauty ideal that they are bombarded with is impossible to achieve, especially if you have had a baby. In addition, their postpartum body is being described as ugly, deformed, and abnormal. Because women's value is tied to their beauty, they need to pursue the beauty standard. If they do not, they are evaluated unfavorably, and in this case, as bad mothers. As offered by the media and cosmetic surgeons who constantly show "healthy" and "deserving" mothers, the cure for a mother's body dissatisfaction and poor parenting skills is the mommy lift, a technology of health. Yet, "[S]tudies have repeatedly shown that people who have cosmetic surgery are happy that a body part has been fixed, but they are not happier with their lives and don't feel better about themselves." [45] In fact, taking part in cosmetic surgery indicates a woman will continue to experience body dissatisfaction because she has internalized beauty standards; thereby, she will continue to compare herself to the standard and find herself inadequate.

In addition to the psychological issues, the mommy lift creates physical ones. Cosmetic surgery is major surgery. It is not a simple procedure where one day a woman looks one way, and the next she looks different as portrayed by makeover television programs.[46] Cosmetic surgery takes weeks of recuperation and has numerous risks and potential side effects, including death. (Kanye West's mother recently died from cosmetic surgery.) As presented on the ASPS Web site, it takes at least eight weeks to recuperate from a tummy tuck procedure, and it has the following risks: unfavorable scarring, bleeding, infection, fluid accumulation (although a plastic tubing may be placed in the incision to allow drainage), poor wound healing, skin loss, blood clots, numbness, anesthesia risks, skin discoloration and/or swelling, fatty tissue found deep in the skin might die, major wound separation, asymmetry, recurrent looseness of skin, persistent pain, deep vein thrombosis, cardiac and pulmonary complications, persistent swelling in the legs, nerve damage, possibility of revisional surgery, and suboptimal aesthetic result.[47] There is also discrepancy regarding the safety of a mommy lift. Having three major surgeries at once increases risks and recuperation time. Although a plastic surgeon's August 2008 press release tries to dispel the discrepancy indicating that the complication and revision rates for women who underwent mommy lifts were similar to the rates for women who underwent just one surgery, the rates are still impressionable. In this surgeon's study of 268 patients, 34 percent experienced complications and 13 percent required revision surgery to correct a complication.[48] And, as even argued by a cosmetic surgeon, the

"cute" marketing term [mommy makeover] that packages surgical procedures . . . tends to trivialize a combination of major surgical procedures . . . [and] may encourage correction of a deformity that was previously of little concern. In other words, a woman seeking a tummy tuck, although not particularly concerned about the appearance of her breasts, may be influenced to have breast surgery just because it is part of "the package."[49]

Finally, the mommy lift is not permanent. As the body ages, breasts will continue to sag and, depending on diet, exercise, and genes, fat will continue to collect. Therefore, to maintain the results of the surgery, additional surgery will be required.

Economically, cosmetic surgery is costly and very rarely covered by insurance. The average surgeon fee for a mommy lift—breast lift, tummy tuck, and liposuction—is $12,500. If a breast augmentation is included, that will increase the average to $16,500.[50] These fees are only the surgeon fees. Of course, the exorbitant amount of money women spend to be beautiful is nothing new. Makeup companies long ago convinced women it is their job to be beautiful and the makeup company, at a price, would be a partner in a woman's pursuit of beauty.[51] In 2007, makeup sales alone (only face, eye, lip, and nail products) generated $6 billion.[52] The mommy lift, however, ups the ante—the costs, the health risks, the perpetuation of a classicist, racist beauty ideal. Because cosmetic surgery is costly and not affordable to many women, the beauty ideal promised to women is primarily only for upper-class women and most likely Caucasian women. Yet, cosmetic surgeons seem to want to help all women achieve the most beautiful you, so many offer a $99 per month credit plan. And the ASPS offers suggestions on how to pay for the surgery, including cash, savings, and credit. Not to be outdone, cosmetic surgeons in Southeast Asian countries advertise rates at a substantially lower rate than American surgeons.

Despite the horrendous psychological, physical, and economic effects, the number of mommy lifts being performed is dramatically increasing. Why? Money. In our society, women's value is tied to beauty, so women have to pursue it no matter what the cost. Furthermore, in our society, bodies are commodified—bodies sell things and are sold themselves, so it is culturally acceptable to cut into the body to make it more marketable. One of the best ways to get women to spend thousands of dollars on beauty is to pathologize their bodies, in this case the postpartum body, and offer a cure. If mothers are told their bodies are deformed and diseased, they will pay to fix the deformity and get well, just like women will pay for the latest diet or exercise fad. Since the 1980s, motherhood has become one of the biggest media obsessions,[53] and since our contemporary culture is obsessed with a youthful appearance, cosmetic surgeons have simply targeted a new market. And the marketing strategy—the pathologization of the postpartum body—is working. In 2007, three of the five top cosmetic surgery procedures were breast augmentation, liposuction, and the tummy tuck—postpartum procedures; and cosmetic surgeons raked in $12.4 billion.[54]

Although motherhood is praised as the most valuable position a woman can hold, our society works to devalue mothers. The mommy lift serves as a literal and figurative example of that. It reminds mothers to, "Cut it out!"—to not get too big for our britches as our increased physical size symbolizes an increase in power. The mommy lift also demonstrates how in our society women's actual capital is being wasted. Instead of setting up retirement accounts, or paying down home mortgages, or putting money into kids' college accounts, mothers are investing in their own downsizing. Perhaps it is time for our society to create a new economy—one based less on the obsession to maintain youth and more on the realization that we can do better for ourselves and our children. What would the twenty-first-century American economy look like without its relentless appeal to women's bodily insecurities? What would happen if the cosmetic surgeon industry asked for a bailout on the same grounds as the car industry is now doing? Would we tolerate that? And, yet we currently support the industry.[55]

NOTES

1. Laurie Tarkan, *Fit Pregnancy*, http://www.msnbc.msn.com/id/25583034 (accessed August 21, 2008).

2. Karen Murphy, comment on StrollerDerby Blog, as qtd. in Natasha Singer, "Is the 'Mom Job' Really Necessary?" *The New York Times*, http://www.nytimes.com/2007/10/04/fashion/04skin.html (accessed August 31, 2008).

3. Susan J. Douglas and Meredith W. Michaels, *The Mommy Myth: The Idealization of Motherhood and How It Has Undermined Women* (New York: Free Press, 2004), 4.

4. Patricia Heaton, as qtd. in Douglas and Michaels, *The Mommy Myth*, 5.

5. Douglas and Michaels, *The Mommy Myth*, 4–5.

6. Ibid., 6–7.

7. Ibid., 109 and 113.

8. "New Mom Diet Secrets: How They Get Thin Fast!" *US Weekly*, August 11, 2008, cover.

9. "Body Watch: Bikini after Baby," *People*, July 28, 2008, 108.

10. http://www.plasticsurgery.org (accessed November 17, 2008).

11. Singer, "Is the 'Mom Job' Really Necessary?"

12. "More Women Getting 'Mommy Makeovers,'" http://www.msnbc.msn .com/id/25583034/ (accessed September 5, 2008).

13. "2000/2006/2007 National Plastic Surgery Statistics," http://www.plastic surgery.org/media/statistics (accessed November 17, 2008).

14. "2007 Average Surgeon/Physician Fees," http://www.plasticsurgery.org/patients_consumers/planning_surgery/Procedure-costs.cfm (accessed November 17, 2008).

15. "Plastic Surgery Procedures Maintain Steady Growth in 2007," http://www.plasticsurgery.org/media/press_releases/, March 25, 2008 (accessed November 17, 2008).

16. Anne Balsamo, "On the Cutting Edge: Cosmetic Surgery and New Imaging Technologies," *Technologies of the Gendered Body: Reading Cyborg Women* (Durham, NC: Duke University Press, 1997), 56, summarizing Carole Spitzack, "The Confession Mirror: Plastic Images for Surgery," *Canadian Journal of Political and Social Theory* 12, no. 1–2 (1988): 38–50. In her article, Spitzack argues that cosmetic surgery uses three mechanisms of control: inscription, surveillance, and confession. The surgeon's examination is a surveillance of a woman's "deformities" and level of adherence to beauty norms. In order to acquire "treatment" or surgery, the patient has to confess her "flaws" so that she can be "fixed" or "treated." And due to cultural standards, women are inscripted to seek cosmetic surgery because if they do not try to adhere to beauty standards they are perceived as refusing to be healthy.

17. J. S. Zubiri, "Correction of the Oriental Eyelid," *Clinical Plastic Surgery* 8 (1981): 725.

18. Bradley Hall, Richard C. Webster, and John M. Dobrowski, "Blepharoplasty in the Oriental," in *Plastic and Reconstructive Surgery of the Head and Neck* (Proceedings of the Fourth International Symposium of the American Academy of Facial Plastic and Reconstructive Surgery), *Vol. I: Aesthetic Surgery*, ed. Paul H. Ward and Walter E. Berman (St. Louis: C. V. Mosby, 1984), 210.

19. As qtd. in Joan E. Rigdon, "Informed Consent? Plastic Surgeons Had Warnings on Safety of Silicone Implants," *Wall Street Journal*, March 12, 1992, Eastern edition: A4.

20. Balsamo, *Technologies of the Gendered Body*, 63.

21. Ibid., 56.

22. William H. Huffaker, www.stlcosmeticsurgery.com, as qtd. in Singer, "Is the 'Mom Job' Really Necessary?"

23. David Stoker, as qtd. in "More Women Getting 'Mommy Makeovers.' "

24. Dr. Koger, as qtd. in "Mommy Makeover with Liposuction, Breast Augmentation and more," http://www.cosmeticsurgery.com/articles/archive/an~61/ (accessed September 5, 2008).

25. http://www.lovermecenter.com/html/mommy-makeover.html (accessed July 24, 2008). Dr. LoVerme calls his doctor's office the Radiance Medical Spa, not a clinic or office, implying that cosmetic surgery is a relaxing treatment, just like a massage or pedicure.

26. www.loveyourlook.info (accessed July 25, 2008).

27. Sharlotte Brikland, as qtd. in Singer, "Is the 'Mom Job' Really Necessary?"

28. Traycee Jones, as qtd. in Charlotte Triggs, Thailan Pham, and Ashley Williams, "Plastic Surgery for Real People," *People*, June 16, 2008, http://web.ebscohost.com/ehost/detail?vid=13&hid=114&sid=5815c7 (accessed September 12, 2008).

29. http://www.drteitelbaum.com/get_your_body_back.html (accessed September 10, 2008).

30. http://www.docshop.com/education/cosmetic/body/post-pregnancy (accessed July 24, 2008).

31. Balsamo, *Technologies of the Gendered Body*, 56.

32. http://www.drpollock.com (accessed November 21, 2008).

33. http://www.docshop.com and http://www.drteitelbaum.com.

34. "Ben's Mom Confesses: It's Baby No. 2," and "Who's Going to Be Next?" *Life & Style*, August 4, 2008, 24–25, 29.

35. "On the Cover—Exclusive: Angie's Secret Tummy Tuck," October 9, 2008, http://www.starmagazine.com/new/14697 (accessed October 9, 2008).

36. Andrew Stephen, "Look Closely: Some People Are Not Real," *New Statesman*, March 4, 2002, http://web.ebscohost.com/ehost/detail?vid=141 &his=102&sid=5815c (accessed September 12, 2008).

37. Helen S. Edelman, "Why Is Dolly Crying? An Analysis of Silicone Breast Implants in America as an Example of Medicalization," *Journal of Popular Culture* 28 (1994): 23.

38. Balsamo, *Technologies of the Gendered Body*, 62.

39. Ibid., 62.

40. "Cosmetic Plastic Surgery Procedures for Ethnic Patients up 13% in 2007," http://www.plasticsurgery.org/media/press_releases/Plastic-Surgery (accessed November 17, 2008).

41. In *The Mommy Myth*, Douglas and Michaels argue that among other things "new momism" creates division in mothers, creating a good mom vs. bad mom polarization. Wealthy, Caucasian women are positioned as good moms and poor, African American women are bad ones. Douglas and Michaels devote a chapter of the book to the demonization of the African American mother by media that consistently, yet erroneously, presented the African American mother as the "welfare mom."

42. K. Jordan, R. Capdevila, and S. Johnson, "Baby or Beauty: A Q Study into Post Pregnancy Body Image," *Journal of Reproductive and Infant Psychology* 23 (February 2005): 19–31. This article includes an overview of research on post-pregnancy body image.

43. Ellen Astrachan-Fletcher, Cindy Veldhuis, Nikki Lively, Cynthia Fowler, and Brook Marcks, "The Reciprocal Effects of Eating Disorders and the Postpartum Period: A Review of the Literature and Recommendations for Clinical Care," *Journal of Women's Health* 17 (March 2008): 227.

44. Michael P. Levine and Kristen Harrison, "Media's Role in the Perpetuation and Prevention of Negative Body Image and Disordered Eating," in *Handbook of Eating Disorders and Obesity,* ed. J. K. Thompson (New York: John Wiley, 2003), 711. This article is a comprehensive examination of current research "concerning media influences on weight and body shape in girls and women," 696.

45. Diana Zuckerman, as qtd. in "More Women Getting 'Mommy Makeovers.' "

46. A. H. Gallagher and L. Pecot-Hebert, " 'You Need a Makeover!': The Social Construction of Female Body Image in 'A Makeover Story,' 'What Not to Wear,' and 'Extreme Makeover,' " *Popular Communication* 5 (2007): 57–79. This is one of several excellent articles discussing, among other things, the unreality of the reality makeover show.

47. http://www.plasticsurgery.org/patients_consumers/procedures/Abdomino plasty.cfm.

48. http://www.24-7pressrelease.com/press-release/study-of-plastic-surgery-after-pregnancy-confirms-safety-of-combined-procedures-59552.php.

49. http://www.drpollock.com.

50. "2007 Average Surgeon/Physician Fees."

51. Gallagher and Pecot-Hebert, "You Need a Makeover," 57.

52. "Make-up in the United States: Industry Profile" (New York: Datamonitor, November 2008), 3. Not included in this makeup classification, but part of the cosmetic industry would be hair, hand, and body care.

53. Douglas and Michaels, *The Mommy Myth*, 6–7.

54. http://www.plasticsurgery.org.

55. Many thanks to Beth Sullivan for her input on this article.

CHAPTER 9

The Bioethics of Designing "Disabled" Babies

Alina Bennett

INTRODUCING DEFORMERS

At 4:12 in the morning on December 5, 2006, the *New York Times* published an online article by Darshak M. Sanghavi, M.D., titled: "Wanting Babies Like Themselves, Some Parents Choose Genetic Defects." [1] The article discussed disabled women using reproductive technologies to ensure that their children will share their same disabilities, a population later termed "Deformers" by the popular press. [2] Within 12 hours, 176 people had posted responses including: "This is far worse than eugenics and 'playing God.' This is playing Devil," and "I'm all for protecting our children from deadly diseases but making them in their own image, freaks!" [3] Using reproductive technologies to choose embryos that will develop into disabled people invoked disparate responses from disability community members and sparked an alarming backlash on a global scale. The ensuing debates have been taken up by the public at large, scholars, and legislators trying to flesh out the resulting economic, medical, and criminal complexities. These debates have centered a moral line of questioning, namely, is it right or wrong to choose an embryo that will become a disabled person? Diluting the controversy to the binary of "right" and "wrong" forecloses a more nuanced and interesting question that I begin to address here: what is at stake in choosing disability within an ableist culture? Disabled women's desires to use reproductive

technologies to select for disabled children is read as a refusal to conform
to ableist notions of "appropriate" motherhood. Restricting reproductive
technologies for the sole purpose of creating "ideal" citizens ensures a
kind of sterilization for disabled women who are always already produced
as corporeally unsound. As such, disabled women's refusal to comply
with ableism results in the discursive production of disabled women as
traitorous mothers and failed citizen subjects.

The global aim of this essay is to further destabilize ableism, which is
the systemic privileging of able-bodied people and the simultaneous
domination of disabled people. Specifically, this chapter seeks to interrogate popular materials such as blog postings and television shows in addition to scholarly works. The data demonstrate how disabled bodies have
become a flash point for a culture that attempts to manage increasingly
ambiguous and messy bodies.[4] Rather than discussing the disabled bodies
being produced or the disabled bodies doing the producing, I am more
interested in ways power circulates throughout discourses about choosing
disability. Choosing discourse as my object of study interrupts the pattern
of objectifying the bodies of people with disabilities that is taking place
within the discourses. This oppositional move challenges the contemporary and historical attempts to position people with disabilities as
"the problem."

Historically, disabled bodies have been objects of a two-prong attack with
science and medicine dissecting all that are positioned as "abnormal."
Science has been the mechanism used to establish the inferiority of disabled bodies in accordance with eugenic standards; these standards then
fueled clinical efforts to contain, constrain, and, ideally, eradicate such
bodies. I argue that unprecedented pharmacological, surgical, and
genomic advances in the last century have crystallized around the body
as not only more knowable but more controllable than ever before. Despite
the public rhetoric of equality and diversity, contemporary cultures are
increasingly anxious about bodily difference to such an extent that obviously eugenic practices are embraced on a global scale. Bodily anxieties
are being managed by scientific and medical practice in no clearer example than the area of reproduction and fertility, and more specifically, within
the deformer debates. This chapter aims to interrogate the panic that
resulted when technologies meant to eradicate disabled people were suddenly being used to create disabled people, and I hope my intervention
can further bolster the foundational work begun by other disability studies
scholars. In this essay, I interrogate how the stakes of choosing disability
are discursively taken up within artifacts of popular culture. But first, a

quick note on terminology. Throughout this work I vacillate between the terms able bodied/nondisabled and disabled people/people with disabilities in an effort to recognize the multitude ways in which people self-define and are defined by others across experience, culture, language, and oceans.[5]

Throughout the discourses of popular culture, Michel Foucault's techniques of power help flesh out what becomes thinkable.[6] To understand a thing as thinkable is to accept and recognize it as possible, and to some extent, "true," within the discourse or system of meaning. In the United States today, it is thinkable that women have the right to vote. This was unthinkable within the discourse, or public systems of meaning, 200 years ago. In terms of the discourses of popular culture, as each discourse establishes what is thinkable, it has simultaneously constructed the unthinkable. As one blogger wrote in response to disabled women choosing to implant embryos that would develop into people with disabilities: "This is so crazy, so cruel, so unthinkable." [7] The popular culture artifacts will show how thinkable and unthinkable notions of motherhood are built upon a small set of repeating themes or codes including: mental illness, economics, criminalization, science, and physicians. Finally, I will discuss the ways in which pop culture is infused with a disability rights perspective concerning the propriety of certain kinds of mothers.

SETTING THE STAGE

"I belong to a new underclass, no longer determined by social status or the color of your skin. We now have discrimination down to a science." Within the world of fictional negative utopias, the 1997 film *Gattaca* is canonical.[8] These words are uttered by Ethan Hawke's character, Vincent Freeman, and serve as an introduction to a "not-so-distant" future in which he is one of a small handful of "faith birth" babies conceived through sexual intercourse. Unlike geneticist created "vitro" babies, the Vincent character is condemned to life in the underclass just seconds after his birth when blood tests reveal a condemning 98 percent chance of cardiac failure at 30 years of age. *Gattaca* describes a world in which reproduction and genetic testing are explicitly linked and works as a cautionary tale against the dangerous conditions of an overscienced society, specifically in terms of reproductive consequences. The notion of science falling into the wrong hands or being used for the wrong ends is one of the most dominant refrains within the public response to Deformers and is a primary site of normalization in terms of both setting and requiring standards when creating the "right" kinds of citizens. But first, a bit of explanation about the technologies being discussed is required.

The chapter leans heavily on the *New York Times* article referenced at the beginning of this chapter, which discusses the use of preimplantation genetic diagnosis (PGD) to select and implant embryos that will become disabled people. On its Web site, London's Guy's and St. Thomas' NHS Foundation Trust, a leader in PGD, explains it as the process during which a number of laboratory fertilized eggs (embryos) each have a single cell removed to analyze DNA and chromosomes for various disorders.[9] Two "unaffected" (read: nondisabled) embryos are then implanted and Guy's and Thomas' boast over their 100 successful births. Guy's and St. Thomas' do not clarify what successful actually means, and it could be understood to simply mean live births or more sinisterly, live unaffected births. Regardless of their intentions, the uses of the PGD procedure are at the heart of the Deformer controversy being debated in national news. The *Times* article was written by Dr. Darshak M. Sanghavi, a pediatric cardiologist at the University of Massachusetts Medical School, and features interviews with various physicians and patients. Dr. Sanghavi addresses the 2006 Fertility and Sterility study conducted by the Public Policy Center at Johns Hopkins University, which revealed that of the 190 U.S. PGD clinics surveyed, 3 percent had used PGD to select and implant embryos that would develop into disabled people.[10] Let me be clear that these embryos have not been "given" disabilities; they were produced "naturally" via fertility treatments. It is not the case that a given embryo was at one point going to be average sized, but was then manipulated into being a Little Person—it is simply that these embryos are being selected for implantation rather than being routinely deselected in favor of "better" embryos. The Sanghavi article uses the Hopkins study to reveal the fact that reproductive technologies are currently being used to select future-disabled embryos. Rather than an exercise in hypothetical ponderings, it was the reality of this practice that received the most vehement responses in service to normalizing ends.

The study, "Genetic Testing of Embryos: Practices and Perspectives of U.S. IVF Clinics," is much more nuanced in its findings than that which is presented in the Sanghavi article. For instance, PGD is used by 74 percent of the respondent fertility clinics, but it accounts for only 4–6 percent of IVF cycles. It is within these 4–6 percent that 3 percent of the clinics are using PGD to select for disabled, or "affected," embryos. That is to say that out of the 3,000 IVF cycles reported in 2005, approximately 150 used PGD and just 6 out of those 150 used it to select for a disability.

A noteworthy absence in the article's discussion of the study is the finding that 42 percent of the clinics used PGD for "non-medical sex selection," meaning people are using this technology to choose whether they have a boy or girl as determined by personal preference, not to avoid genetic diseases that are sex-specific. Based on the 2005 sample from above, 18 out of the 150 PGD cycles were used to choose an embryo based on sex. Feminist scholars have aptly demonstrated that absence is as significant as presence, so it is no accident that the nonmedical sex selection figures are absent from the *Times* article. This absences serves to reinforce the cultural belief that science and technology are exclusively being used toward culturally sanctioned ends, namely, locating and removing the future disabled. This belief is maintained by disavowing the technology's other uses, including sex selection while simultaneously positioning the people who would use such technology to select for disability as "mentally ill."

MENTAL ILLNESS

Disabled parents who want to select embryos that will develop into disabled people are discursively positioned as "mentally ill." Invoking mental illness is a successful strategy, in part, because of larger cultural attitudes and value systems built around mental fitness. In fact, the call to mental illness has been particularly useful at derailing claims to civil rights. Throughout the last century, U.S. civil rights struggles have been negatively impacted when the opposition began labeling the marginalized population as mentally ill or claiming that gaining equal rights would create mental illness among the oppressed.[11] In terms of the current manifestation within the Deformer debates, mental illness serves to delegitimize the claims made by Deformers as the ramblings of "crazy" people, thus negating any serious engagement with those claims.

The bloggers responding to the Sanghavi article called to mental illness, saying that Deformer parents need psychiatric help, and in classificatory ways claiming that the practice "should be flat out rejected with out [sic] any other consideration other than putting the people who propose it in a mental institution to protect us all and especially the children who will not be given any choice." [12] The act of choosing a future disabled person over a future nondisabled person is so heinous as to result in the removal from society at large. Restricting the freedoms of people with disabilities is not new in the United States as rights have historically been restricted based on the argument that people must be able to show a capacity to exercise those rights.[13] Choosing disability is positioned as demonstrating the incapacity to handle those rights that will effectively be removed with institutionalization. These comments seek to demonstrate that there are implicit standards guiding parental behavior by showing how Deformers are failing to meet said standards. Discursively producing these would-be parents as "sick" people trying to enlist physicians to help them accomplish "insane" acts justifies institutionalization arguments on the basis that Deformers are a danger from which the public needs protection, thus accomplishing classification via segregation.

The comments about mental health are particularly frightening because the call to punishment is so severe. Blogger Michelle L. discusses how the selfishness of Deformer mothers demonstrates their need for psychological help but ends by saying that they should be tossed to the lions in order to eliminate the disabled gene pool altogether.[14] In response to the notion that being part of the Deaf community is positive, another blogger wrote: "Why go through the trouble of intentionally creating new life that is rich and varied when it is so much easier to enrich and vary existing life by giving such parents a lobotomy with a sledge hammer [sic]." [15] Lobotomies performed with an ice pick have historically been a treatment for various behaviors considered indicative of mental illness, but more than positioning Deformers as mentally ill, the message here is that these parents should be killed. Invoking such a brutal and often horrifying surgical procedure is more than problematic, but the image of executing such a procedure with a sledgehammer is beyond reprehensible.

Reading these comments in conversation demonstrates a wider cultural attitude about the retribution facing women who challenge traditional notions of motherhood. Rather than extreme aberrations, the repeated call to violence in these statements speaks to a very real desire to police and punish mothers who refuse conformity to motherhood as sanctioned by the status quo. In the United States, taking a person's life is considered the ultimate penalty, reserved for the very worst criminals. Disabled women who want to implant an embryo that will become a person with a disability are now among that select population of criminals whose actions are punishable by death. The cultural panic discernable within these artifacts of pop culture indicates the way in which cultural investments in ableism are authorized through public discourse. Public discourses are a site of production powerful enough to call out other people's insanity, to institutionalize, and even to murder those women who would go so far as to undermine culturally sanctioned motherhood.

ECONOMICS

The crux of the economic argument is that people with disabilities cost the state too much money. Though all citizens cost the state money via public works funds and roadway services, disabled people are presented as those who cannot care for themselves. Though there are indeed people with disabilities who are supported in various ways, the false notion of total dependence simultaneously produces the equally false notion that nondisabled people are completely independent. This construction is fueled by rugged individualism that values economic self-reliance above all else.[16] However false, this construction is useful because it builds the case against people who would want disabled children by positioning them as backwards, self-interested, and willing to exploit the state. Such is the side effect of ableist notions of a responsible citizenry where neoliberal independence reigns supreme.

In *Powers of Freedom*, Nikolas Rose argues that neoliberalism and responsibilization work in tandem where social responsibilities are shifted from the state to the subject so that she becomes increasingly free to such a degree that solely she bears responsibility for her life and economic participation/situation.[17] The state is no longer responsible for the individual, though always present through self-regulation and self-surveillance. Neoliberalism's ideal subject is thus an agent in her own life course that works to become respectable by managing her own behavior, labor, capital, and health.[18] Representing people with disabilities as a drain on the economy positions them as enemies to the neoliberal state. Disabled women interested in having disabled children are positioned as traitors to the system because of their refusal to self-regulate and self-survey in ways deemed appropriate; namely, they should be using reproductive technologies for the sole purpose of producing children who are not "burdened" by such "conditions." The state's ideology effectively argues that if disabled women are going to reproduce, they should be responsible enough to do everything in their power to create ideal, read: nondisabled, citizens.[19] As long as disability is undesirable according to the capitalist state, women who want disabled children will be discursively produced as failed subjects incapable of being socially responsible.

Evidence from public discourse reinforces the success of the belief that disability is an economic drain. The wide range of blog responses varied in venom, one blogger writing: "Sure, go ahead, maim your kid for your own selfish reasons! Just don't expect society (or your insurance company) [*sic*] to pick up the tab for your insanity." [20] Another blogger addressed similar financial concerns:

> Call me a Eugenicist, but with the way healthcare costs are skyrocketing, the rate of debt our nation is accumulating, and the rate the numbers of disabled people are accumulating and I tell you that we as a nation cannot afford to indulge in frivolously creating and maintaining children with major birth defects that will increase the cost on our already overburdened system.[21]

The message is that society does not mind "picking up the tab" for those who are "naturally" born with disabilities, but choosing to implant an embryo that will become a disabled person is just economically irresponsible. The implicit, yet unspoken, message is that implanting "normal" embryos will result in a kind of unparalleled economic independence. This message completely ignores the reality that many in our "overburdened system" are currently covering the costs of many nondisabled children through state-funded foster care. In many cases, it matters more who your parents are than the kind of body into which you are born in terms of requiring financial support from the government. Disabled parents wishing to use reproductive technologies have access to economic privilege because none of these procedures are reimbursable due to their "elective" designation by insurance companies. Despite this reality, the pop culture story is that the economy is barely hanging on under the crushing costs of health care and thus our citizens must be the best, most perfect workers who will remain economically independent forever. And this best, most perfect worker is never disabled.

The unchallenged assumption that accompanies the use of genetic testing is that the lives of people with genetically related disabilities are not valuable and are a social burden that members of the public should not have to endure. The option of aborting a fetus in order to avoid the birth of a disabled or potentially disabled baby is constructed as a choice. In our contemporary moment of insurance companies working to contain rising health care costs, the "option" to abort suspect fetuses may soon become more of a requirement in terms of the medical definition of "what constitutes an acceptable or an unacceptable child in American culture." [22] The move from reproductive freedom to eugenic quality control babies has resulted in the venomous backlash against women with disabilities attempting to become mothers of disabled children.

Let me be clear that in terms of abortion, women should be the sole decision makers about their bodies, at all times, in all scenarios. However, positioning abortion as the solution to positive preimplantation genetic diagnoses for disabilities is a construction that needs to be undermined. In part, the reason that Deformer desires are considered so shocking is because embryos that will develop into disabled people have been held up as justification for abortion rights. Rosemarie Garland-Thomson critiques this position saying: "I am not suggesting abortion restrictions here; rather, I am questioning the myth of 'free choice' regarding the bearing of congenitally disabled infants in a society in which the perceived attitudes about disabled people tend to be negative, oppressive and unexamined." [23] Abortion has been one of the ways proposed to eliminate the presumed economic impact of people with disabilities, which again underscores the subversive nature of the Deformer movement.

CRIMINALIZATION

The move to criminalize people who choose to implant embryos that will develop into people with disabilities has been headed up by the British Parliament via the Human Fertilization and Embryology (HFE) Bill. This bill is similar to many bills passed by the U.S. Congress in that it covers a wide range of issues related to reproduction including: abortion regulations, birth documentation, creation of cytoplasmic hybrid embryos, and the implantation of embryos that will develop into people with disabilities. For the purposes of this chapter, I will only address the restrictions on embryo implantation.

The British Parliament debated the HFE bill from November 2007 through October 2008 and on November 13th, Queen Elizabeth granted Royal Assent to the bill, thus making it an Act of Parliament. The exact language of Clause 14 of the bill states:

> (9) Persons or embryos that are known to have a gene, chromosome or mitochondrion abnormality involving a significant risk that a person with the abnormality will have or develop—
>
> (a) a serious physical or mental disability,
>
> (b) a serious illness, or
>
> (c) any other serious medical condition, must not be preferred to those that are not known to have such an abnormality.[24]

Choosing and implanting an embryo that will develop into a disabled person is now a criminal act. Conversely, embryos that will develop into non-disabled people are now the only embryos available for implantation. This legislation has legalized designing able-bodied babies under the guise of selecting against disability. In addition, the HFE bill now requires that any embryo found to be future disabled will be eradicated or donated to scientific research. The message is clear that while nature may go her own way in terms of producing people with disabilities, science will work toward oppositional ends by ensuring that such people are undesirable. Deaf women who require assisted reproductive technologies will now legally be forced to implant an embryo that will becoming a hearing child. I argue that this use of reproductive technologies results in a kind of specialized sterilization for disabled women. The sterilization is not total in the sense that they can still reproduce, but their wombs can only carry babies deemed culturally valuable, regardless of their corporeal dissimilarities or personal wishes. Although many Deaf mothers may not regard having a hearing child as the kind of difference that makes a difference, however, the impact of this legislation should not be overlooked by focusing on some fantasy of how "good" mothers would not care about what kind of embryo gets implanted.

The impact of the HFE bill cannot be overstated because it is a direct attack on women's reproductive freedoms. This is not some move to reinstate traditional notions of "natural" childbirth where the role of technology in the birth process is being questioned; this is a specific regulation meant to ensure that technology be used strictly for the production of "ideal" citizens. The law positions these "ideal" (read: nondisabled or nondifferent) citizens as legally cognizable to the exception of all others. Being normatively able bodied has been expanded to include the embryonic stage and is now a prerequisite for existence at least in terms of the use of reproductive technology. Standardizing reproduction in this way authorizes the already endemic able-bodied privilege rampant within popular culture as is evidenced in the blog responses to the 2006 *New York Times* article. Standardized reproduction is legally facilitated, thus authorizing specific kinds of motherhood as state sanctioned while simultaneously criminalizing those positioned as oppositional to the state's interests.

A number of responses address criminalization by arguing that the practice should be illegal and violators should face criminal assault or be severely punished for their "evil" behavior. By far the most telling argument made for criminalization supports a more direct version of the HFE bill saying: "And parent's [*sic*] who could be shown to have deliberately selected such a child should be charged with maiming, *permanently sterilized* by the government, and never permitted to ever raise or care for children." [25] Going beyond the reach of the HFE, the writer points to a possible conclusion for eugenic-thinking-turned-legislation. Though outside the scope of this paper, I would like to briefly nod to the fact that this legislation was passed just days after the United States elected Barack Obama president and Arkansas passed Act One restricting adoption and foster care to married couples. Because of the state's pro-heterosexual legislation, queer couples can no longer adopt or foster children.

My point is that even in this most progressive moment, parenting and reproduction are being further claimed as the territory of those deemed normative, valued citizens. The clear message is that disabled people are not worthy and this legislation authorizes the eugenic taming of disabled women's most dangerous capability: their ability to reproduce. Disability Studies scholar Marsha Saxton argues that "By denying our rights to be mothers and fathers, it is not only our competence to care for our young, but our very existence, our desire to 'reproduce ourselves' that is forbidden." [26] Though this book focuses on motherhood in U.S. popular culture, the HFE bill should be seen as the example of ideology being made "real" through legislation.

SCIENCE AND PHYSICIANS

Rogue physicians and "mad" scientists dot the terrain of reproductive technology, at least according to the discourses of popular culture. These caricatures are particularly present in "new genetics" debates regarding the creation of admixed or "true" hybrid embryos, which contain one human gamete (either an egg or a sperm) and one nonhuman gamete (also egg or sperm). In debating the Human Fertilization and Embryology Bill, Baroness Tonge of the British Parliament's House of Lords said: "What of rogue scientists acting outside the law and creating monsters? There have always been rogue scientists, which is why the law and regulations must be in place to ensure that they are caught and stopped." [27] Bloggers responded with similar concerns about physicians calling for the American Medical Association to prohibit doctors from implanting future disabled embryos. The Hippocratic Oath received a large amount of blogging mileage, and physicians willing to implant "abnormal" embryos were discussed as deserving the revocation of their medical licenses.[28]

Bloggers argued that science should be used to advance society and increasing the number of disabled people is an evolutionary step backwards upon which Darwin would frown.[29] These comments illuminate the role of science and technology as the thing that can be used for either good or evil where disability is always positioned as evil. Disability Studies scholar Susan Wendell argues that people expect science to create generalizable, normative bodies and "for the able-bodied, the disabled often symbolize failure to control the body and the failure of science and medicine to protect us all."[30] In short, science must be used to both eradicate unruly, devalued bodies and produce disciplined, "superior" bodies.

Positioning science and technology as safeguards against disability further naturalizes normative bodies as ideal which has implications for both those who have not yet been born as well as those disabled people living today. Disability Studies scholar Simi Linton writes: "What I find most troubling about the impulse to eliminate, cure or contain disability is the ascendancy of that idea over accommodation and integration." [31] The lack of cultural investment in ending oppressive conditions for people with disabilities results in the science as emancipator conflation and serves to reinforce the notion that technology must produce specific kinds of socially valued bodies. Women's bodies and their abilities to mother become the symbolic battleground where discourses, resistances, and contradictions crystallize as science and technology operate on an ever-invasive scale. The ability to control one's reproductive choices has and is being contested in U.S. popular culture at an unprecedented level as genomic medicine grows increasingly commonplace. U.S. popular culture operates as a discursive site where the science of motherhood is being produced and must be critically interrogated. Critical interrogation is necessary to unhinge ableist notions about "appropriate" motherhood and the ideal mother's body as they exist in the everyday artifacts of pop culture.

DISABILITY RIGHTS

One of Michel Foucault's primary contributions is his theory of power as that which circulates (top to bottom and bottom to top) is discursively productive and always inscribes resistance. Resistance shows up in U.S. popular culture discourses around disabled people who want to implant embryos that will develop into disabled people. So rather than undermining my argument, these resistances should be read as necessary for the circulation of power. Disability communities are ambivalent about Deformers but cultural, social, and technological advances have created possibilities that were unthinkable 100 years ago. Being Deaf or a Little Person affects people's lives in radically different ways due to the hard-won battles of the disability rights movements. Regardless of the ways in which the lives of people with disabilities have changed and on many levels improved, disability is still positioned as something to be avoided. While much of the larger culture does not understand Deformers' desires, hence the panic in pop culture discourses, there are examples of counternormative resistance that position disability as a site of possibility. The counternormative resistances challenge ableist notions of "ideal" motherhood, health and disease, and difference within the medical and social models of disability as demonstrated in one of the most popular cop dramas on television today.

On January 22, 2008, *Law and Order: Special Victims Unit* aired episode 14 of their ninth season, a show entitled "Inconceivable." This program discusses the theft of a canister of embryos from a fertility clinic and features a number of interviews between detectives Stabler and Benson and the donors whose fertilized eggs were stolen. In the fertility clinic within the show, the stolen embryos came from women with a range of fertility issues and are considered to have varying "street values." The clinic's lead physician says that each client spends tens of thousands of dollars, but the embryos that screened positive for disabilities and were marked for disposal would have been "priceless" to a researcher. A laboratory technician responsible for performing preimplantation genetic diagnosis to "make sure we only implant healthy embryos" is responsible for allowing the thief into the restricted lab because she was "giving the bad news" about an embryo's positive disability diagnosis. The plot thickens when the fictional "Values Defense League" offers to accept the stolen embryos no questions asked. This fundamentalist Christian organization believes all embryos should be implanted regardless of status, a position found to be deplorable by Detective Benson because kids should be given a fighting chance, and thus no embryo with markers for a condition like Tay-Sachs should be implanted. Beyond the obviously problematic positioning of disability as an indicator of "unhealthy" and thus disposable embryonic status, it is here where counternormalization discourses critique these ableist constructions.

An interview with an egg donor begins with a woman's story of using preimplantation genetic diagnosis to weed out embryos with homozygous achondroplasia because "it is humane to get rid of the defective ones." She tells the story of having her daughter dying in her arms as a result of complications from the disease. At this point the camera pans out to reveal that the conversation taking place is the result of the donor speaking to the detectives from a shelving ladder because she is a Little Person (LP). She then goes on to describe how she is suing the clinic because the doctor refused to implant one of her "healthy embryos." The detectives mistakenly assume that the doctor is discriminating against her because of her size. The donor says that it is her baby's size that is the problem because her doctor was refusing to implant an embryo that will become a Little Person. She is met with the detective's inaccurate question "you want to purposely create a child with a disability?" and responds by saying that size is not a disability and LPs have normal life spans and lives so she should be able to have a baby who looks like her just like everybody else. In the entire episode, this unnamed character played by actress Meredith Eaton offers the sole critique of both the construction that being a Little Person is a disability and the policing around reproductive technologies being used to implant future Little People.

This critical voice within this two-minute segment is subsumed by the overwhelming presence of normalizing discourses constructing disability as undesirable and reproductive technologies being used to ensure that such undesirables are never implanted. The unnamed Little Person character is interrogated and offered no words or gestures of support during her interactions with recurring characters. Other potential, yet still nontraditional, mothers are accepted and supported in ways not extended to the disabled mother. The cancer survivor and the woman going through a divorce are presented as sympathetic characters for whom the audience should be rooting. Normalizing the experience of other nontraditional mothers further establishes the boundaries of appropriate motherhood as stopping short of including disabled mothers choosing to implant future-disabled children.

The blog responses to the *New York Times* article are similarly normalizing, with a mere 22 out of 175 responses speaking against ableist notions of disability. A number of counternormative comments call the question the definition of "defect," saying that difference is not a defect.[32] Others write that: "Dwarfism is not a 'disease' People [*sic*] don't 'have' dwarfism. Deaf people have a very definite and defined culture. Both of these genetic mutations have cultural history and solidarity." [33] Upending traditionally ableist notions of difference and disease has been critical to the success of disability rights struggles in attempting to unhinge the medical model in favor of the social model.[34] The medical model posits that disability lies in the individual pathology of a person who has a condition that keeps him or her from enjoying all aspects of life. This model is treatment and cure oriented and thus medically grounded. The social model calls for a rethinking of disability as having social rather than biological roots. A prime example is that a person who uses a wheelchair is not kept from buildings by their biological conditions or impairments but rather by the material and socially sanctioned conditions of the space. It is the stairs that are disabling, not the person's corporeal particularities.

The resistances within pop culture discourse evidences the useful elements of the social model for critiquing the overdetermined way in which disability is linked to medical management. The overwhelming efforts to continually reinscribe disability as something one would never choose demonstrates how unthinkable such resistances actually are. To undermine the conflation of impairment and disability is critical to the disability civil rights project, which resists such ableist notions. Obviously, the resistances are speakable, but that which is called for by those who resist is firmly unintelligible in our contemporary culture where ableist ideologies are entrenched in medicalized, capitalist, neoliberal frameworks.

CONCLUSION

Some may question the reason for an analysis of this situation. Given the cost, this technology is used by a small but very privileged sect. While the number of interested parties is small, the legislative and pop culture reaction is taking place on a disproportionately large scale. The desires of these women with disabilities must be policed because they want to create illegitimate subjects according to ableist ideologies. Disabled babies are positioned as illegitimate subjects under neoliberal and capitalist frameworks that deliver the rights of social citizenship to those it recognizes as measurable and "independent" producers. Connecting ableist notions of responsibility to citizenship has increased the "privatization of social disadvantage [thus] transforming disabled people into non-rights-bearing citizens." [35] Positioning people with disabilities as non-rights-bearing is no new occurrence, despite the sleek packaging of twenty-first-century medical discourse. Historically, eugenic science has rationalized social policy then used as a weapon by nondisabled people and has had horrifying consequences as was demonstrated in Hitler's Germany. Economics and social responsibility are the repeated refrain, and though disabled women do speak and sign back to power, their resistance is ultimately unintelligible because in an ableist culture, disability can never be chosen.

In closing, a few questions about what exactly is at stake in removing disabled women's reproductive rights and criminalizing motherhood that challenges ableist ideologies. How far are we from a complete restriction on birth for any person deemed "disabled"? The anti-Deformers argue that we should give our children the best start in life and in an ableist world that means being born nondisabled. How long will it be before brown and black women are only able to use reproductive technologies to have white babies? After all, in the white supremacist culture in which we live, it is, for all intents and purposes, "easier" to be white. The Human Genome Project has charted new territories and many of those discoveries have made their way into genomic medicine. Perhaps we will one day identify a "gay" gene. Will embryos with that marker also be positioned as unimplantable? Make no mistake, I am making a direct connection between the oppression of multiple marginalized populations, all of which share a common history of domination under eugenic science. I understand these populations as mutually constitutive, each bleeding, blurring, and fusing across fictional boundaries. In short, we all have reason to be concerned that women with disabilities are not free. Removing the right of disabled women to have children with disabilities is only possible because they are not full citizens and thus do not deserve the freedoms and privileges that nondisabled women enjoy. Restricting motherhood to those who are culturally valued is certainly a move in which science gets positioned as judge, jury, and eradicator. Pop culture discourse demonstrates how crisis ensues when science fails to emancipate "us" from the "problem" of disability, a situation being rectified by invoking ableist ideologies and criminalizing those who challenge the ableist party line. The popular panic around designing disabled babies is really about capital "S" Science helping to produce failed citizens and, thus, disability remains unintelligible and undesirable.

NOTES

1. Darshak M. Sanghavi, "Wanting Babies Like Themselves, Some Parents Choose Genetic Defects," *The New York Times*, December 5, 2006, http://www.nytimes.com/2006/12/05/health/05essa.html?_r=1 (accessed December 5, 2007).

2. William Saletan, "Deformer Babies: The Deliberate Crippling of Childen," *Slate*, September 21, 2006, http://www.slate.com/id/2149854/ (accessed December 4, 2007).

3. "Readers' Comments," *The New York Times*, December 5, 2006, http://news.blogs.nytimes.com/2006/12/05/wanting-babies-like-themselves-some-parents-choose-genetic-defects/ (accessed December 5, 2007).

4. Both "disability" and "deformer" are troubled. It is unclear whether or not "deformer" is a self-identity for the women in question; however, it is a term prevalent in the discourse that is my object so I use this term intermittently. Members and allies of Deaf, Little People, and other communities self-identify as

"disabled" or consider height and hearing to exist along a spectrum of differences. I use disability in this piece in part because of my position within the academic discipline of disability studies, but I know how dodgy this term can be. I use disability not in quotes because the discourses being interrogated are producing specific notions of disability, outside of community and self-definitions that trouble, rework, or refuse the term.

5. This is a subtle nod to the specific history of these terms as they have been differently constructed and interpreted primarily by U.S. and British scholars. The U.S. use of "people with disabilities" (PWDs) is an effort toward "people first" language and as a reaction to the historical abuses of PWDs under medical models of disability. The British use of "disabled people" speaks to identity constructions that privilege disability as a valued experience, also used in reaction to the subsuming of disability by medical discourses and an embrace of the social model of disability.

6. Thinkability is a concept introduced to me by Patti Lather that points to how something becomes culturally knowable in a specific place and time.

7. Caterina C., comment on "Readers' Comments," *The New York Times*, comment posted at at 9:33 AM, December 5, 2006, http://news.blogs.nytimes.com/2006/12/05/wanting-babies-like-themselves-some-parents-choose-genetic-defects/ (accessed December 5, 2007).

8. Andrew Niccol, *Gattaca*, DVD, October 24, 1997, Columbia Pictures, 1997.

9. "Preimplantaion Genetic Diagnosis," Guy's and St. Thomas' NHS Foundation Trust, http://www.guysandstthomas.nhs.uk/services/managednetworks/womensservices/acu/pgd.aspx (accessed November 1, 2007).

10. Susannah Baruch et al., "Genetic Testing of Embryos: Practices and Perspectives of U.S. IVF Clinics," Genetics and Public Policy Center, http://www.dnapolicy.org/pub.bib.html (accessed January 15, 2007).

11. Douglas Baynton, "Disability and the Justification of Inequality in American History," in *The New Disability History*, ed. Paul Longmore and Lauri Umansky (New York: New York University Press, 2001), 33–57.

12. R. Downs, comment on "Readers' Comments," *The New York Times*, comment posted at 2:21 PM, December 5, 2006, http://news.blogs.nytimes.com/2006/12/05/wanting-babies-like-themselves-some-parents-choose-genetic-defects/ (accessed December 5, 2007).

13. Marcia H. Rioux, "Disability, Citizenship, and Rights in a Changing World," in *Disability Studies Today*, ed. Colin Barnes, Len Barton, and Mike Oliver (Cambridge, U.K.: Polity Press, 2002), 210–227.

14. Michelle L., comment on "Readers' Comments," *The New York Times*, comment posted at 9:01 AM, December 5, 2006, http://news.blogs.nytimes.com/

2006/12/05/wanting-babies-like-themselves-some-parents-choose-genetic-defects/ (accessed December 5, 2007).

15. Roy, comment on "Readers' Comments," *The New York Times*, comment posted at 1:35 PM, December 5, 2006, http://news.blogs.nytimes.com/2006/12/05/wanting-babies-like-themselves-some-parents-choose-genetic-defects/ (accessed December 5, 2007).

16. Ruth Hubbard, "Abortion and Disability: Who Should and Who Should Not Inhabit the World?" in *The Disability Studies Reader,* ed. Lenny Davis (New York: Routledge, 1997), 197–204.

17. Nikolas Rose, *Powers of Freedom: Reframing Political Thought* (Cambridge, U.K.: Cambridge University Press, 1999), 82.

18. Ibid., 82.

19. I see a strong connection between this argument and one made in much of Dorothy Roberts's scholarship on critical race and critical legal theory. Her 1991 piece, "Race and Parentage," published in Vol. 209 of the 1995 *University of Chicago Law Review*, forecasts a future where black and brown women's bodies will be purchasable as surrogates for the production of white babies. This directly mirrors the current situation in England where disabled women using reproductive technologies must implant embryos with no discernable disabilities.

20. Liz, comment on "Readers' Comments," *The New York Times*, comment posted at 9:09 AM, December 5, 2006, http://news.blogs.nytimes.com/2006/12/05/wanting-babies-like-themselves-some-parents-choose-genetic-defects/ (accessed December 5, 2007).

21. Dr. Zinj, comment on "Readers' Comments," *The New York Times*, comment posted at 9:40 AM, December 5, 2006, http://news.blogs.nytimes.com/2006/12/05/wanting-babies-like-themselves-some-parents-choose-genetic-defects/ (accessed December 5, 2007).

22. Rayna Rapp. "The power of 'Positive' Diagnosis: Medical and Maternal Discourses on Amniocentesis," in *Feminist Approaches to Theory and Methodology: An Interdisciplinary Reader,* ed. Sharlene Hesse-Biber, Christina Gilmartin, and Robin Lydenberg (New York: Oxford University Press, 1999), 289.

23. Rosemarie Garland Thompson, *Extraordinary Bodies: Figuring Physical Disability in American Culture and Literature* (New York: Columbia University Press, 1997), 145.

24. British Parliament House of Commons, *Human Fertilisation and Embryology Bill: Amendments of the Human Fertilisation and Embryology Act 1990*, http://www.publications.parliament.uk/pa/cm200708/cmbills/120/08120.i-iv.html (London: House of Commons, 2008). [Author's bold.]

25. Dr. Zinj, comment on "Readers' Comments," *The New York Times*, comment posted at 9:40 AM, December 5, 2006, http://news.blogs.nytimes.com/

2006/12/05/wanting-babies-like-themselves-some-parents-choose-genetic-defects/ (accessed December 5, 2007).

26. Marsha Saxton, "Reproductive Rights: A Disability Rights Issue," in *Women's Lives: Multicultural Perspectives*, ed. Gwyn Kirk and Margo Okazawa-Rey (New York: McGraw-Hill, 2007), 144.

27. British House of Commons, *Human Fertilisation and Embryology Bill: Amendments of the Human Fertilisation and Embryology Act 1990*, http://www.publications.parliament.uk/pa/ld200708/ldhansrd/index/071119.html#contents (London: House of Commons, 2008).

28. Ann Scott, comment on "Readers' Comments," *The New York Times*, comment posted at 2:54 PM, December 5, 2006, http://news.blogs.nytimes.com/2006/12/05/wanting-babies-like-themselves-some-parents-choose-genetic-defects/ (accessed December 5, 2007). Dr. Zinj, comment on "Readers' Comments," *The New York Times*, comment posted at 9:40 AM, December 5, 2006, http://news.blogs.nytimes.com/2006/12/05/wanting-babies-like-themselves-some-parents-choose-genetic-defects/ (accessed December 5, 2007).

29. Loren DuBois, comment on "Readers' Comments," *The New York Times*, comment posted at 4:14 PM, December 5, 2006, http://news.blogs.nytimes.com/2006/12/05/wanting-babies-like-themselves-some-parents-choose-genetic-defects/ (accessed December 5, 2007). Joseph Huttner, comment on "Readers' Comments," *The New York Times*, comment posted at 12:50 PM, December 5, 2006, http://news.blogs.nytimes.com/2006/12/05/wanting-babies-like-themselves-some-parents-choose-genetic-defects/ (accessed December 5, 2007).

30. Susan Wendell, "Toward a Feminist Theory of Disability," in *The Disability Studies Reader*, ed. Lenny Davis (New York: Routledge, 1997), 255.

31. Simi Linton. *Claiming Disability: Knowledge and Identity* (New York: New York University Press, 1998), 110.

32. Katie Willilams, comment on "Readers' Comments," *The New York Times*, comment posted at 4:57 PM, December 5, 2006, http://news.blogs.nytimes.com/2006/12/05/wanting-babies-like-themselves-some-parents-choose-genetic-defects/ (accessed December 5, 2007).

33. Alexis Alexander, comment on "Readers' Comments," *The New York Times*, comment posted at 2:14 PM, December 5, 2006, http://news.blogs.nytimes.com/2006/12/05/wanting-babies-like-themselves-some-parents-choose-genetic-defects/ (accessed December 5, 2007).

34. Shakespeare, Tom. "The Social Model of Disability," in *The Disability Studies Reader*, ed. Lenny Davis (New York: Routledge, 1997), 197–204.

35. Marcia Rioux, "Disability, Citizenship and Rights in a Changing World," in *Disability Studies Today*, ed. Colin Barnes, Lend Barton, and Mike Oliver (Berkeley: University of California Press, 1995), 221–227.

CHAPTER 10

"Real" Motherhood: Changing Perceptions of Adoption in American History

Kathleen L. Riley

Real isn't how you are made, said the Skin Horse. It's a thing that happens to you. When a child loves you for a long, long time ... REALLY loves you, then you become Real.[1]

Margery Williams's *The Velveteen Rabbit*, first published in 1922, has achieved the iconic status of a classic in children's literature. The tale of "How Toys Become Real" has been a source of delight for generations of children, and a story of sentimental inspiration for the mothers who read it to their beloved children. When viewed as a prism reflecting the history and changing notions of family in American society, it can also shed valuable light on the subject of adoption, identity, and the definition of motherhood. Over time, perceptions about adoption have evolved along more optimistic and affirming lines, with a narrative that focuses on themes of redemption as well as rescue—for mothers as well as their children—and the real and genuine attributes of adoptive motherhood.

Those who become mothers through adoption often face a more challenging task of creating and fostering the "ties that bind" that are taken for granted, or come "naturally," to women who follow the standard route of childbirth. But along with the challenges come many joys, joys known only to women who become "real" mothers by finding a child to love who will grow to love them back. As illustrated by the popular "Adoption Creed"—inscribed on thousands of greeting cards and plaques—adoptive mothers often strive to overcome their image as "second best" and their own defensive posture by proving themselves equal to, or even better than, more traditional mothers. Rather than focusing on blood lines—flesh and bone—adoptive mothers take comfort in the miracle of loving their children without the biological connection, and making their children feel the special bond of adoption as well: "Never forget for a single minute that you didn't grow under my heart, but in it." [2]

Even the standard language associated with adoption tends to draw attention to the differences between mothers who give birth and mothers who adopt children. Historically, the vocabulary and public images associated with adoption tended to be focused on deficiencies: second choice or "second best," a reluctant alternative to the "natural" method of becoming a mother. Over time, however, the tide has turned in a more positive direction for many adoptive families: an emphasis on affirmation rather than abandonment, and striking a balance between losses and gains. A focus on what satisfaction mothers have "found" in the search for their children, as opposed to what may have been "lost" along the way, is a good sign in much of the current literature on adoption. Despite this spotlight on the happy endings, the "special" characteristics of adoptive motherhood remain, along with the unique challenges they face.

For example, just about every mother invests in the traditional "how-to" motherhood manuals: Dr. Spock, and maybe Penelope Leach or T. Berry Brazelton. They come in handy, especially in the case of emergencies. Benjamin Spock's authoritative *The Common Sense Book of Baby and Child Care* offered advice on "Adopting a Child" in 1946. The central question was whether to tell a child he was adopted, and how and when:

> All the experienced people in this field agree that the child should know. He's sure to find out sooner or later from someone or other, no matter how parents think they are keeping the secret. It is practically always a very disturbing experience for a child of any age, or even for an adult, to discover suddenly that he is adopted. It may shatter his sense of security for years.[3]

This negative view of adoption in terms of secrecy and security risks is a far cry from the "open" climate of adoption that prevails today. In the case of international or transracial adoptions, an increasingly popular trend in the decades following World War II, secrecy is usually a moot point—for it is readily apparent that the child and the mother are not biologically related in terms of appearance. In addition to the warnings, however, Dr. Spock weaves a common thread into his discussion of adoption, advising parents to be careful of overemphasizing their love: "Basically, the thing that gives the adopted child the greatest security is being loved, wholeheartedly and naturally." [4] Extending the blanket of "natural" love to a mother and her adopted child is very telling, de-emphasizing, perhaps, the classic "nature-nurture" dichotomy that is a special issue for adoptive mothers.

Over 40 years later, in *Families: Crisis and Caring*, Dr. Brazelton wrote about the "adjustment required" of adoptive parents, and he recommended support groups to lessen their "anxiety." His advice is a mixed bag, with a well-meaning prescription for those who successfully want to get past their struggles with infertility: giving up the "imaginary" or dream baby is necessary in order to successfully "bond with" and be "available to" the real baby.[5] It is noteworthy that the good doctor extends the term "real" to the adoptive baby, and, by implication, to the mother as well. And he extends the invitation to adoptive mothers to consider themselves to be just like "regular" mothers. For like parenthood in general, "adoption is a lifelong job—infinitely rewarding but tough at times." [6]

Along with the standard child-raising guides, there is a special genre of books that apply only to adoptive mothers. One of these, *Raising Adopted Children: A Manual for Adoptive Mothers*, promotes itself on the cover as "The First Child Care Manual for Adoptive Parents." [7] Acknowledging that "many outsiders view adoption as second best," Melina speaks from personal experience about the unique benefits of adoption: "In addition to the other joys parents know, we who have adopted sometimes marvel at the serendipitous creation of our family . . . and have become a family with deep attachments to one another." [8]

Accentuating the positive, the author responds to the commonplace remark that those who chose adoption get their children "the easy way" by arguing that "people come into adoption having had their decision to raise a child tested and affirmed." In fact, adoptive mothers enjoy a distinct advantage, for "one task of parenthood is reconciling expectations with reality," [9] and much of that process has been performed before the longed for child arrives.

In another book of advice, *How to Raise an Adopted Child: A Guide to Help Your Child Flourish from Infancy through Adolescence*, the co-authors take the long view, and open with a frank assessment and a touch of humor: "Our premise is that adoptive families are in some ways different from birth families ... where is our Dr. Spock?"[10] They strike just the right sense of balance that adoptive mothers need, and provide reassurance:

> Adoption is both the same and different from raising a birth child ... unfortunately, the mass media often focuses on the exception rather then the norm ... The good news is that the basic requirements for raising adopted children, for the most part, are the same as for parenting a birth child—love, empathy, patience, trust and understanding.[11]

Although the public image of adoption has changed for the better, often depicted in the press as "a common everyday phenomenon," myths and misconceptions remain, with some element of "stigma" persisting, for adopted children and their mothers are "somehow less than real."[12]

The book closes with reflections on the beneficial side effects of the new views on adoption, championing the experience of adoptive parents who know, better than their "non-adoptive peers ... how much the family has borne the weight of change in our society." So, adoption provides some women with a unique vantage point as well as the standard rewards of child rearing and blessings associated with becoming a mother. These creative and lucky ones are building "new traditions" in the ever-shifting "frontiers of expanding family possibilities"—pioneers on the cutting edge of the motherhood landscape.[13]

Exploring the history of adoption in the United States sheds valuable light on changing myths, attitudes, and perceptions associated with those who become mothers through adoption rather than childbirth. Quite simply, the emphasis has shifted from "secrecy, shame and stigma"[14] toward openness, honesty, and pride; rather than seeing adoption as something to be ashamed of, the trend has been toward celebration. The shift did not occur overnight or suddenly; rather, it evolved in response to changing societal norms and values.

Julie Berebitsky's *Like Our Very Own: Adoption and the Changing Culture of Motherhood, 1851–1950* offers the best insights, in terms of both a narrow angle of vision focusing on mothers and children, and the larger ramifications for society in terms of family and identity.[15] Writing in the year 2000, Dr. Berebitsky notes that "today, adoption is at the center of many diverse, even rancorous debates that reflect the ever-increasing politicization of the family."[16]

Traditionally, starting in the nineteenth century, adoption was often treated as "a private family matter ... largely a woman's issue" with corresponding measurements of what constituted "real" and "idealized" motherhood:

> Adoption may have supplied a woman with a child to mother, but it did not necessarily provide her with an identity as a "real mother" ... adoptive mothers occupied a place on the edges of the ideal from which they pleaded for cultural acceptance of a maternity based on nurture.[17]

Relying on mass circulation magazines as her richest source of information, Berebitsky acknowledges the complications and contradictions of trying to come up with a definition of motherhood in a time when "magazines presented adoption in terms of sentiment, and social workers in terms of science." In reality, it was a current version of the perennial "nature vs. nurture" debate, as adoptive mothers were "struggling to build families that were just as good as the 'real thing.' "[18]

In the early twentieth century, adoption was cloaked in "service to society" garb in the pages of *The Delineator*, the third largest women's magazine in the country. This was "the first time adoption was discussed in an ongoing publication and popular forum; it gave a voice to the experience, demystified it, and made it visible ... ultimately, the series played an important role in popularizing adoption and promoting an expanded definition of motherhood."[19]

These gains, in terms of honoring the role of adoptive mothers, continued when Theodore Dreiser took over the role of editor. Countless mothers wrote letters testifying to the fact that they had needed their children as much as their children had needed them. These mothers "spoke" in spiritual terms, of motherhood as "their highest achievement ... a holy task and a privilege."[20] At one and the same time, adoptive mothers performed a valuable civic duty, rescuing lost children, and finding great purpose and satisfaction in life once their maternal longings were fulfilled.

From the rhetoric of rescue, it was a logical step for this evolving view of mothers to proceed to redemption. The care and commitment they practiced conferred upon them a status and identity they could be proud of as they gave of themselves to their "chosen children":

> The miracle of bearing a living baby is no more astonishing than the companion miracle of finding a small person adrift in the world without a mother, and bringing him triumphantly home ... an adopted child rewarded a mother's love just as richly as does the baby Mother Nature sends haphazardly.[21]

This example demonstrated that some adoptive mothers were beginning to see themselves as just as good as natural mothers—maybe even better. Overcoming their feelings of inferiority could progress toward conferring a superior, even heroic, status upon themselves. But the underlying matter of perception, and how they continued to be considered by others as "different," remained a source of concern.

With a greater emphasis on common bonds that united all mothers, adoptive mothers nevertheless had to acknowledge that finding a child was not the same as giving birth to a child. But "the travails of adoption could be just as intense as the pains of labor." [22] So, life was not always perfectly "sunny" on the other side of the street. In seeking to prove their worth, mothers of adopted children oscillated between feelings of being better or worse, oftentimes settling for "good enough" in the same company as mothers who gave birth to their children. There were compensations and challenges that came with motherhood, no matter what road one had traveled to achieve it. Over time, an understanding of adoption in the United States had developed into one "in which new parents benefited as much as the child." [23] This balanced view of adoption proved to be a mutually beneficial one—for parents, children, and the nation at large. By the middle of the twentieth century, adoption was often portrayed in terms of its "radical potential" and "transformative power," [24] an institution with positive contributions to make to American society, and gifts that extended well beyond the bonds of mother and child.

A spate of recent books and collections of articles—written from the perspective of social science as well as literature and popular media—elaborate on this idea of the potential of adoption to change society as well as to open up vistas of possibility and hope for mothers. Common themes and language abound. Barbara Melosh writes as both an adoptive mother and historian, grounding her observations in the fact that "the pluralistic ideology and ethnic diversity of a 'nation of immigrants' rendered American society more open to adoption." [25] Her treatment of "rainbow families" (international and transracial adoption) focuses on the fact that the language of adoption is a "revealing index of its anomalous status" [26]—at once optimistic and limited in its optimism. The very difference associated with adoption makes it a "clarifying lens," especially in regards to Korean children, "by far the most numerous single group of persons adopted from abroad." [27] Navigating the complicated path of international adoption is not always easy; many adoptive mothers remember well the anguish they felt when NBC's Bryant Gumbel, covering the 1988 summer Olympics in Seoul, commented on the *Today* show that the fact that Korea exported so many of its children was "embarrassing, perhaps even a national shame." [28] Mothers in waiting, as well as those who had already adopted their children, protested en masse, sending letters and telegrams to NBC. They were fearful that Gumbel's "off the cuff" observation would cause the Korean government to respond by ending the long-term relationship that had fulfilled the dreams of thousands of American mothers. This story is illustrative of the centrality of the "narrative of rescue" in adoption circles. The act of rescue is a two-way street, and it applies to mothers as well as children; children are rescued and become members of American families, while their adoptive mothers are rescued from a lifetime of failure and thwarted desire to have a child to love. Those who have adopted children see it as a "win-win" case; Gumbel's remarks were uncalled for, especially since he had no personal experience and did not know what he was talking about, and failed to consider the damage he might cause.[29]

Collections that cast a wider net across the sea of changes of adoption are *Cultures of Transnational Adoption*,[30] *The Maternal is Political: Women Writers at the Intersection of Motherhood and Social Change*,[31] and *Imagining Adoption: Essays on Literature and Culture*.[32] Many of these authors sound common themes. Shari MacDonald Strong opens her introductory essays with a quotation from William Ross Wallace: "The hand that rocks the cradle is the hand that rules the world." In addition to conferring power, she notes that the inclusive aspect of adoptive motherhood "bears gifts: patience, the necessity of being present, the sharpest sense of compassion . . . and the secret that the lines we erect to partition ourselves off from others, to protect ourselves against the heaviness of human experience, are arbitrary." [33] Also arbitrary is a restrictive definition of motherhood that recognizes only biology and genetics, rather than the power of nurture and love.

In her introductory essay on "Imagining Adoption," Marianne Novy points to the "paradox of adoption," which "establishes a parental relationship which is not genetic; thus, it forces either a redefinition of parenthood or the definition of adoption as pretense or fiction." [34] The literature she examines, which ranges from *Oedipus* to Barbara Kingsolver's *Pigs in Heaven*, is "filled with unhappy, as well as happy scenarios." [35] Nevertheless, when told from the perspective of mothers of "chosen" and "cherished" adopted children, the stories are most often positive and affirming. Toby Alice Volkmann deals with "new geographies of kinship," highlighting issues of "belonging, race and culture" as well as "identity, family and roots." [36] In many cases of adopted Asian children, she offers examples of the "infuriating questions of strangers," such as "are they really yours?... are they really sisters?" [37] She concluded that adoptive parents "live daily with the ambivalences and ambiguities of adoption." [38] Nevertheless, the joys outweigh and compensate for the challenges of becoming a mother by choice and design rather than chance.

A very balanced perspective is offered by Katrina Wegar, the editor of a book entitled *Adoptive Families in a Diverse Society.*[39] Wegar's introduction sounds just the right note: "adoption can serve as a catalyst, not necessarily for competing, but rather for complementary understandings of family, kinship and identity." [40] While acknowledging the special difficulties that can accompany adoption, she does so with a comforting thought that emphasizes what unites all mothers rather than what divides them into categories: "the institution and process of adoption and the lives of adoptive family members are not void of contradictions and conflicts. Then again, few people's lives are." [41] Adoption, then, is simply another piece in the puzzle known as the human condition. One of the articles in Wegar's book offers a fresh, feisty perspective, apparent in the title: "Real Mothers: Adoptive Mothers Resisting Marginalization and Recreating Motherhood." A trio of authors expresses their sentiments about certain societal beliefs that "place a burden of doubts, presumptions and responsibilities on us as adoptive mothers that separate us from biological ones." [42] They prefer to focus on resilience and recovery rather than the sense of loss that can affect all members of the "adoption triangle" (birth mother, adoptive mother, and child). Theirs is a perspective that celebrates the many possibilities opened up by adoption, and welcomes all into one great "Mother's Club": "Adoptive mothering offers unique challenges, opportunities for growth and experiences of risk and adventure in the embracing of diversity and the creation of family relationships." [43] One of the mothers, Mary Watkins, goes on to argue that "love requires a commitment to the advent and nurturing of difference," a comforting prescription for many adoptive mothers.[44]

Seeing adoptive motherhood as an "adventure" is a motif that has resounded in the twenty-first century, from popular news coverage of celebrity adoptions to more thoughtful ruminations offered by several writers and columnists. In "'Adoption Fever' Among Celebrities—Good or Bad?" Stacy Jenel Smith[45] addresses the controversies swirling around high-profile adoptions by Madonna and Angelina Jolie and Brad Pitt. Questions about fairness have been raised in terms of the ability of the "rich and famous" to adopt as they please, while there is a long waiting list and more obstacles to overcome for the "average" parents in waiting. Adoption appears to be especially "trendy" in Hollywood these days, though it is actually nothing new under the sun. Like many other Americans suffering from infertility, or simply motivated by the desire to provide a home for orphans and children otherwise consigned to a life of poverty, Hollywood has a long history of adoptions, going back to the days of Ronald Reagan and Jane Wyman, and André Previn and Mia Farrow. The variations on a theme seem endless, ranging from single and divorced mothers, such as Diane Keaton and Meg Ryan, adopting both at home and abroad, and "phase two" of the Mia Farrow adoption "adventure." Farrow, in addition to giving birth to four biological children, "reached out to adopt ten more from all around the world, some with disabilities." [46] These family lines became seriously messy and crossed when one of her children, Soon-Yi Previn, had an affair with Woody Allen, Farrow's longtime lover. Soon-Yi then became Mrs. Woody Allen, and the happy couple, tainted by the scandal, nevertheless was able to adopt two children themselves. Sensational publicity such as this has not been very helpful to the cause of adoptive parenthood.

Still, adoption remains a wonderful option for many families today, and most of these stories, often inspiring, develop along more normal lines, and successfully carry on the "good news" associated with adoptive mothers. Syndicated columnist Ellen Goodman wrote as the step-grandmother of Chloe, rescued from an orphanage in China, in a column dated July 4, 2003. Her family's experience hit many of the high notes of the adoption "symphony" being performed in today's world. Goodman uses her skills as a writer to sing the praises of adoption, tying in motherhood with the celebration of the national day of independence and moving her readers to poignant sighs if not tears:

> ... this little girl with shiny black hair ... has come to America and to us. We have embraced her with a loyalty that is all the more tenacious for not having been preordained by biology. We have the sort of attachment that the word "adoption" cannot begin to describe ... in a single moment, a year-old child was transferred from one set of hands to another, and from one fate to another. The entire arc of her short life was transformed from being abandoned to being treasured.[47]

Another treasured child from China came to be the adopted daughter of Maureen Corrigan and her husband. As National Public Radio's "Fresh Air" book critic, Corrigan incorporated her adoption saga into the story of her love affair with books, *Leave Me Alone, I'm Reading: Finding and Losing Myself in Books*.[48] In a section of her book devoted to "Women's Extreme Adventure Stories," she tells the reader how she set off on one of her own, calling Part I "The Infertility Saga" and Part II "The Adoption Saga." [49] In a voice both witty and poignant, she recalls the story of her late-in-life marriage, the trials and tribulations of infertility treatments and miscarriages, and the pot of gold at the end of her rainbow, her daughter, Molly. Making her way through several "Adoptionvilles," suburbs of the "Normative World," on her way to her final destination of China, she recognized that parenthood itself was a "crapshoot," whether pursued through the biological or adoption route. Remembering the telephone call from the adoption agency operative who spoke of "news of your daughter," Corrigan speaks the words "MY daughter," recalling the feelings that came over her: "I don't think that any words anyone will ever speak to me will be so simultaneously unreal, frightening and magical." [50] For she was not dealing with a hypothetical baby any more, but "her," a real child, MY baby ... "Molly was a devout wish made flesh." [51] Maureen Corrigan's quest for motherhood had a happy ending. Taking her daughter to a McDonald's years later, she recalls the words of the man cleaning the tables—not the stuff of rude commentary, but a kind and simply stated truth: "You wanted to be a mother, and she needed a mother. You are beautiful." This generous stranger was right: "We found each other, and that is a miracle I will never get over." [52] Adoption and the journey to motherhood, then, are often the stuff of miracles as well as adventure. Many adoptive mothers insist that no matter what path they followed, the destination and reward was well worth the effort.

Many of the divergent roads and perspectives associated with adoption were explored in an online blog published by the *New York Times* during the months of November and December in 2007. Entitled "Relative Choices: Adoption and the Family," it provided a forum for mothers and their children to examine and reflect the images reflected by contemporary adoptive families. Hollee McGinnis, an adoptee from South Korea, wrote several pieces. In "Who Are You Also Known As?" she covers familiar ground. In the movements associated with adoption, "there are both losses and gains":

> At its best, inter-country adoption demonstrated to me the greatness of our human spirits to love across race, nationality, and culture. But I also know that it takes a lot more than just love to make a success; it requires courage, honesty and commitment.[53]

In a follow-up post, she argues "that blood is thicker than water, but love can be thicker than blood." [54]

An adoptee from Vietnam states that "perhaps the role of the adoptive parent could be viewed, not so much as a bridge, but as a builder of bridges, connecting their children to themselves and to their ethnicities." [55] Another contributor, Adam Wolfington, addresses the fact that he is different, a black kid adopted into a white family. But he feels lucky. His mother is outspoken: "when people ask if she is my "real mother," she responds: "What do I look like, a hologram?" [56] Another adoptive mother, Tama Janowitz, speaks for herself in "The Real Thing." Her tone is a bit defensive, even strident, in expressing her love for her daughter and her identity as a mother. She states that "I know that there are some women who have given birth who believe that the type of love they have for their child is more intense, more real, than the love I have for my kid, because they hatched it themselves. This argument makes no sense to me." The real proof of her motherhood is found in the bonds she has forged with her daughter: "And my kid knows I'm her real mother. Not biological, but real. It doesn't get any realer than this." [57]

Truly, the most apt metaphor in today's world for adoption, and the corresponding relationships that blossom as a result, is that of a kaleidoscope rather than just a prism. A kaleidoscope, composed of two plates and mirrors, produces an endless variety of patterns. For mothers and the children they have found and chosen, those patterns comprise a rich tapestry of love, and in the words and experience of Maureen Corrigan, "fate and effort and will." [58] The ties that bind these mothers and children in adoption are made stronger by the efforts, sometimes valiant, which are put into the process of creating a family. In answering the question of how one determines whether a mother is "REAL," a good source for words of wisdom can be found in Margery Williams's Skin Horse, who counsels the Velveteen Rabbit: "It doesn't happen all at once ... You *Become* ... but once you are real, you can't become unreal again. It lasts for always." [59]

The process of becoming a mother though adoption, then, might be viewed in today's world as simply another way of forming a family, sharing similarities with the more traditional biological method, but also creating a unique set of challenges and rewards. If families function as "havens in a heartless world," [60] the hopeful expectation is that they will endure and prevail, regardless of how they came to be. As perceptions of adoption have shifted in a more positive direction in recent decades, mothers have become more adept at celebrating the differences rather than apologizing for or ignoring them; celebrations of Adoption Days and Airplane Arrival Days bring joy and attention to parents as well as their children. These annual rituals testify to the evolution of popular images of families formed by adoption—progressing from families besieged by their differences to families that honor and nurture them. From the nineteenth-century perspective, which often focused on the Biblical metaphor of adoption as a journey from feeling lost to being found and loved, the history of the transformative power of adoption has come full circle in the twenty-first century. Becoming a "real" mother through adoption opens up a whole new world of possibilities, and the myriad promises of redemption both now and in the future.

NOTES

1. Marjorie Williams, *The Velveteen Rabbit or How Toys Become Real*, in *The World Treasury of Children's Literature (Book I)*, ed. Clifton Fadiman (Boston: Little Brown & Company, 1984), 246.

2. The author of this poem, frequently reproduced and quoted in adoption circles, is Fleur Conkling Heylinger.

3. Benjamin Spock, *The Common Sense Book of Baby and Child Care* (New York: Duell, Sloan and Pearce, 1946), 505.

4. Ibid., 507.

5. T. Barry Brazelton, M.D., *Families: Crisis and Caring* (Reading, MA: Addison-Wesley Publishing Co., Inc., 1989), 200, 210.

6. Ibid., 201.

7. Lois Ruskai Melina, *Raising Adopted Children: A Manual for Adoptive Parents* (New York: Harper & Row/A Solstice Book, 1986).

8. Ibid., ix.

9. Ibid., 2.

10. Judith Schaffer and Christian Lindstrom, *How to Raise an Adopted Child: A Guide to Help Your Child Flourish from Infancy through Adolescence* (New York: Penguin Group/A Plume Book, 1989).

11. Ibid., 2.

12. Ibid., 7.

13. Ibid., 289.

14. See Adam Pertman's essay, "Adoption in the Media: In Need of Editing," in *Adoptive Families in a Diverse Society*, ed. Katrina Wegar (Piscataway, NJ, and London: Rutgers University Press, 2006). Pertman refers to the "corrosive combination of secrecy, stigma and shame that has enveloped adoption for centuries," 60.

15. Julie Berebitsky. *Like Our Very Own: Adoption and the Changing Culture of Motherhood, 1851–1950* (Lawrence: University Press of Kansas, 2000).

16. Ibid., 2.

17. Ibid., 8–9.

18. Ibid., 15.

19. Ibid., 51.

20. Ibid., 57.

21. Kathleen Norris, novelist, writing in the April 1930 issue of *Ladies Home Journal*, as cited in ibid., 83–84.

22. Ibid., 90.

23. Ibid., 2.

24. Ibid., 167. The "radical potential" reference is credited to Margaret Mead.

25. Barbara Melosh. *Strangers and Kin: The American Way of Adoption* (Cambridge, MA: Harvard University Press, 2002), 166.

26. Ibid., vii.

27. Ibid., 192.

28. Ibid., 193.

29. Twenty years later, the fallout has finally materialized. In a story in the October 9, 2008, edition of the *New York Times*, "Korea Aims to End Stigma of Adoption and Stop 'Exporting' Babies," Norimitsu Onishu reports that the government of South Korea has stepped up efforts to have Korean children adopted by Korean families at home, phasing out foreign adoptions in the next four years.

30. Toby Alice Volkmann (ed.), *Cultures of Transnational Adoption* (Durham, NC, and London: Duke University Press, 2005).

31. Shari MacDonald Strong (ed.), *The Maternal Is Political: Women Writers at the Intersection of Motherhood and Social Change* (Berkeley, CA: Seal Press/Perseus Books Group, 2008).

32. Marianne Novy (ed.), *Imagining Adoption: Essays on Literature and Culture* (Ann Arbor: The University of Michigan Press, 2001).

33. Strong, *The Maternal Is Political*, 66.

34. Novy, *Imagining Adoption*, 2.

35. Ibid., 2.

36. Volkmann, *Cultures of Transnational Adoption*, 5–6.

37. Ibid., 15.

38. Ibid., 18.

39. Katrina Wegar (ed.). *Adoptive Families in a Diverse Society* (Piscataway, NJ, and London: Rutgers University Press, 2006).

40. Ibid., 2.

41. Ibid., 5.

42. Betsy Smith, Janet L. Surrey, and Mary Watkins, "Real Mothers: Adoptive Mothers Resisting Marginalization and Recreating Motherhood," in Wegar, *Adoptive Families in a Diverse Society*, 147.

43. Ibid., 149.

44. Mary Watkins, "Adoption and Identity: Nomadic Possibilities for Reconceiving the Self," in Wegar, *Adoptive Families in a Diverse Society*, 271.

45. Stacy Jenel Smith, "Adoption Fever Among Celebrities—Good or Bad?" http://channels.isp.netscape.com/celebrity/becksmith.jsp?p=bsf_celebadoption, November 23, 2008.

46. Ibid.

47. Ellen Goodman, "Welcome to the Party," *The Seattle Times*, July 4, 2003, http://seattletimes.nwsource.com/cgi-bin/PrintStory.pl?slug=goodmano4&date =20030704.

48. Maureen Corrigan, *Leave Me Alone, I'm Reading: Finding and Losing Myself in Books* (New York: Vintage Books, A Division of Random House, 2005).

49. Ibid., 34–35.

50. Ibid., 39.

51. Ibid., 37–40, 44.

52. Ibid., 50.

53. Hollee McGinnis, "Who Are You Also Known As?" *New York Times*, November 13, 2007.

54. Hollee McGinnis, "Blood Ties and Acts of Love," *New York Times*, December 4, 2007.

55. Sumeia Williams, "I Am Not a Bridge," *New York Times*, November 19, 2007.

56. Adam Wolfington, "Being Adopted, and Being Me," *New York Times*, November 16, 2007.

57. Tama Janowitz, "The Real Thing," *New York Times*, November 12, 2007.

58. Corrigan, *Leave Me Alone, I'm Reading*, 57.

59. Williams, *The Velveteen Rabbit*, 246–247.

60. See Christopher Lasch, *Haven in a Heartless World: The Family Besieged* (New York: W. W. Norton and Company, 1977).

CHAPTER 11

Moms.Com

Dennis Hall

Last time I looked (September 10, 2008), the domain name "Moms.com" was still for sale at Moniker Marketplace with an asking price of $4,900,000, which, with Moniker's modest 15 percent service fee, makes the total something like $5,635,000, but I am not sure how sales taxes function in this realm. The ad at Moms.com includes a photograph of a slim woman, wearing a pink-tinged white suit; she is holding a baby and carries a large, black "designer" bag over her left shoulder, over which her long hair falls; the photo is cropped such that the woman is visible only from her knees to her shoulder; the heads of baby and mother are not visible. The focus here is upon what has become known as the "millennial mom."

Both the photo and the accompanying text argue that this sum is warranted, in Moniker's view, because "Moms.com" has, at four characters, excellent name length, is memorable (and, I would add, can be understood as both a plural and a possessive), has excellent marketability through clear ties to its perceived uses, has the highest "dot value" as a dot-com name rather than a dot-net or dot-org or other dot-extension, and exhibits excellent development potential.[1]

Whether or not this price is inflated, I leave to Internet entrepreneurs to argue, but I do think it reasonable to see this price tag as an index of the increasing presence of "moms" online and of the increasing traffic in and complexity of their interests, personal as well as commercial. Moreover, while an entirely defensible definition of "moms" as people or as a category may not be possible, "mom" in the first decade of the new millennium is culturally if not linguistically a great deal more than an abbreviated term for "mamma" or "mother," which lexicography suggests emerged in the 1890s. References to "moms" in 2008, wherever they appear, carry a cluster of associations distinct from those of 50 or 20 or perhaps even 10 years ago. A considerable portion of this resonance is both reflected and constructed online.

*

The proliferation of virtual communities or perhaps more accurately, as Howard Rheingold suggests in his revision of *The Virtual Community*, "online social networks" [2] is apparent even to the casual online explorer. Rheingold points out that "[T]here is no such thing as a single, monolithic online subculture; it is more like an ecosystem of subcultures, some frivolous, others serious. . . . You can use virtual communities to find a date, sell a lawn mower, publish a novel, conduct a meeting," [3] as well as engage in scientific discourse, psychotherapy, political activity, religious devotion, among very many other human undertakings. The list of common interests around which people aggregate online is seemingly endless, including not all but nearly all the things people do in their lives. Moreover, these networks commonly do not exhibit taxonomical rigor, and so they mix and match a wide diversity of interests and discursive practices with a singular alacrity. "Virtual communities," as Rheingold defines the term, "are social aggregations that emerge from the Net when people carry on those public discussions long enough, with sufficient human feeling, to form webs of personal relationships in cyberspace." [4] That "moms" should collapse interests in knowledge and feeling to join together online is, dare I say, only natural.

A Google search of "moms" yields nearly 30 pages of more or less mainline mom sites before falling into addresses where "mom" or "moms" is a remote extension in the URL. [5] Many of these sites, quite predictably, are simple sales pitches to moms, often co-opting the cyberspacial look and playing with the rhetorical feel of virtual community. Momagenda.com sells day planners "guaranteed to help eliminate chaos," as does Moretimemoms.com. Instylemoms.com features baby wear and hip maternity fashions "you can wear anywhere, anytime, designed for this incredible time in your life." Amominredhighheels.com is a blog-like commercial site dedicated to "empowering moms through beauty and style." Momsmaternity.com sells breast-feeding products and provides an "exclusive breast pump comparison chart" to help make the choice. Momsfavoritestuff.com provides " 'real moms' reviews of everything for mom, baby, and child" and provides links to where the stuff can be purchased online, while Mom's Best Friend (mbfagency.com) places nannies and household staff. Momsrewards.com is a guide to "Quality Freebies Rewards and Resources for Mom." Healthymomsfitness.com, which describes itself as an "organization dedicated to enhancing the physical and psychological well-being of women before, during and after pregnancy," also provides a link on its home page to its "Licensee Program!": "Have your own Healthy Moms fitness business—we've got *everything you need* to get started and to keep you going!" And lest one overlook a mom-oriented commercial site, Swankymoms.com, "where hip moms hang out," provides an exhausting directory and a list of the "Top 100" sites, reputedly based upon participant ratings.

Many of these commercial sites work the borders between simple selling—if there is any such thing anymore—and group participation, preaching a gospel of one ilk or another and organizing, reflecting that "ecosystem of subcultures, some frivolous, others serious" that Rheingold points to.

Mealmakeovermoms.com, for but one example, is tied to a book, *The Mom's Guide to Meal Makeovers: Improving the Way Your Family Eats One Meal at a Time*, by Janice Bissex and Liz Weiss, two registered dietitians, copies of which are available via a link to Amazon.com along with the invitation to join the authors' free "Moms Club." [6]

This simple platform is conventionally constructed. Head-shot pictures of the authors—very attractive but not too dishy women, old enough to warrant confidence but young enough to garner trust—adorn the top banner. To the right is a search-the-site button and a slot for the email address if one wishes to "join," next to which appears a brief account of membership benefits: bimonthly electronic newsletter, opportunity to submit recipes, organized shopping lists, and "Articles about the Moms in the News!" Despite the opportunity to submit recipes and the ubiquitous "Contact" link, Mealmakeovermoms is substantially a one-way street with the authoritative dietitians providing useful knowledge to an interested, possibly even eager, audience, whatever its size. The left column has links to Home, The Book, Recipes & Tips, Moms' Club, About Us, The Kitchen Links, and Contact. Below the links are three small, very discreet, advertising logos: for Amazon, for eggs, and for beef. Below the logos is a link to a copy of an article they have written on "Veggie Love" and a link to MealMakeoverTV.com, a large collection of brief "cooking shows" and lectures on dietary practices by the authors that are easy to access and have high production values for material of this sort. The middle of the page provides links to their podcast, "Cooking with the Moms," to their blog, to a description of their book, and to the recipe of the month. The "About Us" page establishes their academic as well as journalistic and maternal credentials. "The Kitchen Links" page is a long list of links to organizational and commercial food-related sites, at least some of which presumably support this extensive Web structure.

Author Jonni McCoy's Miserlymoms.com applies essentially this same Web strategy to a broader target audience:

> Welcome to Miserly Moms. It is my goal to help people (especially moms) get the tools that their family needs to spend more time together. Through the use of the tips I share and the other resources recommended, I hope that many people will be able to afford to cut back on working hours or quit altogether in order to spend more time with their family.
>
> I believe this can be done because it happened to us. I was a successful business woman with a career in Silicon Valley. After my son was born, I wanted to be at home full-time with my children. I didn't believe that I could afford to quit, because we were living in the expensive San Francisco Bay Area, and I was bringing home 50% of our income. But I did it anyway because my family was my priority. I realized that being a stay-at-home mom was the best for my children.
>
> I had to learn quickly how to stretch a dollar—especially in our grocery budget. I had little training in frugality, having grown up in an affluent surrounding. We didn't sell our home or cars. Our household expenses remained the same (except those for childcare). I did my homework, learned from trial and error and the experiences of other frugal moms who had gone before me.[7]

Other sites engage a common, sometimes very narrowly shared interest. Spinabifidamoms.com provides remarkably detailed information on spina bifida from a Management of Meylomeningocele Study conducted by a consortium of major medical centers, which seeks to recruit study participants as well as to inform. Msmoms.com offers support in managing multiple sclerosis. Custodyprepformoms.org is "a support site provided by those that have been through the process" for women involved in child custody litigation. LDSmissionarymoms.com provides support for "LDS parents who have sons or daughters serving or preparing to serve full time missions for the L[atter]D[ay]S[aints] Church." Sites also focus upon specific religious groups: Christian Moms (at Justmoms.com), Modernjewishmom .com, and Catholicmom.com, among many others. Goldstarmoms.com is the official site of the organization founded in 1928 by women whose sons had died in World War I. Militarymoms.net, Marinemoms.us, Marinemomsonline.net, and Sgtmoms.com, "The Internet site for Military families Since 1996 " (which is considerable history in this environment) are among the many sites supporting military moms and families.

The scope of moms sites, however, inevitably widens, making categorization difficult if not nearly impossible. Many moms sites are, for want of a more precise term, what has become known as "values-oriented." Emphasisonmoms.com is a "ministry for moms with family values," Mainstreetmom.com is "the online magazine for modern mothers with traditional values," which offers a substantial "spirituality" section. Justformom.com's slogan is "touching each mom's life, one mom at a time" and declares "finally a place that's just for mom," enunciating a common claim to uniqueness despite the ubiquity of moms sites and their remarkably conventional content. Momswhothink.com declares an intention to provide "thoughtful discussions and intelligent debates on today's issues," but, despite its name, this site exhibits greater interest in baby names than in social or political issues.

Several sites, however, actually do focus on social and political activism, among them Mothers Movement Online (Mothersmovement.org), Mainstreet Moms (Themmob.org), Mothers Acting Up (Mothersactingup.org), Mothers & More (Mothersandmore.org). Utahmomsforcleanair.org is one of many sites that focus on a single issue. Perhaps the most distinct site of this kind is Momsrising.org, co-founded by Joan Blades who with her husband created the famous (at least in California) MoveOn.org. *Ms. Magazine* has characterized Blades as the "mother of cyberspace mobilization," and "... she is trying to build an army of citizen activists to push for paid family leave, flexible work and better access to quality child and healthcare...."[8]

Some moms sites are situational in their orientations as, for example, Singlemom.com and singlemoms.org. Midlifemom.com is a site

> dedicated to the health, wealth and needs of the mature mom. If you find yourself pushing 40, and either already are or about to become a mom, come right on in, because your [sic] in good company.... This site was born after weeks of surfing, & searching for information and support for us over 40 mom's [sic]. We found very little. But today we are here for you. We are here for your, education, entertainment, and support.

A very large category of sites and a common theme among more generally oriented moms sites is working moms, either WAHMS—work at home moms (Bizymoms.com, Jobsformoms.com, Internetbasedmoms.com,

Merchantmoms.com)—or moms struggling to "balance" (a contested term) the demands of work in the conventional workforce and motherhood. The primary focus of Emptynestmoms.com is on the processes of reentering the workforce. Momstown.com aims at "Helping Entrepreneurial Moms Make Money." The Moms in Business Network (Mibn.org) is a "National network dedicated to supporting and actively promoting working mothers and their businesses." Planetmoms.com is a site that claims to put "the world of moms at your fingertips," with a search engine and Web directory "serving moms and work at home moms." And moms increasingly blog. Workitmom.com, for example, is a directory of working-mom blogs as well as a free membership site, while Themomblogs.com is a directory of "moms who blog" about whatever they wish.

Another large category of moms sites are those tied to place: Hawai imoms.com, Lamorindamomsclub.org, MomsinMadison.com, East baymom.com, DCurbanmom.com, Gulfcoastmoms.com, Springfieldmoms .org, RenoTahoemoms.com, IndyMoms.com, Milwaukeemoms.com, Hunterdonmoms.com, Bigcitymoms.com and Minglingmoms.com (NYC), Musiccitymoms.com, Acadianmoms.com, Michiganmoms.com, and Kentuckianamoms.com, among very many others. A recent list of 75 currently available "moms domain names" for sale were all regional.[9]

* *

A way to begin to understand a cultural phenomenon of this magnitude is to consider the observations of people relatively unfettered by ideology—apart from the profit motive; that is, the marketers of goods and services to moms. Mothers, always a crucial commercial market, became increasingly so in the decades after World War II, as their social and economic roles changed. Moms of the 1950s have given way to Boomer Moms to Soccer Moms to Gen X Moms to Gen Y Moms, aka Millennial Moms, and marketing researchers have been tracking their evolution with increasing efficiency.

Moms are, for one example, Maria Bailey's specialty, resulting in *Marketing to Moms: Getting Your Share of the Trillion Dollar Market* and *Trillion Dollar Moms: Marketing to a New Generation of Mothers*.[10] Bailey declares "Farewell Soccer Moms. Hello GenXers and Millennial Moms." [11] Central players in this phenomenon she describes as Mom Mavens: "Moms who have earned the respect of their peers, the "Go-To" mom for answers and information," what marketing in the 1960s called "leading consumers." The Mom Maven Matrix™ includes managing some formal or informal network of communication, having established access to media, being involved in some form of education, having more than one child, parenting a child with some special need, being an author or owning a business, maintaining at least one leadership role in her community, demonstrating a passion for some cause, and surviving a challenge or crisis.[12] A mom with a cluster of these characteristics will influence her peers. Marketers, Bailey contends, need to harness the influence of Mom Mavens upon, presumably, moms ordinaire through "word of mom," and the most effective word of mom initiatives are based upon relationships— relationships between moms and relationships between mom and brand. "The most effective Word of Mom Relationships include:

- Memberships to a group that elevates her rank among peers
- A brand she can attach to her resume
- Simple ways to share messages that are impressive to her peers
- Gives mom an exclusive nugget of information
- Empowers her child within his/her circles." [13]

While Bailey is not engaged in what academe might characterize as an analysis characteristic of "cultural studies," her research does reveal the heavy use of email and participation in virtual communities and in online learning and sharing among this demographic known as Millennial Moms.[14] Becky Ebenkamp reports that

The U.S. Census Bureau defines millennials as those Americans born between 1978 and 1994. There are currently about 9 million Millennial Moms in the U.S. ... Gen Y moms are projected to have more kids—and at a younger age—than both their Gen X and baby boomer predecessors.[15]

Many more of these women are college educated and acclimated—to the point of genuine comfort—to the use of computers and especially to being online than their predecessors. Bailey finds that "eighty-two percent go online for fast updates" and that they

- Want fast ideas, tips, and quick advice
- Want to hear from a peer mom
- Are more likely to call or email for help
- Are more likely to remain loyal to a company that provides them with valuable/useful information.[16]

Moreover, she finds that

- Moms want help making decisions
- Moms are knowledge seekers in parenting and business
- Moms as consumers seek relationships
- Moms value a company that can change with their life stages and roles
- Moms are moved by emotions and an inherent sense of nurturing[17]

These generalizations are, of course, subject to exception, but presumably are based upon calculations of some statistical significance.

Moreover, Bailey points to an important distinction that Millennial Moms commonly make between "benefits" that goods and services provide to her and to her family and the once commonly touted "features" of such goods and services—a real difference between an orientation to use, problem solving, and experience, rather than an orientation to the thing itself or, as Wallace Stevens might have said, to the idea of the thing. And whatever the strength of her research, this market analyst, and many of her professional colleagues, point to many of the values and behaviors associated with the prevailing sense of "mom" in the first decade of the new millennium, a sense of mom to a considerable degree constructed by life lived in part online.

"The Post-Soccer Mom," Becky Ebenkamp reports in June 2008 in *Brand Week*, has "stepped aside to make way ... for a new mother in the house [with] a more relaxed attitude about the kids [who has discarded] some of the strictures her mom raised her with ... [because] some of what defines them is in reaction to being raised by them." [18] While their mothers sought a "balance" between the obligations of motherhood and work or the other parts of their lives, the New Millennials seek an "integration." "Integrating is [a] better [figure of speech]. When you are balancing, you always have to make an artificial choice, a compromise that could be a false compromise. When all is said and done, you have to unify, which is the integration of body and mind." [19] This sense of integration reflects a desire for control. And what have become known in some circles as "social technologies" are increasingly recognized as and used as instruments of control.

Ebenkamp breathlessly observes:

Ah yes, you knew that Web-has-changed-everything stuff would be coming, didn't you? But in the case of Millennial Moms, there's actually a lot of meat there. Not only have tech tools and the Internet changed how many young moms live, they've changed what they expect from marketers in terms of content, delivery and even product development. It's why savvier marketers have started responding with Gen Y mom-specific initiatives from brand-sponsored online meetups for new mothers, to mom-fueled word-of-mouth campaigns, to promotional partnerships with the growing ranks of young mom bloggers.[20]

Ebenkamp also notes that "Everyday, about 10,000 moms are starting blogs ... And that, of course, doesn't touch the separate world of virtual communities." [21] And Amanda Natividad reports that while Gen X and Gen Y Moms share interests, they use the Net differently.

Gen Y moms most often use the Internet to connect and commune with other moms, usually through blogs, social nets, and creating and sharing videos. Their Gen X predecessors, on the other hand, tend to gravitate toward task-oriented activities, such as surfing photo sites, product ratings and reviews, and online shopping ... from a common goal, exploring child-rearing issues online. The data from 847 moms visiting Parenting.com also found: 149 Gen Y versus 71 Gen X women own a blog, 160 versus 86 read others' blogs, 148 versus 78 maintain an online profile, 154 versus 96 create/share their own videos, [and] 156 versus 105 participate in an online community.[22] This last datum is to my mind significant and an online practice to which I will return directly.

A partial explanation is also geographical. "Millennial Moms don't always live near their folks, so peer-to-peer support and information gathering is critical. ... Moms look for other moms to network with. Community is their mantra." [23] Some of these moms may have themselves been abused or neglected as children, women who now have children of their own and are in desperate need of information and models of behavior they did not have growing up. And some Millennial Moms may well seek an escape from—or at least seek an alternative to—the advice of "their folks," particularly their moms, who may be perceived as hopelessly old-fashioned or even dangerously out of touch with current and rapidly changing developments in child care and rearing. Many Millennial Moms have never heard of Dr. Benjamin Spock's *The Common Sense Book of Baby and Child Care* (first edition 1946) or Haim Ginott's *Between Parent and Child* (first edition 1965), or the other authorities their mothers may have consulted, and might well be appalled were they to read them, finding them insufficiently current, or even unfashionable.

But Bailey points to perhaps a more salient factor: "Because they were raised on technology, they [Gen Yers] know they can have things when they want them, that it can help them customize a lifestyle on their own terms. . . . These moms want a relationship with marketing rather than 'Just flash an ad in front of me.' They want to be part of the peer group with marketers." Indeed, Bailey says, "If I had written *Marketing to Moms* today, I would call it *Marketing WITH Moms*. They realize they have a voice and that it's empowering to invoke change." [24]

* * *

The degree to which the access to computer technology and the desire for aggregation and participation—which for many people since time out of mind has simply been a part of the human condition—actually yields online communities is a matter of continuing speculation and debate, and far more contentious is the debate over the character and function of such communities. But the construction of something of the kind, whatever its character and function, is increasingly acknowledged. As Nicole Brown suggests, the persistent use of the term "community" itself serves to ". . . identify, describe, and construct online contexts and groups—online communities [which are] . . . constructed by the discourses and actions of online groups." [25] She points, for instance, to the contributions of online communities, to one degree or another and in one way or another, to the creation of what critical theory has for some time recognized as "interpretive communities," "discourse communities," and "knowledge communities." While this theoretical turf is still hotly contested (see Andrew Feenberg[26] and everything Howard Rheingold has written, among others), the consensus is moving toward recognition of the palpable reality of online communities, virtual communities, online social networks—call them what we will—even as our understanding of their character and function remains in flux.

Understanding how virtual communities work, much less what they may mean as a popular cultural phenomenon, may not now be knowable with any satisfaction. While we will better understand the phenomenon 50, 25, even 10 years from now, Constance Elise Porter has bravely taken a useful first step in "A Typology of Virtual Communities: A Multi-Disciplinary Foundation of Future Research," a mercifully succinct article in this realm that provides a more inclusive definition of virtual community than has been common practice and seeks to develop "a classification system that is useful to researchers from various disciplinary perspectives." [27] "A virtual community" Porter defines ". . . as an aggregation of individuals or business partners who interact around a shared interest, where the interaction is at least partially supported and/or mediated by technology and guided by some protocols or norms." [28] Virtual Communities are marked by five key attributes:

1. *Purpose (Content of Interaction)* This attribute describes the specific focus of discourse, or focal content of communication, among community members.

2. *Place (Extent of Technology Mediation of Interaction)* This attribute defines the location of interaction, where interaction occurs either completely virtually or only partially virtually.

3. *Platform (Design of Interaction)* This attribute refers to the technical design of interaction in the virtual community, where designs enable synchronous communication, asynchronous communication, or both.

4. *Population (Pattern of Interaction)* This attribute refers to the pattern of interaction among community members as described by group structure (e.g., small group or network) and type of social ties (e.g., strong, weak, stressful).

5. *Profit Model (Return on Interaction)* This attribute refers to whether a community creates tangible economic value where value is defined as revenue generation.[29]

Trying to understand how the relatively narrow category of moms sites might work in this larger, seemingly chaotic, environment is a little like trying to define the characteristics and functions of a new literary or artistic subgenre as it struggles to emerge from a plethora of competing forms. One can begin—with all due respect to the much maligned New Criticism—with individual texts, with close readings of particular moms sites, and so gradually accumulate understanding.

A place to begin is with moms sites tied to place, apparently the largest and currently fastest growing category of moms sites. While far from uniform, they are often very much alike, in part the result of the sponsorship or ownership by local newspapers whose decline in circulation—2007 being the worst year on record—has driven them to the Net in an increasing variety of forms in desperate pursuit of readership and advertising revenue. The *Courier-Journal* of Louisville, Kentucky, for but one of many instances, owns and operates several niche Web sites, including KentuckianaPets.com, www.rednbluefans.com (University of Louisville and University of Kentucky sports), DerbyCityBrides.com, and, of course, Kentuckianamoms.com (Louisville, Kentucky, and Southern Indiana).[30]

An advertisement for Kentuckianamoms.com in *Velocity* (July 9, 2008), a weekly free paper distributed in bins across the city and also published by the *Courier-Journal*, shouts beneath a picture of three diverse (White, African American, Latin) moms embracing three children, "Hey Mom, check it Out! Your Local Connection ... Just for Moms! Meet New Friends Mom to Mom Chats and Play Dates Photo Galleries Find Great Sales Book Exchange and Reviews Family Friendly Event Listings Give-aways, Prizes, and Coupons. KentuckianaMoms.com."

The content of interaction, to use Porter's taxonomy, is clearly focused upon "moms," in that the site's content and virtual conversations converge on the interests and needs for knowledge of the mothers now known as moms. While the site is open to unmarried women, older women, and grandmothers—pretty much to anyone as long as the site's rules are obeyed—the community is not made up exclusively of Millennial Moms. The data available at Quantcast, a site that reports on Web site traffic and demographics, are "sparse" because KentuckianaMoms is a relatively new undertaking, but the data to hand suggest the largest group is 18–34 years old (64 percent), but this group is strongly reinforced by those 35–49 (16 percent) and those over 50 (14 percent); the 41 percent with household income from $30K–60K is reinforced by 22 percent with household income $60K–100K and another 22 percent with over $100K, which in Kentucky is high. Sixty-one percent have some college or are college graduates and 14 percent have graduate education, which in Kentucky is a remarkable concentration of educated people.[31] Natividad reported that the smallest disparity between Gen X and Gen Y in their use of online resources was in participation in an online community (156 versus 105). When those communities are regional, the disparity may be even less, and the contribution of Gen X to the development of Gen Y may be greater in this environment than in other online communities.

Although not completely virtual, technology seems to dominate the mediation of the interaction of participants on this site. Opportunities for moms and for moms and children to meet in person are promoted and seem to occur, but the degree is difficult to assess, and the action in this community seems principally to be online. The site, however, seems keen to promote person-to-person interaction and to sustain a blended community, or at least the appearance of one. Moreover, since the site is very much tied to place and local activities and concerns and since Louisville is a small city, the opportunities of connecting online blending into person-to-person "connections" are greater than on moms sites with either larger or narrower constituencies of interest. Finally, even if this blending does not occur, the site is able to capture the feel of a blended site. Exhibiting this resonance is a synecdoche; whatever the reality, it stands for person-to-person contact and represents a degree of intimacy satisfying to many.

The platform of KentuckianaMoms is well-designed and includes most of the conventional technical features online users have come to expect. When one signs on, for example, one takes a name, one assumes an online identity, and one is discouraged from revealing her actual identity online. An FAQ link orients newcomers to the conventions of life online, even providing a glossary of the shorthand terms and abbreviations used on the site. The site does not, however, offer the chat-room technology that supports real-time connection; rather it maintains "email-based forums [that] allow members to view and respond to messages at their convenience rather than in real time." [32] The site performs, in a variety of technical ways, principally two functions: the posting of information and advertisements, and the enabling of "members" to "connect" and respond to one another, most commonly in a "Moms to Moms" forum. The site's manager also runs a news-like blog—an odd mixture of announcements, crowd control, and thinly disguised advertising. The forum, however, is the heart of the community and is remarkable for its exhausting categorical structure. Click on *Activities*, for example, to connect to subcategories on Sports, Lessons, Camps & Programs, Crafts, Parties and Celebrations, Playgoups & Clubs, and from each of these subcategories one may link to individual posts and responses to those posts. A link at each post allows one to see the poster's "profile," which indicates the date that person joined, the total number of posts that person has made (including the percentage of total posts and the average of posts per day, and, if supplied by the member, a link for a private message and the person's general location, Web site, occupation, interests, email address, and the like). The forum is topically organized in good parallel fashion: *Activities*, *Behavior* (Attitudes, Drugs, Alcohol & Sex, Habits, Potty Training, Sleep), *Education and Development* (Babies & Toddlers, Preschool, Elementary, Middle & High School, College, Home School, Workshops & Classes), *Entertainment* (Books, Events, Movies & TV, Museums & Parks, Music, Vacations, Shopping), *Food* (Eating Out, Nutrition, Recipes Meals Snacks), *Health* (Common Illnesses, Long-term Illnesses, Allergies & Asthma, Dental, Eyecare, Fitness, Special Needs Children), *Motherhood* (Fertility & Conception, Pregnancy, Labor & Delivery, Adoption, Breastfeeding, Multiples, Single Moms, Stepmoms, Name My Baby, Natural Parenting, Grandparenting), *My Life*

(Family, Finances & Money, Grief & Loss, My Stories, Religion & Beliefs, Romance & Sex, Working, Politics), *Random Thoughts* (Parents Lounge, Kentuckiana Moms yard sale, *Newcomers* (Welcome our newcomers), and *Contests* (Win free stuff).

While patterns of interaction are changeable and tricky to assess, the pattern of interaction at KentuckianaMoms appears to be an uneven mixture of small groups with strong ties and larger groups with weak ties that Porter calls "virtual publics [which] are computer-mediated spaces, whose existence is relatively transparent and open, that allow groups of individuals to attend and contribute to a similar set of computer-mediated interpersonal interactions." These interactions vary and are likely to include strong, weak, and stressful ties. KentuckianaMoms as a consequence adopts a highly structured platform and, apparently, a closely monitored set of norms for participation. The statement of "Registration Agreement Terms" reserves the right of the "moderators of this forum" to remove or edit any generally objectionable material," insists that all posts express the opinions of the author, and asks that participants agree not to post "any abusive, obscene, vulgar, slanderous, hateful, threatening, sexually-oriented" material. The site also insists upon a good many other of the increasingly detailed conventions of online community etiquette, such as prohibiting arguments from one thread spilling over into others, hijacking a thread into unrelated topics, gossip about members, and long back-and-forth arguments. These restrictions notwithstanding, the conventions tend to be liberally applied so that the forums are open and free and the patterns of interaction communal as they focus on matters of concern to moms.

There is no knowing at present what "tangible economic value," as Porter puts it, the virtual community at KentuckianaMoms generates or for whom. If it does not generate revenue for the *Courier-Journal* and its advertisers, presumably the site will cease to exist, at least in its present form. The "community," however, through its sharing of knowledge, may well provide tangible economic value to its members, many of whom may well participate out of a strong sense of money-saved-is-money-earned and as well as out of an apparently more powerful need, in the parlance of our times, "to connect."

* * * *

Moms are a subset of humanity to one degree or another immobilized by their maternity. And Millennial Moms—women who have enjoyed unprecedented social, political, and economic mobility—are people singularly in need of the consolations of cyberspace. "High-resolution screens and broadband communication channels aren't widget-making machinery," Howard Rheingold observes, "but sense capturing, imagination stimulating, opinion-shaping machinery." [33] And sites like KentuckianaMoms, I suggest, create something akin to that territory ahead for which Huck Finn "lights out"—space to move around, space in which to act and to discover self and relationships, and so to restore a sense of independence, particularly when enduring the severe dependence created by motherhood and/or work. Rheingold has also observed that "At the heart of V[irtual] R[eality] is an *experience*—the experience of being in a virtual world or a remote location." [34] The experience of this virtual location lies on something like a Foucauldian axis of knowledge and power, discipline and control, but focused upon self rather than upon society or bureaucracy.

The *Courier-Journal* on July 5, 2008 (J4), ran a full-page color (mostly light purple) ad for KentuckianaMoms.com, picturing a grade-school-age Asian girl with a pink backpack slung over her right shoulder and a big book under her right arm, sporting a pleasant expression, but not the big smile characteristic of cute-kid pictures. The very large type to the right reads "Yesterday it was a rattle. Tomorrow, spreadsheets." The smaller type immediately below reads: "There are some things moms only understand. And there's a new place to connect with moms just like you: KentuckianaMoms.com. Come as you are and make new friends."

Here, I submit, is the territory ahead. This image at once represents both the promise posed by a future dominated by "technology" and the anxiety posed by the need to keep pace with technology. The use of an Asian child in the picture further complicates this representation, for Asian children are currently the favorite adoption choice in the Louisville area and the reputation of Asian children for scholastic achievement endures. The implications of this image are among "the things moms only understand." KentuckianaMoms.com seeks to provide the territory in which moms can share and refine those understandings.

NOTES

1. "Profile—Moms.com." http://marketplacepro.moniker.com/profile/property _id/15674482/?return=moms.com, June 24, 2008. For a brief account of the rationale for domain name evaluations, see "Sample Domain Name Appraisal and Explanation," http://www.renewlife.org/RenewLAppraisValue.pdf, June 24, 2008.

And some sense of the market may be had at "Buy Domains.Com: Business Starts Here," http://www.buydomains.com, July 7, 2008.

2. Howard Rheingold, *The Virtual Community: Homesteading on the Electronic Frontier*, Rev. ed. (Cambridge, MA: MIT Press, 2000), 359.

3. Ibid., xvii.

4. Ibid., xx.

5. While Google is pretty good about segregating online searches under the heading of "moms," it is easy to stumble upon what are known as MILF sites with names like BadSoccerMoms, MyBestMom, MomsArchive, and the like, most of which are commercial pornography outlets. Some communal sites, however, are beginning to cater to this interest—as, for example, Louisville Mojo: The M.I.L.F.S of Mojo (http://www.louisvillemojo.com/Live/Group.cfm?BID=1262). This phenomenon, however, is a different chapter in the saga of virtual community.

6. "Meal Make Over Moms," http://www.mealmakeovermoms.com/, July 3, 2008.

7. "Miserly Moms," http://www.miserlymoms.com/, July 3, 2008.

8. Katherine Seligman, "The Motherhood Movement: Can a group like MomsRising finally foment policy change in America by harnessing a citizen army of mothers?" *The San Francisco Chronicle*, May 20, 2007, CM10, http://sfgate.com/cgi-bin/article.cgi?f=/c/a/2007/05/20/CMGCEPG9UE1.DTL, June 3, 2008.

9. "Family Friendly Domains," http://www.familyfriendlydomains.com/, http://www.localizeddomains.com/moms.html, June 24, 2008.

10. Maria T. Bailey, *Marketing to Moms: Getting Your Share of the Trillion-Dollar Market* (Roseville, CA: Prima Publishing, 2002); Maria T. Bailey and Bonnie W. Ulman, *Trillion-Dollar Moms: Marketing to a New Generations of Mothers* (Chicago: Dearborn Trade Publishing, 2005).

11. Maria T. Bailey, "Trillion Dollars Moms: Marketing to a New Generation of Mothers" (BSM Media 50 slide PowerPoint presentation), http://www.idfa.org/meetings/presentations/smartmkt2006_bailey.ppt, June 27, 2008, Slide 2.

12. Ibid., Slide 39.

13. Ibid., Slide 37.

14. Ibid., Slide 35.

15. Ebenkamp, Becky, "The Post-Soccer Mom," Brandweek.Com, June 23, 2008. http://www.brandweek.com/bw/content_display/current-ssue/e3i1bbfaf7a505146051dd14dd93925df26, June 24, 2008 [page 2 of 7].

16. Bailey, "Trillion Dollars Moms," Slide 30.

17. Ibid., Slide 31.

18. Ebenkamp, "The Post-Soccer Mom" [page 1 of 7].

19. Ibid. [page 2 of 7].

20. Ibid. [page 2 of 7].

21. Ibid. [pages 2–3 of 7].

22. Amanda Natividad, "Gen X, Gen Y Moms Share Interests But Use Net Differently: Survey," Content Next.com, http://www.paidcontent.org/entry/419-older-and-younger-moms-using-net-to-explore-childrearing/ContentNext.com, June 27, 2008.

23. Ebenkamp, "The Post-Soccer Mom" [pages 2–3 of 7].

24. Quoted in ibid. [pages 4 of 7].

25. Nicole R. Brown, " 'Community' Metaphors Online: A Critical and Rhetorical Study of Online Groups (Focus on Research)," *Business Communication Quarterly* 6, no. 2 (June 2002): 92–100, http://bcq.sagepub.com/cgi/content/citation/65/2/92, July 2, 2008.

26. Andrew Feenberg, *Critical Theory of Technology* [TofC and Chapter One], http://www.sfu.ca/~andrewf/CRITSAM2.HTM, June 24, 2008.

27. Constance Elise Porter, "A Typology of Virtual Communities: A Multidisciplinary Foundation for Future Research," *Journal of Computer-Mediated Communication* 10, no. 1, Article 3 (November 2004), http://jcmc.indiana.edu/vol10/issue1/porter.html, July 2, 2008, "Objectives."

28. Ibid., "Defining Virtual Communities."

29. Ibid., "Attributes."

30. "Kentuckiana Moms," http://www.kentuckianamoms.com, July 9, 2008.

31. Quantcast, "Kentuckianamoms.com," http://www.quantcast.com/kentuckianamoms.com, July 10, 2008.

32. Porter, "A Typology of Virtual Communities."

33. Howard Rheingold, *Smart Mobs: The Next Social Revolution* (New York: Perseus, 2003), 184.

34. Howard Rheingold, *Virtual Reality* (New York: Summit Books, 1991).

CHAPTER 12

Jewish Mothers: Types, Stereotypes, and Countertypes

Jessica Prinz

The subject of Jewish mothers touches upon the following different approaches and disciplines: folklore, psychoanalysis, anthropology, film history and theory, literary criticism and theory, art and art history, Holocaust studies and Jewish history, ethnic studies and American culture, both high and low. My argument below concerns the way Jewish women are portrayed in literature, video art, and popular culture, including the extremes of Holocaust remembrance and Jewish joke cycles. These widely divergent views somehow coexist: the stereotypes established in jokes, and the countertypes conveyed in more complex and serious works of literature and art. I make a number of assumptions here: (1) That the history and nature of the Jewish Mother stereotype is best illustrated in the joke cycles concerning her;[1] (2) That psychoanalysis is central to the stereotype; (3) That some of the most poignant and powerful images of the Jewish Mother from Dan Greenburg, Philip Roth, Woody Allen, and Thane Rosenbaum bear out Freud's ideas and express an Oedipal conflict in some way, even as they problematize it; (4) That first generation Holocaust literature, the works by survivors, is too serious to joke about, yet it is also centrally concerned with mothers, maternity, and motherhood; and (5) That second generation Holocaust literature, film, and art move beyond the stereotypes to present countertypes: mothers as themselves complex and conflicted. I will conclude by analyzing how mothers are portrayed in a variety of second generation Holocaust genres, including the graphic novel, *Maus*, the films, *A Call to Remember* and *A Secret*, and the creative video work of Israeli artist Maya Zack titled *Mother Economy*.

"YOU DON'T HAVE TO BE JEWISH TO BE A JEWISH MOTHER, BUT IT HELPS"

Certainly, all sorts of ethnicities such as Greek, Italian, Polish, and Chicana overlap with the Jewish stereotypes and share characteristics and jokes. The prevalence of Jewish jokes and the preponderance of Jewish comedians suggest some of the complex attitudes that formulate and underlie the joke cycles in general: ambivalent feelings of love and hate, self-hatred and self-love, anger, aggression, and attraction; comic responses to tragic situations, survival and coping mechanisms; processes of criticism and denigration along with the desire for and experience of pleasure. Every image of a Jewish mother in the media, literature, and/or comedy addresses in some way a prevailing Jewish Mother stereotype that can be defined by the following traits: excessive worrying about her offspring; overprotecting them; taking excessive pride in them; nagging them, inflicting guilt and food upon them; and smothering them, even if they are grown up. A selection of the most popular Jewish Mother jokes will follow, with some brief running commentary about what each joke or joke cycle contributes to the stereotype.

There is an entire joke cycle that concerns famous people in history and what their Jewish mothers would have said to them if they had had Jewish mothers at all:

Mona Lisa's Jewish Mother:
"This you call a smile, after all the money your father and I spent on braces?"

Christopher Columbus's Jewish Mother:
"I don't care what you've discovered, you still should have written!"

Michelangelo's Jewish Mother:
"Why can't you paint on walls like other children? Do you know how hard it is to get this junk off the ceiling?"

Napoleon's Jewish Mother:
"All right, if you're not hiding your report card inside your jacket, take your hand out of there and show me!"

Abraham Lincoln's Jewish Mother:
"Again with the hat! Why can't you wear a baseball cap like the other kids?"

George Washington's Jewish Mother:
"Next time I catch you throwing money across the Potomac, you can kiss your allowance goodbye!"

Thomas Edison's Jewish Mother:
"Of course I'm proud that you invented the electric light bulb. Now turn it off and go to sleep!"

Paul Revere's Jewish Mother:
"I don't care where you think you have to go, young man, midnight is long past your curfew!"

Albert Einstein's Jewish Mother:
"But it's your senior photograph! Couldn't you have done something about your hair?"

Moses' Jewish Mother:
"That's a good story! Now tell me where you've really been for the last forty years."

This cycle turns mostly on the characteristics and stereotypes of historical personages and the clichés concerning them, including Lincoln's hat, Einstein's hair, Napoleon's famous stance, and Mona Lisa's smile. The Jewish mother continues to be unimpressed by the accomplishments of her "children," and generally disavows the power and prestige traditionally accorded these famous figures.

The Jewish Mother stereotype, as it is expressed by the jokes below, is centrally an American phenomenon, first studied and conceptualized by the famous anthropologist Margaret Mead,[2] which then entered mainstream culture, via jokes of the following kind:

A young man begs his mother for her heart, which his betrothed has demanded as a gift; having torn it out of his mother's proffered breast, he races away with it; and as he stumbles, the heart falls to the ground, and he hears it question protectively, "Did you hurt yourself, my son?"

Below is a sampling of Jewish mother jokes, emphasizing different aspects of the stereotype:

Q: Why don't Jewish mothers drink?
A: Alcohol interferes with their suffering.

Q: Why do Jewish Mothers make great parole officers?
A: They never let anyone finish a sentence.

Q: What is a Jewish Mother's favorite position?
A: Facing Bloomingdale's.

Q: Where does a Jewish husband hide money from his wife?
A: Under the vacuum cleaner.

Q: What did the waiter ask the group of dining Jewish mothers?
A: Is ANYTHING all right?

Q: What is the difference between a Rottweiler and a Jewish Mother?
A: Eventually, the Rottweiler lets go.

A Jewish boy comes home from school and tells his mother he has been
given a part in the school play.
   "Wonderful. What part is it?"
   The boy says, "I play the part of the Jewish husband."
   The mother scowls and says, "Go back and tell the teacher you want a
speaking part."

These jokes are obviously demeaning and derogatory, suggesting that the
Jewish mother, among other things, is lazy (does not vacuum), vicious and
possessive (like a Rottweiler), and critical of her husband (and his presumed silence). The most famous of all Jewish Mother jokes is this:

Q: How many Jewish mothers does it take to change a light bulb?
A: (Sigh) Don't bother. I'll just sit in the dark.

The famous folklorist Alan Dundes wrote an article about "screwing light
bulb" cycles of jokes, concluding that generally they concern sex and sexuality ("screwing") and the possession and lack of knowledge and insight
("light").[3] He did not address this Jewish version (though he had much to
say about Jewish Mother jokes in general—to which we will return); but
clearly the force of Dundes's analysis applies here: The Jewish mother is
NOT "screwing" in the light bulb; hence she is not sexy or sexual. Furthermore, she is sitting in the dark, unenlightened and lacking even a minimal amount of knowledge, information, and understanding (light).
   A whole cycle of jokes expresses the Jewish mother's ambitions for her
sons: namely entering the professions of law or medicine. She takes

excessive pride in their accomplishments, inflates their achievements, and often brags about them to others, emphasizing, of course, their success as doctors or lawyers.

There is a big controversy on the Jewish view of exactly when life begins. In Jewish tradition, the fetus is not considered viable until after it graduates from medical school.

A Jewish mother was seen running along the beach screaming, "Help! Help! My son, the doctor, is drowning!"

Nadine, Joyce, and Sylvia are sitting on a park bench, talking about their children.
Sylvia: Well, friends, I have good news and bad news.
Nadine: Nu?
Sylvia: My Michael called me up on the phone last night and told me he was gay.
Joyce: Oy, Sylvia, vey iz mir! And after all you did for him! You were such a wonderful mother. Don't blame yourself.
Nadine: Of course she was wonderful! No nu? That's the bad news. Let's hear the good news.
Sylvia: Well, he's marrying a doctor!

Another cycle of Jewish jokes emphasizes how long-suffering is the mother, and how guilty (therefore) are her children:

Lovely nose ring—Excuse me while I put my head in the oven.

Jewish telegram: "Begin worrying. Details to follow."

My mother is a typical Jewish mother. Once she was on jury duty. They sent her home. She insisted SHE was guilty.

Is one Nobel Prize so much to ask from a child after all I've done?

And Jewish Mother jokes often take place in the "divide" of language, in which the old world, and Yiddish, meets the new, and English:

A young Jewish Mother walks her son to the school bus corner on his first day of kindergarten.
"Behave my bubaleh" she says, "Take good care of yourself and think about your mother, tataleh!"
"And come right back home on the bus, schein kindaleh."
"Your mommy loves you a lot, my ketsaleh!"

At the end of the school day the bus comes back and she runs to her son and hugs him. " So what did my pupaleh learn on his first day of school?"

The boy answers, "I learned my name is David."

And what would a collection of Jewish jokes be without food? Jewish mothers are seen cooking enormous quantities of food, serving huge portions, force-feeding their children (no matter what age they are), and generally much like their Greek counterparts foisting food upon their offspring. "Are you hungry?" the mother asks in *My Big Fat Greek Wedding*, "No? Okay, I'll fix you something."

Never leave a restaurant empty-handed.

What is the difference between a Jewish mother and an Italian mother?

The Italian mother says to her child, "eat this or I'll kill you" while the Jewish Mother says to her child, "eat this or I'll kill myself."

Testing the warm milk on her wrist, she beams—nice, but her son is forty.

The mother in these jokes is overprotective and infantilizing. She is concerned with the welfare of her offspring to such an extent that it becomes ridiculous, calling them on a daily basis and wondering if they have been "eating well" or doing their wash. On one hand, the mother is loud, demanding, clingy, and manipulative; on the other, she is devoted and warmhearted, taking pride in the accomplishments of her children. She is ambitious, not for herself, but for her children and lives vicariously through them. Filled with love, she is also hypervigilant and hypercritical, worrying constantly about her children and their relationships and spouses:

Three Jewish women get together for lunch. As they are being seated in the restaurant, one takes a deep breath and gives a long, slow "oy."

The second takes a deep breath as well and lets out a long, slow "oy."

The third takes a deep breath and says impatiently, "I thought we agreed that we weren't going to talk about the children."

What is the Jewish definition of "genius"?

A "C" student with a Jewish mother.

A young Jewish man excitedly tells his mother he's fallen in love and that he is going to get married.

He says, "Just for fun, Ma, I'm going to bring over three women and you try and guess which one I'm going to marry."

The mother agrees.

The next day, he brings three beautiful women into the house and sits them down on the couch and they chat for awhile.

He then says, "Okay, Ma, guess which one I'm going to marry."

She immediately replies, "The one on the right."

"That's amazing, Ma. You are right. How did you know?

The Jewish mother replies, "I don't like her."

The child in these jokes is on one hand an angel who can do no wrong and also a disappointment who can do no right. Significantly, there is no distinction made (by the mothers) between young children and children who are adults. Dundes discusses the way the Jewish Mother joke cycles became the point of departure for Jewish American Princess (J.A.P.) jokes, which he argued were produced largely in response to the movements of feminism and critiques of patriarchy in the 1970s and 1980s (Q: "Have you seen the newest Jewish American Princess horror movie?" A: "It's called *Debbie Does Dishes*.").[4] The following is a good example of how the Jewish American Mother (J.A.M.) jokes anticipated the preoccupations and concerns of their progeny, the J.A.P., and these are pretty ugly and demeaning views:

Three Jewish mothers met for lunch:

"Oy Oy have I had a week!" the first cried. "On Monday my daughter's husband of 15 years, the father of my three grandchildren, announces he's leaving her for another woman!"

"You think you've got problems?" exclaimed the second lady. "My son has left his wife to set up home with the man next door."

"That's nothing!" Declared the third, "I've lost my cleaner!"

Also influencing later J.A.P. jokes, many J.A.M. jokes concern shopping:

A woman in Brooklyn decided to prepare her will and make her final requests. She told her rabbi she had two final requests. First, she wanted to be cremated, and second, she wanted her ashes scattered all over the shopping mall.

"Why the shopping mall?" asked the rabbi.

"Then I'll be sure my daughters visit me twice a week."

A Jewish mother's advice:

If you have to ask the price, you can't afford it. But if you can afford it, make sure to tell everybody what you paid.

Some theorists argue that the Jewish Mother joke cycles were responses to the clash of cultures Jews experienced as they immigrated from Eastern Europe to America at the turn of the past century. Both Alan Dundes and

Beverly Gray Bienstock[5] argue that the role of the woman in *shtetl,* Eastern European village, life was very different from what normal "American" culture allowed for her. In the *shtetl,* women raised children and also ran businesses, while their husbands spent all their time reading and studying the Torah (Bible). A very troubling work that gives voice to this conflict in cultures is Anzia Yezierska's novel, *Bread Givers* (1925),[6] in which the father remains self-centered and self-righteous despite his loss of prestige and respect in the new world. Many people did adapt, though, to the new cultural imperative of America in which the husband works and makes a living, while avenues for women's ambitions and accomplishments dwindled and disappeared until the rise of feminism in the 1970s, 1980s, and 1990s.

In the joke cycles of the 1950s, 1960s, and 1970s, though, the Jewish woman is somehow very out of touch with society. She seems to belong to a previous or different world and remains very much out of place in everyday, American culture. Certainly, there is a big gap (sometimes generational), between the realities of the world and how she experiences them, as in the following:

> Did you hear about the bum who walked up to the Jewish mother on the street and said, "Lady, I haven't eaten in three days." "Force yourself," she replied.

> A Jewish grandmother was watching a football game. She observed half a dozen burly and aggressive men seeking to tackle the Jewish quarterback and exclaims: "Look at these anti-semites trying to attack that Jewish boy!"

As a segue into the next section of this paper which is on Freud, I will conclude this discussion with Jewish Mother jokes that all relate to psychoanalysis in some way:

> Dear Abby—
>   My forty year old son has been paying a psychiatrist $150.00 an hour every week for two and a half years. He must be crazy.

> Without a Jewish mother, who would need therapy?

> Three Jewish mothers are sitting on a beach in Brent Cross shopping center talking about (what else?) how much their sons love them.
>   Sadie says, "You know the Chagall painting hanging in my living room? My son, Arnold, bought that for me for my 75th birthday. What a good boy he is and how much he loves his mother."

Minnie says, "You call that love? You know the Mercedes I just got for Mother's day? That's from my son Bernie. What a doll."

Shirley says, "That's nothing. You know my son Stanley? He's in analysis with a psychoanalyst on Harley Street. Five sessions a week. And what does he talk about? Me!"

"OEDIPUS SCHMOEDIPUS! A BOY SHOULDN'T LOVE HIS MOTHER?"

This rather quick-witted retort to Freud on behalf of Jewish mothers is at once critical of the psychoanalytic project (as a whole) and at the same time a good joke, according to Freud's own analysis in *Jokes and Their Relation to the Unconscious*.[7] The most surprising aspect of Freud's study is that there are no Jewish American Mother (J.A.M.) jokes within it. The J.A.M. joke developed in a different country and at a different time (with the Jewish Mother first theorized in the 1950s and 1960s, and the Jewish Mother joke formulated as an object of study in the 1980s). Nevertheless, the generic Jewish joke was central to Freud's theory, including a lot of schnorrer jokes, or Jewish Beggar jokes, for instance.[8] The kinds of jokes he describes are those concerning rabbis, students, marriage brokers, and a variety of different ethnicities. He addresses in general the "pleasure in nonsense"[9] that is shared by all jokes, and he studies the following jokes, which along with others serve his purposes of analysis:

> A doctor, as he came away from a lady's bedside, said to her husband with a shake of his head: "I don't like her looks." "I've not liked her looks for a long time," the husband hastened to agree.[10]

> Two Jews met in the neighborhood of the bath house. "Have you taken a bath?" asked one of them. "What?" asked the other in return, "is there one missing?"[11]

Basically Freud argues that the joke does the same work as the dream. Like a dream, the joke expresses feelings, desires, and aggressions that have been repressed and that are brought to consciousness in some more acceptable form. Also like a dream, the joke works by means of condensation (multiplying the meanings of one thing, image, or idea) and displacement (diverting attention from one thing to another) to disguise its own real meaning (sometimes hostile and often obscene)[12] and therefore shifting the content so that it appears in a more "acceptable" form to the conscious mind. While the dream seeks to avoid "unpleasure," the joke enables and yields pleasure.[13] Civilization and education are among society's repressive forces, and jokes provide the means of "undoing" the renunciation (or repression) and the "retrieving of what was lost." [14] Jokes, thus, circumvent repression by expressing "forbidden" and "hidden" desires and/or antagonisms.[15] A joke will allow us to exploit something ridiculous, which we could not bring forward because of social or psychological restrictions; the joke "will evade the restrictions and open sources of pleasure." A good example of this dynamic is marriage broker jokes, "which have something forbidden to say." [16] The joke allows the truth(s) about marriage to slip out in an "unguarded" moment, allowing the joker to be free of pretense for a brief moment.[17] As a result, jokes are good for attacking the (socially) great, dignified, and mighty (who, of course, cannot be disparaged outright) and are by nature a way of saying one thing and meaning another.[18] Like the dream, the joke has "something forbidden to say." Thus humor reduces inhibiting forces (like the mother) and offers psychic relief.[19] As Sander Gilman points out, Freud himself used jokes, and his study of them, to assuage his own anxiety and insecurity as a Jew in fin de siècle Vienna. By this means, Freud himself "exorcizes [his social] anxiety." [20] And since the next section of this chapter will address the Jewish mother from the sons' perspective(s), we might also emphasize that the mother is an agent of repression, while the Jewish mother jokes become a means of evading that censure.

Oedipus Wrecks

In what follows, I discuss the work of contemporary male authors who all express some kind of Oedipal complex in their works. Woody Allen's pun on Oedipus "Rex" conveys some of the ambivalence with which these sons view and treat their mothers. The maternal figure looms large, as an object of veneration and disparagement both. These are powerful women capable of repression and coercion, as seen by their very vulnerable, troubled, and conflicted sons. While Philip Roth's work is pretty well-known (and will be dealt with rather briefly here), Thane Rosenbaum's fiction has a very small audience and these issues are at the center of his work. Woody Allen has received attention for the way he treats "the shiksa (WASP) girlfriends" in his films;[21] but the work that deals centrally with the Jewish Mother in the film *Oedipus Wrecks* deserves more attention and analysis.[22]

The Jewish Mother came to the forefront of popular American culture with a small paperback that hit the best-seller lists in the 1960s. It was titled, *How to Be a Jewish Mother*, written by a Jewish son, Dan Greenburg[23] (first published, 1964). It perpetuated all of the stereotypes associated with the figure of the mother, and as the cover says: "It is responsible for bringing the term, Jewish Mother, into our everyday language." It was throughout an affectionate and charming view with the subtitle: "A Very Lovely Training Manual." The back cover says it all: the photograph of a middle-aged woman spoon-feeding her adult son, with an insert showing the same mother and son 20 to 30 years before doing exactly the same thing. The mother certainly has not changed, nor has the son, except, perhaps, in years!

I will not describe all of the attributes of the Jewish Mother that concern Greenburg in this brief text, but it is effective and especially funny in places where diagrams and illustrations take the place of words. So we find "The proper form for administering the second helping." [24] This technique for serving second helpings is performed whether the son wants a second helping or not, and with the right motions of hands and wrists the mother can effectively serve her son a huge "sliver" of potatoes while disregarding everything that he says.

The most famous author treating this dynamic of an Oedipal conflict between the son with his Jewish mother is certainly Philip Roth, whose portrayal of the tensions between these figures borders on self-hatred and an almost anti-semitic view of the Jewish family in America.[25] First published in 1967, Roth's novel, *Portnoy's Complaint*, takes its title from a new (and fictional) psychoanalytic category designed by Alex Portnoy's therapist, Spielvogel, to describe Alex's neurotic relationship with his mother. The pre-text for the novel includes a definition of "Portnoy's Complaint," including the following sentence: "It is believed by Spielvogel that many of the symptoms can be traced to the bonds obtaining in the mother-child relationship." Much of the narrative is told from the point of view of Alex, as he talks to his analyst, whose name is importantly prefaced by the term, "spiel" or "play," suggesting already the sexual "play" that is the topic of most of Alex's narrative. Roth's "breakthrough" novel has been discussed at length, so there is no need to revisit that scholarship now. I just want to make two or three points that are pertinent to my study of the Jewish mother here.

There is one scene early in the novel that beautifully conveys the characters and conflicts central to this novel, and it might serve as a symbol or synecdoche for the work as a whole. Alex, having claimed to be suffering from a case of diarrhea, is actually in the bathroom masturbating for the fourth time that day, while his mother addresses him from outside the door, accusing him of having upset his stomach by eating too many French fries at the "Chazerai [Unkosher] Palace." A number of underlying assumptions and implications are made here: (1) The mother is associated with food—and nurturing—and she assumes that if there is something wrong with her son, it must have something to do with what and where he is eating; (2) The traditions of Judaism (invoked by the rituals of kosher eating) come into conflict with the eating habits of mainstream American culture (French fries); the mother represents the past and tradition, while the son is associated with the new; (3) The (Jewish) mother is completely out of touch with her son; she represents repression (in the form of obliviousness to the sexuality of her child) and the conflict between them structures the work as a whole and inspires Alex's very vivid hatred and anger for both his parents and Judaism.

I think it is important (and perhaps bears repeating) that Roth invokes the Jewish Mother JOKE to best describe his experience in the Jewish household and the oppressiveness of his mother. He describes to his analyst what it feels like to be caught within such a joke with stereotypical roles being played by himself and his parents:

> Spring me from this role I play of the smothered son in the Jewish joke! Because it's beginning to pall a little, at thirty-three! And also it hoits, you know, there is pain involved, a little human suffering is being felt ... Sure they sit in the Casino at the Concord, the women in their minks and the men in their phosphorescent suits and boy, do they laugh, laugh, and laugh, and laugh—"Help, help, my son the doctor is drowning!"—ha, ha *ha*, ha ha *ha*, only what about the pain ... ! What about the guy who is actually drowning! Actually sinking beneath an ocean of parental relentlessness! What about him— ... who happens to be *me*! ...[26]

The kind of jokes told by the comedians at the Catskill resorts (in the 1950s and 1960s) entertained the upwardly mobile Jewish patrons, who (notably in this passage) laugh enthusiastically in response to the very Jewish jokes that belittle and insult them. Alex continues: "The macabre [black humor] is very funny on the stage—but not to live it, thank you!"[27] The novel as a whole can be summed up in Alex's quip, "LET'S PUT THE ID BACK IN YID"[28] despite the infantilizing intrusions of his parents into his private life:

> A Jewish man with parents alive is a fifteen-year-old boy, and will remain a fifteen year-old boy til *they die*! ... Doctor! Doctor! Did I say fifteen? excuse me, I meant ten! I meant five! I meant zero! A Jewish man with his parents alive is half the time a helpless infant![29]

> I am the son in the Jewish joke—only it ain't no joke! ...

These two are the outstanding producers and packagers of guilt in our time!³⁰

Like Roth's protagonist Alex, the character of Sheldon in Woody Allen's short film, *Oedipus Wrecks* (in the trilogy *New York Stories*, 1989) also concerns the son's relation to a Jewish mother.³¹ In addition to the Oedipal relationship(s) explored in this work, the 50-year-old Sheldon is seen first talking to his psychiatrist about his "difficult" and "loud" mother. Although Roth and Allen share an interest in psychoanalytic theory and processes, Allen's story ends with a more positive, perhaps even fairytale view of the Oedipal conflict at its center.

As in Roth's work, Allen's character is an accomplished lawyer in public life but is treated like an adolescent by his mother. While looking at her photo album with his fiancé, Lisa, the mother, Sadie, mentions his childhood bed-wetting and his cute "little behind," as he sinks into a chair overcome with embarrassment. She visits him at work, and when introduced to one of the partners in the practice, she says, "Oh, you're the one having the affair" (!). She criticizes his name change from Millstein to Mills, and in therapy, he voices the longing of his heart, wishing that she would "just disappear."

Of course, this is exactly what happens, when he and his fiancé, her three children, and his mother all attend a magic show. The magician chooses her from the audience for the "Chinese Box Trick," the only problem being that she literally does disappear—much to everyone's surprise. Three days later, after employing a detective to find her and mourning his mother's absence, he and Lisa make love. With the oppressive/repressive presence of the mother having disappeared or "lifted like a great weight," Sheldon "feels like a new man," and performs "better than ever."

In true Freudian fashion, though, that which is repressed returns with greater vengeance and power. Suddenly Sadie's countenance is huge and hovers above the New York skyline like a middle-aged female deity, pronouncing her advice and criticisms of her son for all of New York to hear. Literally hundreds of people on the ground listen as she admonishes her son not to marry (they have only known each other six months), and describes tales from his infancy (including the fact that he sucked a blanket for many years as a baby). The girlfriend, Lisa, realizes that this figure of the mother is embarrassing her as well, and "saying things about me" from up above.

Sheldon's psychoanalyst resorts to extreme measures for an extreme situation: he sends Sheldon to a psychic for help. She "works" on his case for three weeks, employing various bizarre costumes and rituals, including a comic voodoo doll that actually looks like Sadie. Nothing works. The young, Jewish woman admits failure and starts to cry. They have a "heart to heart" conversation (about her being a fake), which leads to dinner, which leads to what else? Chicken soup! Even more—she sends him home with leftovers.

Sheldon arrives home to find a letter from Lisa breaking off the relationship. As the music reaches a crescendo, and as he holds a chicken leg aloft, Sheldon has an epiphany, expressed by the slowly developing grin on Sheldon's face, concerning his relationship with this young Jewish woman. Cut to the following morning, when Sheldon runs out of the house to introduce his new fiancé to his mother who still hovers in the sky. The young Jewish woman says, "I love your son, he's a doll," at which point the mother miraculously descends and reappears in her normal body. Everybody is happy in the end: the mother seems to have known the truth about her son and is loved again by him; the man meets the "right" woman; the "right woman" loves the man.

If this seems overly optimistic, the film does present some twists in its portrait of the Jewish mother. Sadie begins as a traditional meddling mom, who infantilizes her son, embarrasses him, and generally ignores his own insecurities and feelings. That she should appear as a giant, all-powerful female god in the sky is in keeping with the feelings of insecurity felt by all of these sons as they try to please their mothers and fulfill all of their mothers' expectations and ambitions for them. In one of the most powerful scenes in the film, Sadie, who still floats above the New York skyline, shows off a photo of her son, Sheldon. At this point hundreds of people on the ground stop, pull out their own family pictures, and simultaneously start describing their loved ones to each other. The point, I think, is clear: Sadie is not so very unique, but like most other mothers takes pride in her son and wants to share that pride with others. There are redemptive possibilities in this story by Woody Allen that are unavailable to or unexplored by Philip Roth's Alex Portnoy. Significantly, the Allen piece is also a bit more fantastical and contrived, with a resolution that is finally more ideal than real.

I want to address one more text in this overview of Jewish mothers from the sons' perspectives, namely a short story by Thane Rosenbaum from his collection of linked stories (sometimes referred to as a novel), *Elijah Visible* (1996).[32] All of the stories concern a young man named Adam Posner, who wrestles in various ways with his family inheritance—the suffering of the Holocaust experienced by the previous generation. The story I want to focus on here is titled, "Romancing the *Yohrzeit* Light." Like the other narratives discussed above, the story portrays a conflict between a powerful mother figure and the love "interest(s)" of her son; the difference here is that the mother is actually dead. A *Yohrzeit* candle is a memorial candle, lit by Jews on the anniversary of the death of a loved one. It is a small white candle in a little glass jar that is easy to find in local groceries, as Adam discovers when he decides to light one in his mother's honor.

Adam is an assimilated and disaffected Jew, who is bewildered by Jewish customs, rituals, and prayers (as well as the confusing lunar calendar by which the date of the *Yohrzeit* is determined). He does his best, though, to follow tradition (in his own way), and the candle comes to represent his love and affection for his departed mother. But alas, his devotion to his mother is challenged by his girlfriend (a Swedish fashion model named Tasha), who decides on exactly that same day of the *Yohrzeit* to consummate their relationship. Adam is torn between these two women, and he is so happy to have sex with Tasha that he refrains from explaining the real nature of the strange candle in the room. Although he feels that he is somehow betraying the memory of his mother, Adam's allegiance is finally with his beautiful and sexy girlfriend. The last image in the story has Adam falling asleep under Tasha's Christmas tree.

The imagery of candles is woven throughout the story, creating a leitmotif that actually links the women in Posner's life. In the first instance, we see Adam's mother as she tiptoes up to light the Sabbath candles. In the second related image, Adam lights the *Yohrzeit* candle in her memory. This candle is extinguished by Tasha, who has no idea what it is or what it represents. The final, and perhaps most important, image is of Tasha on her tiptoes as she lights the candle at the top of her Christmas tree. Since the story ends here, we can assume that Adam will continue to be a "lapsed" Jew, one for whom intermarriage is not only tolerated but also accepted.

"BLACK MILK OF DAYBREAK WE DRINK IT AT SUNDOWN WE DRINK IT AT NOON IN THE MORNING WE DRINK IT AT NIGHT ..."[33]

Holocaust literature of the first generation, the stories and experiences of the survivors, somehow coexists with all of these Jewish mother jokes, but obviously the Holocaust literature resists and opposes the humor and lightheartedness that shape the jokes. Those authors most commonly associated with the Holocaust are monumental literary figures most of whom are men—like Primo Levi, Elie Wiesel, Paul Celan, and others. This literature gives voice to the most horrible and the horrifying experiences of the Jews at the hands of the Nazis. Celan's poem, "Death Fugue" (quoted above), suggests that something is terribly wrong— that which usually nourishes is black with the ashes from the crematoria. Survivors have been writing about their experiences, and scholars have been studying that literature for a good 60 years by now, in what is a rich tradition of various kinds of narrative forms and various modes of expression.[34]

What I would like to do here is discuss briefly a work by Cynthia Ozick, titled *The Shawl* (a duo of two short stories published together).[35] Before discussing the work itself, though, the story concerning its creation is significant as well. Following a famous dictum by Theodor Adorno, for a long time Ozick believed that after Auschwitz, there could be no poetry (or art, or literature, or creative pursuits at all). The tragedy, the historical reality defies description and expression. George Steiner, for instance, "insists that the horrors of the Holocaust have so stunned the imagination of the artist that it has been paralyzed: history collaborates with invention to produce—silence." [36]

Ozick also believed that only those who actually experienced the historical events in the camps had a right to discuss them. Yet she wrote her "survivor's story" despite these restrictions. She did not experience the camps herself and thus she violated her own "ethics of expression," by writing about them. She has said:

> Well, I did it [write fiction about the Holocaust] in five pages in *The Shawl*, and I don't admire that I did it. I did it because I couldn't help it. It wanted to be done. I didn't want to do it, and afterward I've in a way punished myself, I've accused myself for having done it. I wasn't there, and I pretended through imagination that I was ... I want the documents to be enough; I don't want to tamper or invent or imagine. And yet I have done it. I can't not do it. It comes, it invades.[37]

What is so spectacular about Ozick's writing in this piece, *The Shawl*, is that it gives voice to that which few authors deem worthy of attention: Jewish mothers and the forms of suffering unique to them in the camps.

The story revolves around a young mother, Rosa, hiding an infant daughter beneath a shawl, which offers the only "warmth" and nourishment available to the baby, Magda. Because she is starving, Rosa's breasts provide no sustenance for her child, who nevertheless is "pacified" by sucking on the cloth, "the shawl's good flavor, milk of linen." As in previous literature, notably Virginia Woolf's *To the Lighthouse*, the shawl itself is a symbol of femininity and life-affirming maternity.[38] Furthermore, it is tied to the Jewish religion by its connection to the *Tallit*, the prayer shawls that men (and now women) wear when praying. Finally, as Daniel R. Schwarz points out, the word "shawl" relates to the word "*Shoah*," a Hebrew term for the Holocaust that means, literally, "desolation."[39]

Because the baby Magda has "Aryan" features, the story implies that this baby is the result of a rape in the camp. Even though Rosa gives her child all of her food, both she and her daughter are slowly starving to death. The shawl is described (at least twice) as "magic" and that it sustains Magda through her infancy is itself a miracle. Magda is mute and does not talk at all, yet she grows into a toddler who "beg[ins] to walk." When the young girl (Stella) steals Magda's shawl because she (Stella) is so very cold, "and the cold went into her heart," Magda goes in search of the shawl on her "pencil legs" into the courtyard controlled by Nazis. At that moment, she says her first word: "Ma," which is short for both "Mama" and "Magda." In the end, the baby is thrown against an electric fence by a Nazi, and the mother stops her own screams by "stuffing" the shawl into her mouth and "tasting the cinnamon and almond depth of Magda's saliva."

It is difficult to find a more poignant or powerful work of fiction concerning the Holocaust than this very brief text. Its central themes go beyond those I will discuss here, including the nature and meaning of survival, death, prejudice, faithfulness, betrayal, and the peculiar experiences of Holocaust victims. If, as some of my students have suggested, Ozick writes "too much about breasts and breastfeeding" in this story, my response to those students is that she is an author concerned with women's experiences and with the special forms of suffering faced by women in dire circumstances like the concentration camps.

THE SECOND GENERATION: TO WHOM DOES THE PAST BELONG?

Here I look at second generation Holocaust narratives and examine just how they respond to the Jewish Mother stereotype, and how they modify and manipulate it, how they exploit and/or counter it.[40] Some scholars believe that the children of survivors (the second generation) have no right to discuss their own lives or presume to speak about their parents' experiences. The term "second generation," thus, refers to the children of survivors and what Marianne Hirsch calls "postmemory": when the survivor parents transfer their own traumas ("wounds") to their children in various ways and in varying degrees:

> Postmemory characterizes the experience of those who grow up dominated by narratives that preceded their birth, whose own belated stories are evacuated by the stories of the previous generation shaped by traumatic events that can be neither understood nor recreated.[41]

Psychoanalysts Nicholas Abraham and Maria Torok, have formulated a related term, "encryptment," to describe secondary inherited trauma of this kind. In this concept a trauma "not one's own becomes the basis for repressed, hysterical behavior,"[42] what Thane Rosenbaum calls "Second Hand Smoke."[43] Alan L. Berger describes the second generation in this way:

> These [works] are significant in visualizing an important transition in the lives of second-generation witnesses. As young adults they are now prepared to confront the anxiety, pain, and uncertainty of growing up in survivor households.[44]

In what follows, I trace these issues as they appear in a variety of genres, including Art Spiegelman's graphic novel, *Maus* (two volumes, in 1986 and 1991),[45] in the films *A Call to Remember* (1997) and *A Secret* (2007), and finally, in the recent video artwork of Maya Zack (2008), titled *Mother Economy*. Critic Efraim Sicher poses the following pivotal questions concerning the second generation: "What attitude, we may ask, toward a traumatic past might enable the next generation to be free of the crippling fears they have inherited and yet bear the burden of memory? *Indeed, whose past is it?*" (emphasis added).[46] Thane Rosenbaum gives eloquent voice to precisely this dilemma:

> My parents, no longer alive but continually reinvented, revised, hostage to my own private therapy. The Holocaust survivor as myth, as fairy tale, as bedtime story. I had created my own ghosts from memories that were not mine. I wasn't there in Poland, among the true martyrs. Everything about my rage was borrowed. My imagination had done all the work—invented suffering, without the physical scars, the incontestable proof.[47]

All of the following works are somehow about the relation of the two generations as each generation struggles in its own way to cope with undeniable and unique forms of suffering.

Critic Sara Horowitz is exceptional for the attention she gives to gender issues in Spiegelman's *Maus*.[48] She argues that the father, Vladek, maintains a fairy-tale conclusion, for at the end, he says, "We were both very happy, and lived happy, happy ever after." A number of details defy this contrived conclusion: Artie's mother, Anja, committed suicide; she suffered from depression her whole adult life; the parents lost a precious son, "Richieu"; Vladek has destroyed his wife's journal (which leads Artie to call his father a "murderer"). Skipped over in many readings of *Maus* is the fact that Anja worked as a spy during the war, translating information for the "communists," which in this work is perhaps short-hand for the "resistance." In any event, she has been involved in "conspirations," [49] which Vladek calls to an abrupt stop. As Horowitz claims, "Anja as activist, selfless, bold, contradicts the portrait drawn by Vladek and Art." [50] Because we get our entire view of Anja from the perspective of her husband, who sees her throughout as a "good girl," we are left to ponder what is not told about Anja in this story and how those narrative gaps would be filled in if she were still alive.[51]

Finally, this story links up with other examples of second generation narratives because its plot concerns what might best be called, "the missing brother" syndrome. *Maus* concludes with Vladek, misspeaking in a significant way, when (at the very end) he calls Artie "Richieu" and mistakes his living son for the son whom he lost in the camps. This theme of a "phantom brother" is shared by at least two other narratives to be dis-cussed here: the films *A Call to Remember* and *A Secret*, both of which portray sons discovering and confronting "ghost siblings" and "previous families" from the past.

The title of the film *A Call to Remember* (1997) is actually a pun that has two very different connections to the plot. On one hand, it refers to the telephone "call" that the mother, Paula, receives, telling her that her son lost in the Holocaust is actually alive and wants to meet her. Tragically, this turns out not to be the case and as a result, she succumbs to a deep depression. Her husband, David, is also a survivor who lost a previous family in Europe; but he is challenged by his young, American kids, Ben and Jake, to describe his previous family; in short, the young men "call" their father "to remember" the past, although the father really does not want to. As in *Maus*, the children sense the existence of some previous and lost siblings, who they want to know more about, and who haunt their present existence and affect their relationships with their parents. The entire trajectory of the film, though, concerns the mother, and whether or not she will be able to survive her depression and rejoin her two sons and her husband as an active member of the family that she still has.

The captivating film *A Secret* (2007) also touches on these themes and concerns, and it is an original family saga that intersects with the Holocaust.[52] In this film, a young, fragile, sickly, and perhaps "wimpy" young boy named Francois has a stunningly beautiful mother, Tania (frequently seen diving from the high board at the swimming pool); he also somehow senses that he has an older brother and actively imagines that his older brother exists. The entire film slowly discloses how this is in fact the case, and that his parents had previous families lost (for various reasons) in the Shoah. There is a special poignancy here, as Francois grapples with the disconcerting possibility of a previous (and equally precious) boy who was perhaps a bit more accomplished than he is (especially in gymnastics—his father's favorite sport). As the story develops, we realize that the postwar son cannot adequately compensate for the previous loss, as exemplified in the differences between the young men. In this film, the parents have a "secret" that concerns their previous marriages, and along with Francois we discover the existence and the tragic death of this "phantom brother."

Once again, in *A Secret*, we get very complex female characters, in the first (Hannah) and then second (Tania) wives of the father figure, Maxime. Both wives are mothers, but not Jewish mothers in any stereotypical way. Hannah, for instance, is a Jewish mother, but one who, recognizing that her husband loves another woman (Tania), turns herself and her young son in to the Gestapo, thus identifying herself as Jewish in the most horrible way possible. Her demise, and that of her son, is the direct result of her religion combined with her depression, her anger, and her "madness" (in both senses of the term). The religion and ethnicity of Tania, however, is an ambiguity in the film. Because of her exquisite "Aryan" features (she is both an athlete and a fashion model), she passes easily as a Christian during the trials of the Holocaust years in France. It is not clear in the film whether or not she is Jewish, though we do know that Maxime and Tania have their son, Francois, christened in the postwar years. The two central women in this film face unspeakable tragedies—the creation of one family out of the violent destruction of another. Their suffering is experienced at various levels, as private sorrows mirror and interconnect with the disintegration and destruction occurring in society as a whole.

The achronological narrative juxtaposes various temporal scenes (and shifts from color to black and white), but the film as a whole centers on two generations and the conflicts between them: the present generation, represented by Francois, who tries to discover and understand the past;

and the older generation (his parents), who try to repress the past and keep it "a secret."

THE JEWISH MOTHER MEETS POSTMODERNISM

The last work I want to discuss here is titled *Mother Economy*, by Israeli artist Maya Zack. Born in 1976, Zack teaches art at Tel Aviv University, and her 19-minute work of video art showed at the Jewish Museum (New York) from July to September 2008. The work won the prestigious "Celeste Art Prize" in Berlin in the same year.[53]

The work bridges many extreme differences, most centrally those between traditional women and their contemporaries, including the various roles available to and actively performed by women. The film raises important questions for contemporary Jewish women—should they reject the old roles associating women and "home economics" to pursue more challenging professions (rabbinate, law, medicine, business, etc.)? Or should they (emphasizing their continuity with mothers and grandmothers) welcome the connection between women and the domestic sphere, along with the "culinary arts" of their forerunners.

One of the central techniques of postmodern art and literature is the sophisticated use of indeterminacy or ambiguity. The work by Zack certainly produces the effect of perplexity in the viewers, one of whom left the room, saying, "I don't understand a thing of this." Were that viewer more familiar with contemporary art, she would not have been so disgruntled, though she would still experience the mysteriousness and the obscurity of the work. Zack's piece is indeterminate at a variety of levels including some of the following: genre, characterization, time, and space.

A discussion of Zack's artwork must be prefaced by acknowledging the ambiguity of its genre. Is it "art" and/or "film" and/or "performance art" and/or "video art" and/or "theater" and/or "cinema," or some odd combination of the above? The sense of time in the piece is equally ambiguous. We get radio broadcasts from Nazi Germany, sound bites from German operettas and British politicians, suggesting that this is a meditation on Holocaust remembrance. The silent and sole protagonist (played by Idit Neuderfer) wears period clothing: including high white laced collar and hair in a bun. To what time period does this strange figure belong? Is she a figure from the past or the present?

Space is also mysterious in this work. Here we are located in a closed place: a small apartment whose main room is the kitchen, and which Zack herself has called a kind of "museum." Does the female figure belong in this space, or does the space "belong" to others? We have no way of knowing. The setting was actually designed by Zack to create a certain self-reflectiveness in the work: to heighten a sense of the superficial and contrived, and that is why the artist chose to create it in a studio. There is a pervading sense of the artificial, especially in the pink, paper-lined walls (a surrogate canvas?), on which the woman draws and traces. Zack (finally) proposes the interconnectedness of housewife and artist. "Every housewife is an artist with her installations," writes Jeannie Rosenfeld about Zack's work. In fact, the voice track includes a comment in German: "She is a miserable housewife, but a wonderful actress."

Likewise, this mysterious protagonist (along with her enigmatic setting) is both familiar and strange: we see her perform traditional activities like sewing and cooking, as well as performing unusual modes of calculation, weighing, counting, and tracing. Some of these mundane actions combine art and domestic activities, like tracing both solid and ephemeral objects (such as cigarette ash), or counting on an abacus, or weighing and measuring on an old-fashioned scale. What she is doing and why she is doing it become ambiguities in the work, although she herself seems to know what she is doing and creates a sense of purposefulness and determination in her activities. As one critic, Sara Ivry, asks, "Does anybody else live there? Are they coming home? Who is this woman? What is her history?" all of which are questions that remain unanswered.

In keeping with postmodernism, too, the central female figure problematizes (and does not resolve) issues of identity and characterization. As Rosenfeld points out in the first review of Zack's work, "[The artist] offers no definitive answers to the central questions of the heroine's identity and motivation." Her strange actions suggest that she is trying to create order of some kind, but how is totally unclear. Is she a housewife? A mother? A detective? An anthropologist? An economist? A mathematician? A housekeeper? An artist? A spy? A curator? Or some unusual combination of these possibilities? The activity of tracing itself connotes drawing, and perhaps alludes to the traditional activities of "visual" artists within the film. Preoccupied with the activities of counting (with an abacus) and measuring (with an outmoded scale), we can certainly say that the woman is somehow "decoding information," though for whom and for what purposes remain unclear. She is both a "mother" and a "machine," as Zack has said: "There's this tension between the mother who is supposed to nurture, and on the other hand, she's this calculating machine." She performs cryptic processes using various measuring devices, such as an abacus, scales, beakers, test tubes, pie charts, and compass. We cannot understand what it is she is doing, but she is translating a language or a mathematical or sign system that occupies her completely and remains a mystery to us.

Zack's short video invokes and then overturns the cliché, "a woman's place is in the home." It ends with the woman, having baked her "kugel" (traditional Jewish noodle casserole)[54] and divided it according to a pie chart using a big compass, placing the traditional food at the center of an empty (but finely decorated) table. This last image invokes the path-breaking work of feminist artist Judy Chicago, whose installation piece titled "The Dinner Party" (1974–1979) was the point of departure for literally hundreds of female artists to follow.[55]

Also in this tradition are performance artists/dramatists studied by Lesley Ferris, like Bobby Baker and Blondell Cummings, who use the kitchen as a setting for theatrical performances. In a way that reflects back on Zack's work, Ferris describes the work of Baker and Cummings in this way:

> By situating their performances in the kitchen, both Cummings and Baker blur the distinction between domestic drudgery and art. No longer hidden and inside, the kitchen becomes a theatrical playground for women's memories, desires, fantasies. They bring conventionally inside space outside; their performances make public those intimate, personal, and often private moments historically consigned to oblivion.[56]

Like these artists, Zack also "performs" the autobiographical subject. It is important that some of her inspiration for the film was a trip she took to discover (or "trace" back) her grandmother's house in Kosice, a city in present-day Slovakia. She was barred from the house, but Zack was inspired to imagine what the interior may have looked like. The video is thus a "sketch" of the past, using period costumes, old objects, and retro furniture.

Additionally, there is throughout a pervading sense of irrationality and surrealism in this piece. It does seem to follow the logic of a dream. At the outset, the female figure (located in the kitchen) slices a lemon and sucks on it, with juice dribbling down her chin. Why? The kugel, which she spends so much time concocting, appears at the top of a cooking pot rather than inside of it, which is odd. Even more, we see the unnamed and silent woman from within the oven, as she peers inside at us, while baking her kugel. Further, she uses an inordinately big compass to cut her kugel, and wears a huge rubber glove to retrieve it from the oven. Objects change size and shape so that absolutely mundane and everyday activities become strange or "de-familiarized" by a pervading surrealism.

There is yet another context in which to view Zack's work: namely, the cookbooks created by concentration camp prisoners, especially at Terezin. These women shared fantasies and recipes (for such things as plum strudel, cream strudel, chocolate strudel, doughnuts, glazed fruits, dumplings, poppy seed cakes, goulash, breast of goose, onion kuchen, etc.), despite the grim horror and starvation of the camp. Thinking about food, recipes, and cooking helped these women cope with their own deprivations. "In Memory's Kitchen" is a profound and beautiful work created by starving women, whose recipes are valuable despite, and because of, their "errors" of memory or transcription.[57]

It is significant that at the end of Zack's piece, the table is empty and her creation, the kugel, goes uneaten. There is something unsettling and unresolved about the way this video concludes. The cook is alone, and the room is empty. The woman in Zack's work does survive, though, despite the sense of violence, injustice, and upheaval filtering in from outside on the radio. This is a woman viewed as isolated and vulnerable (at one point, she trips and falls). Zack's character calls us to look beyond the stereotypes of the Jewish mother, and she raises questions about Jewish women and their survival in a threatening world.

Because of the anachronisms in the work, from Magic Marker to fashions from the 1930s, it is difficult to place the piece and its character. Is she a Jewish Mother? The title suggests that she is. We should perhaps refrain from jumping to any solid (or convenient) answers to this and the other various questions raised in this video. This artwork nevertheless revises and complicates all of the simple stereotypes with which this chapter began. Significantly, there are as many different ways to make kugel as there are Jewish mothers—and there are as many ways to be Jewish mothers as there are mothers in the world. Stereotypes? Or countertypes? Either way, these female figures—both real and imagined—deserve our ongoing attention and perhaps, also, admiration.

NOTES

1. This paper is dedicated to my son, Joseph Prinz, for all the information, insights, and feedback he gives me. Unless noted otherwise, all of the jokes herein are from the site "Jewish Mother Jokes.com."

2. Mead persuaded the American Jewish Committee to fund research at Columbia University, in the early 1950s, on European *Shtetl*. She interviewed

128 European Jews who immigrated to the United States, conceptualizing the category of the "Jewish Mother" for the very first time. The "joke" about the mother and her heart was quoted by Mead. See http://www.slate.com/id/2167961/slideshow/2167764/entry/2167761/.

3. Alan Dundes, "Many Hands Make Light Work or Caught in the Act of Screwing in Light Bulbs," *Western Folklore* 40, no. 3 (July 1981): 261–266, http://www.jstor.org/stable/1499697. See also Alan Dundes, "The J.A.P. and the J.A.M.," *American Folklore* 98, no. 390 (October–December 1985): 456–475, http://www.jstor.org/stable/540367 (accessed December 31, 2008). See also Diane Wiener, "Performativity and Metacommentary in Jewish American Mother Light Bulb Jokes," *M/C: A Journal of Media and Culture* 6, no. 5 (November 2003), http://journal.media-culture.org.au/0311/5-wiener-jewish-lightbulb.php.

4. Sigmund Freud, *Jokes and Their Relation to the Unconscious*, trans. James Strachey (New York: W. W. Norton & Company, Inc., 1963; first published in German, 1905; first English translation, 1916).

5. Beverly Gray Bienstock, "The Changing Image of the American Jewish Mother," in *Changing Images of the Family*, ed. Virginia Tufte and Barbara Myerhoff (New Haven, CT: Yale University Press, 1979), 173–192. See also Avner Ziv and Anat Zajdman, eds., *Semites and Stereotypes: Characteristics of Jewish Humor* (Westport, CT: Greenwood Press, 1993); and especially Judith Stora-Sandor, "From Eve to the Jewish American Princess: The Comic Representation of Women in Jewish Literature," in *Semites and Stereotypes*, ed. Avner Ziv and Anat Zajdman (Westport, CT: Greenwood Press, 1993), 131–142.

6. Anzia Yezierska, *Bread Givers* (New York: A Karen and Michael Braziller Book, Third edition, 2003; First edition, 1925).

7. Sigmund Freud, *Jokes and Their Relation to the Unconscious*, trans. James Strachey (New York: W. W. Norton & Company, Inc., 1963; first published in German, 1905; first English translation, 1916). For a study of women and humor, see Helga Kotthoff, "Gender and Humor: The State of the Art," *Journal of Pragmatics* 38, no. 1 (January 2006): 4–25; ISSN: 0378-2166; DOI: co1016/j.pragma.2005.06.003. Kotthoff observes: "In the past, women were often the objects, but only rarely the subjects of jokes" (5). She continues: "stereotypes bring gender to the forefront of attention in affirmative *or* subversive ways . . . until 15 years ago, women were absent from humor anthologies."

8. Freud, *Jokes and Their Relation to the Unconscious*, 112–113.

9. Ibid., 127.

10. Ibid., 37.

11. Ibid., 49–52.

12. Ibid., 51.

13. Ibid., 180.

14. Ibid., 101.

15. Ibid., 103.

16. Ibid., 108.

17. Ibid., 106.

18. Ibid., 105.

19. Ibid., 127.

20. Sander L. Gilman, *Jewish Self-Hatred: Anti-Semitism and the Hidden Language of the Jews* (Baltimore: The Johns Hopkins University Press, 1986; paperback, 1990), 268.

21. Sam B. Girgus, "Philip Roth and Woody Allen: Freud and the Humor of the Repressed," in *Semites and Stereotypes: Characteristics of Jewish Humor*, ed. Avner Ziv and Anat Zajdman (Wesport, CT: Greenwood Press, 1993), 121–130. See also Richard Freadman, "Love Among the Stereotypes, or Why Woody's Women Leave," in *Semites and Stereotypes: Characteristics of Jewish Humor*, ed. Avner Ziv and Anat Zajdman (Westport, CT: Greenwood Press, 1993), 107–120.

22. The most scholarly and most thorough book to date on the Jewish Mother is by Joyce Antler, *You Never Call! You Never Write! A History of the Jewish Mother* (Oxford, U.K.: Oxford University Press, 2007). It is a complete history, especially of the Jewish mother in popular culture. Concerning *Oedipus Wrecks*, Antler writes: "it hits the bull's-eye with his humorous depiction of this interfering Jewish mother. She is the epitome of the nag . . ." (173). All of the male authors I discuss here (Roth, Allen, and Rosenbaum) express what Antler calls "matrophobia"—a wonderful coinage (173). I do, however, see *Oedipus Wrecks* as much more positive and affirmative in the end, with its mother knowing more about the son than the son himself knows. In my view, it has an amazingly positive ending.

23. Dan Greenburg, *How to Be a Jewish Mother: A Very Lovely Training Manual* (Los Angeles: Price/Stern/Sloan, 1978, 7th printing; first published, 1964).

24. Ibid., 29. Antler also chooses to comment on this illustration in the book, which along with the cover provides crucial visual expressions for the J.A.M. stereotype.

25. Philip Roth, *Portnoy's Complaint* (New York: Random House, 1967).

26. Ibid., 111.

27. Ibid., 112.

28. Ibid., 124.

29. Ibid., 111.

30. Ibid., 36–37.

31. See also Woody Allen, *Woody Allen on Woody Allen: In Conversation with Stig Bjorkman* (New York: Grove Press, 1993).

32. Thane Rosenbaum, *Elijah Visible* (New York: St. Martin's Griffin, 1999). See especially the story "Romancing the *Yohrzeit* Light," 13–34. See also Rosenbaum's novel *Second Hand Smoke* (New York: St. Martin's Press, 1999); and an interview with Rosenbaum by Derek Parker Royal, "An Interview with Thane Rosenbaum," *Contemporary Literature* 48, no. 1 (Spring 2007): 1–28; ISSN: 00107484.

33. From Paul Celan, "Death Fugue," trans. Michael Hamburger, in *Holocaust Poetry*, ed. Hilda Schiff (New York: St. Martin's Griffin, 1995), 39.

34. Here are just a few from the vast number of studies in Holocaust literature: Yehuda Bauer, *Rethinking the Holocaust* (London: Yale University Press, 2002); Bella Brodsky, "Teaching Trauma and Transmission," in *Teaching the Holocaust*, ed. Marianne Hirsch and Irene Kacandes (New York: MLA of America, 2004), 123–134; Jerome Charyn, ed., *Inside the Hornet's Head: An Anthology of Jewish American Writing* (New York: Thunder's Mouth Press, 2005); Paul Eisenstein, *Traumatic Encounters: Holocaust Representation and the Hegelian Subject* (New York: State University of New York Press, 2003); Hilene Flanzbaum, ed., *The Americanization of the Holocaust* (Baltimore: The Johns Hopkins University Press, 1999); Berel Lang, *Post-Holocaust: Interpretation, Misinterpretation, and the Claims of History* (Bloomington: Indiana University Press, 2005); Lawrence L. Langer, *The Holocaust and Literary Imagination* (New Haven, CT: Yale University Press, 1975); Michael Morgan, *A Holocaust Reader: Responses to the Nazi Extermination* (New York: Oxford University Press, 2001); Jonathan Rosen, "The Uncomfortable Question of Anti-Semitism," in *Those Who Forget the Past: The Question of Anti-Semitism*, ed. Ron Rosembaum (New York: Random House, 2004), 3–13; Ron Rosenbaum, *Those Who Forget the Past: The Question of Anti-Semitism* (New York: Random House, 2004); Hana Wirth-Nesher and Michael P. Kramer, eds., *The Cambridge Companion to Jewish American Literature* (Cambridge, U.K.: Cambridge University Press, 2003).

35. Cynthia Ozick, *The Shawl* (1980/1983) (New York: Random House, 1990). See also Cynthia Ozick, "Afterword," in *Those Who Forget the Past: The Question of Anti-Semitism* (New York: Random House, 2004), 595–614.

36. Steiner continues: "The world of Auschwitz lies outside speech . . . ," qtd. Lawrence L. Langer, *The Holocaust and the Literary Imagination* (New Haven, CT: Yale University Press, 1975), 14–15. See also George Steiner, *Language and Silence* (New York: Atheneum, 1966).

37. Ozick, qtd. in Andrew Furman, "Inheriting the Holocaust: Jewish American Fiction and the Double Bind of the Second Generation Survivor," in *The Americanization of the Holocaust*, ed. Hilene Flanzbaum (Baltimore: The Johns Hopkins University Press, 1999), 83–101, especially 87.

38. Virginia Woolf, *To The Lighthouse* (New York: Harcourt Brace Jovanovich, 1989; first published, 1927). In part I, Mrs. Ramsay covers the boar's skull in the children's bedroom with her shawl, a life-affirming gesture that is undone (literally as the shawl unwinds) in the "Time Passes" chapter.

39. Daniel Schwarz, *Imagining the Holocaust* (New York: St. Martin's Griffin, 1999), 306.

40. The second generation is a broad category that includes the following novelists, poets, and filmmakers: David Grossman, Thane Rosenbaum, Arye-Lev Stollman, Anne Michaels, and Melvin J. Bukiet, Sarah Kaufman and Paul Auster, Anne Karpf, Alain Finkeilkraut, Leon Wieseltier, and others. Susan Gubar's chapter, "Children of Survivors," in *Poetry After Auschwitz* (Bloomington: Indiana University Press, 2003), analyzes the following additional authors: Klepfisz, Burton D. Wasserman, Gregg Shapiro, Nadine Fresco, Jason Sommer, Louis Simpson, Sari Friedman, and Hilary Tham. Scholars who have studied these artists, filmmakers, and writers of the second generation follow: Melvin Jules Bukiet, ed., *Nothing Makes You Free: Writings by Descendents of Jewish Holocaust Survivors* (New York: W. W. Norton & Co., 2002); Robert Eaglestone, *The Holocaust and the Postmodern* (Oxford, U.K.: Oxford University Press, 2004); and Lawrence Baron *Projecting the Holocaust into the Present: The Changing Focus of Contemporary Holocaust Cinema* (New York: Rowman & Littlefield Publishers, Inc., 2005), a work about Holocaust film; Anne Karpf, "From the War After," in *Nothing Makes You Free: Writings By Descendents of Jewish Holocaust Survivors*, ed. Melvin Jules Bukiet (New York: W. W. Norton & Co., 2002), 279–293. See also Efraim Sicher's chapter on Second Generation Holocaust authors, especially Art Spiegelman (*Maus*) and David Grossman (*See: Under: Love*), in "Postmemory, Backshadowing, Separation: Teaching Second-Generation Holocaust Fiction," in *Teaching the Representation of the Holocaust*, ed. Marianne Hirsch and Irene Kacandes (New York: Modern Languages Association of America, 2004), 262–273. Eaglestone's canon of Holocaust authors include Bernhard Schlink's *The Reader* (1997), W. G. Sebald's *Austerlitz* (2001), William Styron's *Sophie's Choice* (1979), D. M. Thomas's *The White Hotel* (1981), Thomas Keneally's *Schindler's List* (1986), Martin Amis's *Time's Arrow* (1991), Rachel Seiffert's *The Dark Room* (2001), and Jonathan Safran Foer's *Everything Is Illuminated* (2002); see Eaglestone, *The Holocaust and the Postmodern*, 103.

41. Hirsch, qtd. by Efraim Sicher, "Postmemory, Backshadowing, Separation: Teaching Second-Generation Holocaust Fiction," in *Teaching the Representation of the Holocaust*, ed. Marianne Hirsch and Irene Kacandes (New York: MLA of America, 2004), 262–273, especially 266. See also Marianne Hirsch, *Family Frames: Photographs Narrative and Postmemory* (London: Harvard University Press, 1997), 22.

42. Qtd. in Emily Miller Budick, "The Holocaust in the Jewish American Literary Imagination," in *The Cambridge Companion to Jewish American*

Literature, ed. Hana Wirth-Nesher and Michael P. Kramer (Cambridge, U.K.: Cambridge University Press, 2003), 212–230, especially 217.

43. See Thane Rosenbaum's novel, *Second Hand Smoke* (New York: St. Martin's Press, 1999).

44. Alan L. Berger, qtd. by Lawrence Baron, *Projecting the Holocaust into the Present* (New York: Rowman & Littlefield Publishers Inc., 2005), 161–162.

45. Art Spiegelman, *Maus: A Survivor's Tale*, Vol. 1: *My Father Bleeds History* (New York: Pantheon, 1986); *Maus: A Survivor's Tale*, Vol. II: *And Here My Troubles Began* (New York: Pantheon, 1991).

46. Efraim Sicher, "Postmemory, Backshadowing, Separation: Teaching Second-Generation Holocaust Fiction," in *Teaching the Representation of the Holocaust*, ed. Marianne Hirsch and Irene Kacandes (New York: MLA of America, 2004), 268.

47. In Rosenbaum's short story, "An Act of Defiance," in *Elijah Visible*, 58–59.

48. Sara R. Horowitz, "Gender and Holocaust Representation," *Teaching the Representation of the Holocaust*, ed. Marianne Hirsch and Irene Kacandes (New York: MLA of America, 2004), 110-122.

49. See Spiegelman, *Maus*, Vol. I, 27.

50. Horowitz, "Gender and Holocaust Representation," 114.

51. See Henri Raczymon, "Memory Shot Through with Holes," *Yale French Studies* 85 (1994): 98–105. On the important notion of narrative gaps in Holocaust testimonies and narratives.

52. The film *A Secret* was based on the novel by Philippe Grimbert, *Memory*, trans. Polly McLean (New York: Simon & Shuster: Portobello Books, 2007). Some of the details differ, most notably that Tania has long, black hair in the book. I believe that it is still ambiguous as to whether she is Jewish or not. For an early review, see A. O. Scott, "A Jewish Family Caught in War's Ebb and Flow," Movie Review, *The New York Times*, January 8, 2009. http://movies.nytimes.com/05secr.html.

53. Short, early reviews include the following: Sara Ivry, "Object Lessons: Maya Zack's Singular Take on Home Economics," http://nextbook.org/cultural/feature.html?id=893; Jeannie Rosenfeld, "Reel Life: Israeli Artist Maya Zack Makes a Powerful American Debut," *Forward*, July 13, 2008, http://www.forward.com/articles/13886/; and George Robinson, "Home Economics, Shoah Style," *The Jewish Week*, January 12, 2009, http://www.thejewishweek.com/viewArticle/c344_a13023/The_Arts/Film.html.

54. There is an interesting, but finally unconvincing, essay by Allan Nadler that argues the kugel is totally associated with the male rabbi who cuts and serves it. Nadler makes his argument about the "masculinity" of the kugel in "Holy Kugel: The Sanctification of Ashkenazic Ethnic Foods in Hassidism," in *Food*

and Judaism, ed. Leonard J. Greenspoon, Ronald A. Simkins, and Gerald Shapiro (Omaha, NE: Creighton University Press, 2005), 193–214. Most others agree that "kugel" is linked to women, because they cook and serve it.

55. "The Dinner Party" by Judy Chicago included 39 place settings on a large, triangular-shaped table, first exhibited in 1979, with a companion text published in 1996.

56. Lesley Ferris, "Cooking Up the Self: Bobby Baker and Blondell Cummings 'Do' the Kitchen," in *Interfaces: Women/Autobiography/Image/Performance*, ed. Sidonie Smith and Julia Watson (Ann Arbor: University of Michigan Press, 2002), 186–210, especially 208.

57. See Cara DeSilva, "In Memory's Kitchen: Reflections on a Recently Discovered Form of Holocaust Literature," in *Food and Judaism*, ed. Greenspoon, Simkins, and Shapiro, 105–118.

About the Editors and Contributors

THE EDITORS

Mardia J. Bishop's research focuses on popular culture, body image, and cultural practices associated with the manipulation of the body. In addition, she has extensively published and presented on contemporary theatre. She holds a Ph.D. in theatre history from The Ohio State University and teaches at the University of Illinois' Department of Communication. She is co-editor of *Pop-Porn: Pornography in American Culture* (Praeger 2007).

Ann C. Hall is professor of English at Ohio Dominican University, president of the Harold Pinter Society, and currently a drama series editor for Palgrave-MacMillan. In addition to publishing numerous articles, books, and editions, she has most recently co-edited *Pop-Porn: Pornography in American Culture* (Praeger 2007) and edited *Making the Stage: Essays on the Changing Concept of Theatre, Drama, and Performance* (2008). She is currently at work on a book-length project on Ronald Harwood.

THE CONTRIBUTORS

Alina Bennett is a Lecturer with the Department of Women's Studies at The Ohio State University where she earned her Master's degree in Women's Studies and her Graduate Interdisciplinary Specialization in Disability Studies. She recently published a number of reviews in *Disability Studies Quarterly* and the *National Women's Studies Association Journal*. In 2008, she won the Department of Women's Studies' Joellen Thomas Writing Award for the Outstanding Paper on Women and Disability.

Angela Dancey received her Ph.D. in English from The Ohio State University in Columbus. Her dissertation is a study of the makeover in popular film and culture. Her research interests include beauty culture, the woman's film, female stardom, and celebrity. She has taught film studies and writing at The Ohio State University and Otterbein College in Westerville, Ohio.

Dennis Hall is professor of English at the University of Louisville, where he teaches literature and the odd course in popular culture. He is co-editor with Susan Grove Hall of *American Icons: People, Places, and Things That Have Shaped Our Culture* (Greenwood 2006) and recently published essays on "The Little Black Dress" and "The Watch" as cultural icons. He is currently working on an essay on "Tattoo as Baroque Art."

Katherine N. Kinnick is Professor of Communication and Director of Pre-College Programs at Kennesaw State University. She is the author of numerous publications and presentations dealing with the portrayal of gender and race in the media, including articles in *Women's Studies in Communication* and *Race, Gender & Class*. Recent work includes a chapter on increasing sexual explicitness in media in Mardia J. Bishop and Ann C. Hall's *Pop-Porn: Pornography in American Culture* (Praeger 2007). She received KSU's highest teaching honor, the Distinguished Teaching Award, in 2003. She holds a doctorate in mass communication from the University of Georgia.

Manuel Martínez is an Assistant Professor of Spanish at Ohio Dominican University in Columbus, Ohio. He specializes in contemporary Cuban and Cuban American fiction. He is currently working on translating the collected works of Cuban poet Dr. Gleyvis Coro Montanet.

Craig N. Owens is a member of the English Department at Drake University, where he teaches courses on drama, literary criticism, theory, and writing. He writes and speaks on theater, performance studies, and contemporary American film. At present, he is writing a surrealist play, *Angus*, which explores bovine agricultural crises during the Midwest's past century. He is the editor of *Harold Pinter Etc.*, forthcoming from Cambridge Scholars Publishing. He is a founding member of Steinsemble Performance Group.

Jessica Prinz, Associate Professor of English at The Ohio State University, specializes in art and literature of the twentieth century. Her book, *Art Discourse/Discourse in Art* (Rutgers 1991) concerns how contemporary artists use language. She has written essays on Pound, Pinter, Beckett, Williams, as well as more recent figures such as Laurie Anderson and Jenny Holzer. Her current book project is titled, "Hyperreal and the Advent of Pop."

Kathleen L. Riley, a graduate of the University of Notre Dame, is Professor of History at Ohio Dominican University. She is the objective/historian author of *Fulton J. Sheen: An American Catholic Response to the Twentieth Century* and *Lockport: Historic Jewel of the Erie Canal.* In the interest of fair disclosure, some objectivity was set aside for this essay, as she is the proud mother of Emily (Sun Mee Kim), who arrived from South Korea on August 10, 1990, and is a currently a freshman at Skidmore College in Saratoga Springs, New York.

Robin Silbergleid is the author of the chapbook *Pas de Deux: Prose and Other Poems* (Basilisk 2006). Her current project is a book-length memoir, "Texas Girl," which deals with fertility treatment and single motherhood. She is an assistant professor of English at Michigan State University.

Marjorie Worthington is an Assistant Professor of English at Eastern Illinois University who focuses on Contemporary American fiction. Her writing has appeared in journals such as *Studies in the Novel*, *Critique: Studies in Contemporary Fiction*, *Twentieth-Century Literature*, and *LIT: Literature, Interpretation, Theory.*

Index